Multicultural Education
The Interminable Debate

Multicultural Education
The Interminable Debate

Edited by

Sohan Modgil PhD
Reader in Educational Research and Development,
Brighton Polytechnic

Gajendra K. Verma PhD
Reader in Education,
University of Manchester

Kanka Mallick PhD
Senior Lecturer in Psychology of Education,
West London Institute of Higher Education

Celia Modgil PhD
Senior Lecturer in Educational Psychology,
University of London

 The Falmer Press
(A member of the Taylor & Francis Group)
London and Philadelphia

UK The Falmer Press, Falmer House, Barcombe, Lewes, East Sussex, BN8 5DL

USA The Falmer Press, Taylor & Francis Inc., 242 Cherry Street, Philadelphia, PA 19106-1906

First published 1986

Library of Congress Cataloging in Publication Data

Main entry under title:

Multicultural education.

   1. Intercultural education—Great Britain—Addresses,
essays, lectures.   2. Intercultural education—Canada—
Addresses, essays, lectures.   3. Children of minorities—
Education—Great Britain—Addresses, essays, lectures.
4. Children of minorities—Education—Canada—Addresses,
essays, lectures.   I. Mogdil, Sohan.
LC1099.M836   1985   370.19′6   85-6743
ISBN 1-85000-054-9
ISBN 1-85000-055-7 (pbk.)

Typeset in 10/12 Bembo by
Imago Publishing Ltd, Thame, Oxon

Printed in Great Britain by Taylor & Francis (Printers) Ltd, Basingstoke

Contents

Contributors

Professor Christopher Bagley, University of Calgary
Professor James A. Banks, University of Washington, Seattle
Professor John Berry, University of Kingston, Ontario
Professor Brian Bullivant, Monash University, Melbourne
Mike Cole, Brighton Polytechnic
Professor David Dufty, University of Sydney
Dr Roger Homan, Brighton Polytechnic
Professor James Lynch, Sunderland Polytechnic
Dr Kanka Mallick, West London Institute of Higher Education
Dr Celia Modgil, University of London
Dr Sohan Modgil, Brighton Polytechnic
Professor Bhikhu Parekh, University of Hull
Professor John Rex, University of Aston, Birmingham
Professor Ronald Samuda, University of Kingston, Ontario
Professor Sally Tomlinson, University of Lancaster
Professor Harry Triandis, University of Illinois, Champaign
Dr Gajendra Verma, University of Manchester
Dr Paul Yates, University of Sussex

1 Multicultural Education: The Interminable Debate

Sohan Modgil, Gajendra Verma, Kanka Mallick and Celia Modgil

Introduction

The debate and activities concerning multicultural education have become much more openly acknowledged since 1981. Confusion and contradiction permeate multicultural education.

The ethnic minority child, although not a new phenomenon in British schooling, came to feature in the classrooms of post-war Britain, as the numbers of such children increased in the wake of post-war immigration. At first, provision for the ethnic minority child in the classroom consisted primarily of equipping the child to cope with life in British society; for many of these children provision began with teaching them English. A few years later the focus began to shift away from pure survival to the structures of the education system: could they offer these children the same chance of academic success and success in life in general as that sought by the population at large (Verma and Ashworth, 1985)?

Multiculturalists have sought to establish a new educational consensus. Rejecting assimilationist and ethnocentric philosophies of the 1960s, many have argued for a form of education that is pluralist in orientation and positively embraces a multiethnic perspective. Issues of teacher education, curriculum development, ethnic minority underachievement and the changing of racist and prejudiced attitudes have all received some hard campaigning. However, there has been little serious debate on the political presumptions and possibilities of such issues. Hatcher and Shallice (1983) consider the recent responses of the state to multicultural innovations: 'What are we to make of the strange sight of previously recalcitrant and "colour-blind" LEAs now embracing the very principles of multiculturalism they had previously ignored?' Hatcher and Shallice 'warn against taking such conversions at face value and offer a political analysis of the role of multiracial education and its possible incorporation within reactionary state policies as a whole. They argue that only a close link between anti-racist teachers and community forces will be capable of producing realistic strategies for change' (*Multiracial Education*, 1983).

1

Early government reports offer little consensus of opinion. They add to the momentum of the debate and fuel the disputes further. Policy and practice are at different stages of development. The official reports highlight the currently transient nature of the multicultural debate and 'situations are changing so rapidly that even to stand still is to move backwards'.

The Momentum of Debate

In the early 1970s a project carried out by the National Foundation for Educational Research (Townsend and Brittan, 1972) and sponsored by the Department of Education and Science reported a variety of arrangements being made by local education authorities and schools in relation to the education of immigrant pupils. This diversity reflected varying local situations, differing priorities and the absence of a strong policy lead from central government together with an attitude of 'benign neglect'. The Report of the House of Commons Select Committee on Race Relations and Immigration (1973) echoed the findings of Townsend and Brittan: 'If ... one conclusion stands out above all others, it is that we have failed to grasp and are still failing to grasp the scale of what we have taken on ... it follows that the most urgent task is to measure and face up to the scale of what now confronts us.'

The British Government's support for multicultural education appeared in the 1977 Green Paper *Education in Schools*. This Paper stressed that the presence of ethnic minority groups in Britain has implications for the education of all pupils, and that all schools, whatever their ethnic composition, should give their pupils an understanding both of the multiethnic nature of British society, and of Britain's place in an interdependent world. The Green Paper referred to the needs of this new Britain which should be reflected in school curricula.

The 1980s commenced with a plethora of pronouncements and publications from establishment sources. The Schools Council (Little and Willey, 1981, 1983) survey, established in 1978, constituted the first major investigation of local education authorities' and schools' policies and practices in multiethnic education since that undertaken by Townsend and Brittan. The survey showed that while in some fields there had been little advance, in other respects there had been significant developments. Widespread acceptance in multiracial areas of the need to make arrangements to meet the particular educational needs of minority ethnic groups was reported; although in terms of actual provision this largely meant meeting language needs (English as a second language). Awakenings were identified of curriculum development being seen less in terms of simply adding on special subjects and more as involving a reappraisal of the curriculum as a whole to make it relevant to all pupils. However, there was little evidence of this in schools with few or no minority ethnic group pupils — the wider multiethnic society being seen as having little relevance. However, Little and Willey (1983) report that although there had been significant changes in attitude, there had been less progress in terms of action, and the scale of provision remained very limited. The survey revealed 'a considerable gap between views and policies about what should be happening and some aspects of practice'.

In July 1979 a Committee of Inquiry into the Education of Children from Ethnic Minority Groups was appointed to look at the educational needs and attainments of children from the whole range of ethnic minority groups, bearing in mind factors relating to pre-school experiences and prospects for school leavers. As a first step the Rampton Committee was required to prepare an interim report on the particular needs and attainments of West Indian children, due to concern about their academic underachievement. Considering the various factors which have been said to lead West Indian children to underachieve, the Rampton Report (DES, 1981c) argues strongly that a broadly based 'multicultural' approach to the curriculum should be adopted by *all* schools. The Committee does not 'believe that education should seek to iron out the differences between cultures, nor attempt to draw everyone into the dominant culture' but rather should 'draw upon the experiences of the many cultures that make up our society and thus broaden the cultural horizons of every child.'

Little and Willey (1983) comment that many of the Committee's recommendations 'on reading and language, on curriculum, on books and teaching materials, on examinations, on school and pastoral arrangements, on links between the schools and the community, on teacher education, on the advisory services and on statistics are complementary to the conclusions of the Schools Council Project.'

The Home Affairs Select Committee (House of Commons, 1981) is somewhat sceptical about the role of the Rampton Committee which it describes as 'a symbol of hope for those concerned with ethnic minority children and a shield behind which the Department and the LEAs have sheltered from demands for action on policy pronouncements' (Vol. I, p. 131). Riley (1982, p. 12) comments, '. . . certainly many of the things that Rampton has to say are not new: that West Indian children are being disadvantaged by our educational system and that as they progress through the education system the gap between their performance and that of other children widens . . . The unique contribution of Rampton is to suggest, for the first time, that this disadvantage is caused by factors other than "temporary problems" of adjustment and language. The question of racism within schools is finally raised in an official education document: "we are convinced from the evidence that we have obtained that racism both intentional and unintentional has a direct and important bearing in the performance of West Indian children in our schools".' Riley (*ibid.*) considers that 'the different emphases in the recommendations of Rampton and the Home Affairs Committee on teacher education, reflect the different styles of the two Committees. The Rampton response is cautiously to suggest that Teacher Training Institutions should carry out a "fundamental reappraisal" of their policy. As these Institutions have been asked several times in the past to review their activities, to little avail, another review is unlikely to bring about the changes that are needed.'

The Home Affairs Committee recommendations have much more bite: 'Every initial training course should be examined by its validating body to ensure that it accurately reflects the society in which those who follow the course will be working' (Vol. I, p. 140). Further, 'all teachers should have at least some initial specialized training to enable them to perform effectively in a multi-racial classroom' (Vol. I, p. 142).

The Home Affairs Committee, whilst recognizing that the role of the Department of Education and Science is to 'advise and warn', is scathing about their lack of success in promoting multiracial education in schools: 'We recognise this problem but have the impression that the Department has in the past been more reticent in encouraging good practice in the field of ethnic minority education than in some areas such as home-school liaison, curriculum reform or corporal punishment. . . . HM Inspectorate provide the Department with a wealth of detail which seems to disappear without trace . . . the Department alone are in a position to provide authoritative guidance' (Vol. I, p. 132).

Riley further emphasizes that 'in spite of their shortcomings, the overall effect of Rampton, Scarman, and the Select Committee on Racial Disadvantage is to put the question of "race" and education firmly on the Government's agenda. The urgent task of all those concerned about the education of black children is to ensure that it does not slip *off* the agenda' (pp. 9–10).

Multiracial Education (1982) casts serious doubts concerning the practical implementation of the reports and argues that 'the political will to realise the recommendations of Rampton and the others is clearly lacking, as evidenced by the Government Reply to Select Committee Report on "Racial Disadvantage", and the possibility of a national policy on race relations and education is as remote as ever' (p. (i)).

Sustaining debate, the second phase of the Committee of Inquiry into the Education of Children from Ethnic Minority Groups, under the chairmanship of Lord Swann, is due for publication in Spring 1985. Press notices suggest that the proposed report is pursuing a controversial path. 'Leaks' reported in the press on the recommendations include reference to every school (even those in all-white areas) having to provide courses in such languages as Creole, Gujerati and Punjabi, and to schools with big numbers of ethnic minority children having to offer the whole curriculum in these languages. Commentaries in the various newspapers in September 1984 indicated the controversy likely to surround any such recommendations. The *Daily Mail* (13 September) referred to 'leaked proposals' as 'an unqualified, unremitting and unimaginable recipe for educational and social disaster. And a provocative encouragement to the very phenomenon it seeks to resolve — racism.' 'Reverse discrimination has already been practised in the United States with bitter results. White people who now fail, say, to get a place in a university because the black quota takes priority feel embittered, cheated and not surprisingly hostile to blacks.' Further, 'it is so against the interests of the child not to equip him with the best possible instruction through proper English', and 'a good education is the best possible form of anti-racism . . . you don't find much racism at Harrow — and that's multi-ethnic.' The *Daily Express* (13 September 1984) elaborates: 'Generations of immigrants have been absorbed in these islands precisely because they learned the mother tongue of England and integrated into the community, bringing to it their own strengths and talents.' An extreme recommendation emanates from *The Sun*: 'Our advice to the Education Secretary, Sir Keith Joseph, about what to do with this wretched report is simple. Shove the whole thing — all 1,000 pages of it — in the Whitehall incinerator.' Although these recommendations have no validity and are speculative, the commentaries reflect the underlying issues and conflicts inherent in any positive approach to multiculturalism. The debate continues!

The Strategy of This Book and the Continuation of the Debates: Specific Issues

(i) Multiculturalism

Katz (1982) pleads for a clear definition of multicultural education. Many national groups have provided very useful definitions for all educators. She cites as examples, 'Multicultural education is preparation for the social, political and economic realities that individuals experience in culturally diverse and complex human encounters. . . . Multicultural education could include, but not be limited to, experiences which (i) promote analytical and evaluative abilities to confront issues such as participatory democracy, racism, and sexism, and the parity of power; (ii) develop skills for values clarification including the study of the manifest and latent transmission of values; (iii) examine the dynamics of diverse cultures and the implications for developing teaching strategies; and (iv) examine linguistic variations and diverse learning styles as a basis for the development of appropriate teaching strategies' (pp. 16–17).

The very term is without an agreed definition, and the implementation of the concept appears to depend largely upon the standpoints of individuals, whether they take an assimilationist, cultural pluralist or anti-racist approach. Crozier (1983) maintains that 'the rise in the debate on "multicultural education" may produce a sense of optimism for the development of this concept or practice of education' (p. 53). As Verma (1984) comments, multicultural education has no clear-cut meaning; the term has blind-alley implications which not only take us away from moral and social realities, but direct us towards conceptual confusion.

In this volume Parekh maintains that the idea of multicultural education has gained considerable currency in Britain during the last ten years, and has become a subject of acute controversy. 'For the conservative critics, it represents an attempt to politicize education in order to pander to minority demands, whereas for some radicals it is the familiar ideological device of perpetuating the reality of racist exploitation of ethnic minorities by pampering their cultural sensitivities.' Parekh elucidates the meaning and implications of the concept of multicultural education; demonstrates why multicultural education is desirable and assesses the validity of the criticisms made of it.

Bullivant focuses on the faults inherent in the concept of multiculturalism. The history of education in the English–speaking world since Rousseau's *Emile* has been the search for ideologies of pluralism to legitimate the types of schooling and curriculum made available for status-class, ethno-cultural and racial minorities. Throughout this search two extremes of thought can be detected: utopianism, idealistic, in which wishing prevails over thinking; and realism, hard-headed, and often cynically aware of the realities of power and control in pluralist societies. Bullivant argues that multiculturalism cannot adequately deal with realistic — power — conflict issues posed by race, status-class and even gender differences, all of which involve consideration of the life-chances of children from minority groups. This is partly because multiculturalism tends to stress utopian visions of society by adopting definitions of culture that favour ethno-cultural maintenance of life-styles. He further maintains that selections for the curriculum that encourage children from ethnic backgrounds to learn about their cultural heritage, languages, histories, customs and other aspects of their life-styles, have little bearing on their equality of educational opportunity and life-chances. These are influenced more by structural, social class, economic, political and racist factors operating in the wider pluralist society, and by the control exercised by its dominant groups over access to social rewards and economic resources. 'Thus, to claim, as many romantic utopian multicultural advocates do, that teaching an ethnic child about his or her cultural heritage will lead to greater ethnic self-esteem and therefore better educational attainments and ultimately a better job is simplistic in the extreme . . . .' Teaching *all* children about cultural differences in their societies may reinforce and not reduce their sense of distinctiveness. Bullivant proposes radical multiculturalism as a compromise between utopian and realist views, using a modern definition of culture and a power-sensitive curriculum. Culture can be defined in a way that is much less utopian. 'In essence culture is a form of ever-evolving "survival device" based on adaptive change that enables social groups to cope with the problems of living in a particular habitat. It is *this* kind of culture that children from ethno-cultural groups have to master, rather than a romanticized fossil-culture based on utopian views of pluralism.'

In his chapter on 'Multiculturalism, class and ideology', Bagley presents a European-Canadian comparison. He demonstrates that although the three societies (Canada, Britain and the Netherlands) have similarities in terms of technological and economic change, each of these societies has responded to the problems of ethnicity in a different way. The implication is that the policy of multiculturalism for education varies in form and meaning from one society to another. His analysis clearly shows that the debate about multicultural education is about the values which inform the working of society itself. Considering the current state of multicultural-ism in Canada, Britain and the Netherlands, Bagley concludes, '. . . multicultural-ism in its present forms is little more than a masking ideology with which an artful and ruthless capitalism protects itself.'

In this volume Yates promotes the potential of cultural analysis and eth-nography for providing an adequate theory of culture in relation to multicultural-ism. Ethnography re-examines existing categories which explain phenomena and recategorizes and reconceptualizes the field of study, giving fresh insights into perplexing problems. A programme of small- and larger-scale studies of classrooms, institutions and the communities they serve and of the people, organizations and networks of those who control and direct the education system is required. There is no clear idea of how culture should relate to schooling and that it is a multicultural curriculum that is needed. Prevailing notions of culture need to be submitted to more rigorous analysis than has been the case, and also require a proper empirical grounding. Without this prior basis to innovation, there can be no clear logical connections between the analysis of the problem, the strategy for meeting it and the criteria for education. An ethnography of cultural diversity, which would include indigenous white culture as equally problematic as any other, would provide the necessary context within which hitherto unheard debates could provide us with answers to these most pressing problems, and with them a reliable guide to action.

Verma and Bagley (1984) assert that 'culture' (whatever it is) is not a static entity, a culture is dynamic; it changes over time. Furthermore, a 'culture' is not objective; any description of it must allow for the way in which it is perceived by the individuals living in that particular culture. Personal experience may well dictate a different attitude to a perception of some particular aspect of a shared culture.

Triandis argues that pluralism is the development of interdependence, appreciation and the skills to interact intimately with persons from other cultures. Current attempts at integration, based on a legal framework, disregard individual differences and attempt to eliminate cultural differences. Triandis advocates a shift from that perspective to one that provides for a marriage of the legal framework with our understanding of social psychological principles. Rather than integration, as conceived today, or assimilation, which involves the elimination of cultural differences, Triandis advocates *additive multiculturalism* where people learn to be effective and to appreciate others who are different in culture. Additive multiculturalism is by its very nature something that needs to be developed in the majority rather than the minority of the population. As more members of the minority learn to integrate in jobs and are given a chance to do so, the majority must learn to relate to the minorities with a perspective of additive multiculturalism. 'Within that framework and over a period of many years, we should develop a pluralism that gives self-respect to all, appreciation of cultural differences and social skills leading to interpersonal relationships with more rewards than costs.' Ignorance of multiculturalism is as much a deficiency of educational systems today as ignorance of history or geography.

Samuda notes that multiculturalism in Canada represents a radical shift on the part of the federal government of Canada; further, it represents a recognition of the cultural diversity of Canadian society and the equality of status for the various ethno-cultural groups. Canadian multicultural policy recognizes the existence of two official languages, but no official culture. Cultural pluralism is the very essence of the Canadian identity, based on the notion that every ethnic group has the right to preserve and develop its own culture and values within the Canadian context. 'It represents a sharing of culture — an extension of participation and control of social, political and economic institutions ... more importantly, multiculturalism in Canada means the acceptance of cultural diversity and the abandonment ... of the ... racism and ethnocentrism that formed the basis of government practice ... [However,] the concepts of multiculturalism are not yet integrated into the faculties of education, and many practising teachers still view education from the archaic assimilationist perspective ... ethnocentric teacher training and insufficient emphasis on appropriate curriculum and counselling methods represent the failure of the educational system to adapt to the new Canadian school population.'

Dufty also identifies limitations in the current concept of multicultural education in Australia: the concentration on issues related to ethnicity. A broader concept of society and social education is needed in order for people to become more fully aware of the many dimensions of their pluralistic society. Dufty maintains that these dimensions include differences associated with ethnicity and race; socio-economic class; ideological convictions; gender; age; health; and the region in which people live. It is desirable and possible to do something further about remodelling the images which have been passed down as authentically and typically Australian by the dominant social groups: 'to reconceptualize Australian society and culture in the minds of political leaders, academics, educators and members of the general public ... A more radical viewpoint on pluralism would be that it is not sufficient to change the images through education, even if that is possible; one must change the structures of society as well.'

(ii)   Racism and Radicalism

Hatcher and Shallice (1983) maintain that 'the starting-point of an approach to anti-racism in education has to be an understanding of why racism is today so powerfully rooted in British society. If racism is primarily an ideological anachronism from the days of Empire, then the task of eradicating it is primarily an *educational* one, and the problem is simply one of developing appropriate *teaching* strategies. But if racism is being newly generated at the political, social and economic levels of a society in crisis, if it is a popular ideology which seems to offer a way out of that crisis for millions of people, then it has implications for *education* which multiculturalists have seldom drawn' (pp. 7–8). They continue, 'the fight against racism is primarily a political one, which takes place in every region of social life, including on the terrain of *education*. The success of anti-racism in *education* will depend on how it is inserted into that wider political struggle.'

Green's (1982) paper presents an analysis of conflicting conceptions of multi-racial education. In replying to radical critiques of multiracial education, he argues that the confusion has arisen because of the application of one term to 'include a host of different policies, programmes and political objectives.' Green summarizes: 'The major critiques of multicultural education are those written by Stone, Dhondy, Carby and Mullard. These accounts differ considerably in political perspectives but the central and organizing theme of the latter three is that multiculturalism is primarily about control; it is a strategy to contain black resistance. It involves an attempt by the State to preempt and defuse black struggles (Mullard), to coopt a group of successful black students who will be trained as tomorrow's black bourgeoisie and the vehicle by which the State tries to achieve the political incorporation of the black working class (Dhondy), or simply a ruse by means of which teachers reach a negotiated peace in the classroom. According to Carby "discussions about the nature of curriculum changes that could adequately reflect a multiracial society tend to avoid ... issues of discipline and control which are central to education practice." Dhondy argues that multicultural education was a quite lucid reaction on the part of the State to the political challenge of black youth: "without a renewed effort on the part of the school system, without tipping the balance of forces within the world of school, Britain cannot expect to contain the infectious disease of black youth." Multiculturalism was a response to the struggles of black youth. The pupils demanded black studies so the State provided these to placate them. However, says Dhondy, the " 'co-optation' of this impulse and the demand killed the interest that black youth took in the subject." Mullard argues a similar thesis. Multiculturalism "is none other than a more sophisticated form of social control and it has the effect of containing black resistance." '

However, Green points out that the arguments are marred by the simplification of thinking of multiracial education as a homogeneous entity. Further, there is an analysis that confuses intentions with outcomes and continues with the assumption that the aims of state policy will be realized. Over and above this, schools are not viewed as institutions of struggle and in which outcomes do not occur uncontested. Green advocates a political and explicitly anti-racist teaching practice designed to develop the political strengths of those to which support is directed, together with challenging the racism of institutions. Objectives will differ from official state-sanctioned multicultural education policies, but they will operate within officially recognized bodies, making the rhetoric a reality. Green acknowledges the contradictory situation in which radical teachers are placed: teaching against racism whilst agents of an institutional system that can be said to perpetuate it. However, 'contradiction is the essence of social change and the occupational hazard of political action' (p. 34).

However, Hatcher and Shallice (1983) note that Green does not discuss what the relation is between the different sites of struggle: are they merely adjacent or does the wider struggle play a determining part in what is possible in schools? 'What happens when this thoroughgoing politicisation arouses the rigorous opposition of the DES?' Hatcher and Shallice conclude that 'it is utopian to believe that anti-racist education can steadily spread through the school system by the normal processes of curriculum innovation. It will require powerful forces to push through educational reforms of the character and magnitude of anti-racist education.'

Cole, in this volume, is fervent that anti-racism must be stressed to the exclusion of the traditional concept of multiculturalism (not to be just part of the package to be swamped by more traditional approaches). Racism must be seen as a white problem — the white response to black people living in Britain. Cole maintains that one of the advantages of teaching and learning about the *reality* of race is not only what it tells us about race, but what it tells us about the whole nature of the society in which we live. 'We cannot and must not rely on multiculturalists to protect and further the interests of young blacks. Unless we, as teachers, confront these real issues, unless we address a culture which is relevant and pressing, we have no hope of making meaningful contact with our students.'

(iii)   Teacher Education

Teachers åre consistently blamed for being racist, ethnocentric and unsympathetic towards the culturally plural society. Watson (1984) argues that teachers are less at fault than teacher educators in training institutions and that unless the latter move towards introducing more courses in multiracial/cultural education there is little hope of change. In alignment with the general position in relation to multicultural education, the origin of pressures for preparing teachers for a multicultural society can be traced to the 1970s. In 1969 the House of Commons Select Committee on Race Relations and Immigration (HMSO, 1969, para. 214) urged the government to give consideration to the preparation of all teachers for work in a multicultural society. Even at this stage the point was made that teachers should be equipped to prepare *all* children for a multicultural society, not only in the schools where they meet mixed classes. Subsequent reports and surveys (Schools Council, *Immigrant Children in Infant Schools*, 1970; Townsend and Brittan, 1972, *op. cit.*; James Report, 1972; Select Committee on Race Relations and Immigration, 1972/73; Commission for Racial Equality, 1974; Bullock Report, 1975) have given credence to this requirement.

There was evidence of a number of colleges and schools being influenced by the Bullock Report, which included a chapter emphasizing the language difficulties confronting ethnic minority children together with ethnocentric bias evident in school books and in relation to dialect (cf. Watson, 1984). However, subsequent writings and reports (see above) have focused on the failure of colleges and universities to prepare teachers adequately for the multicultural society.

Craft (1981) comments, 'there emerges the developing repetition of inadequacies in initial and in-service teacher education; it is an indictment not simply of central and local government for failing to give a lead or to make resources available, but also of teacher educators, course validators and schools for failing to respond more imaginatively and with a greater sense of urgency to the growing racial problems and tensions of our day.' (p. 10).

Watson (1984) concludes, ' ... in spite of the rhetoric advocating the preparation of teachers for a multicultural society the reality is different. Most teacher education in the United Kingdom is essentially ethnocentric and very practical. "Specialists" are expected to deal with multiracial/cultural aspects of education which, in any case, are not considered to be essential for all students. The idea of multiculturalism "permeating the whole of the curriculum", as advocated by the Rampton Report and the Commission for Racial Equality, is virtually unheard of . . . . For change to come about, not only must teacher educators themselves be convinced of the value, worth or necessity of preparing teachers for a career in a multicultural society but the Government must also (a) insist on teacher training institutions providing adequate courses in multiracial/cultural education and (b) make additional funds available for both staff and materials' (p. 398). The Swann recommendations will be fervently awaited in relation to this crucial area.

James Lynch, in this volume, seeks to generate an outline typology for the staff development needs of teacher education lecturers, seen as a prerequisite to the effective introduction of multicultural teacher education. Acknowledging the apparent lethargy of British teacher education in introducing multicultural programmes, Lynch draws in particular on the work of Gay in the United States to construct, by extrapolation from proposed programmes of teacher education, the implications for the staff required to implement such programmes. The typology identifies six major dimensions of development needs: cultural/contextual; moral/affective; cognitive; pedagogical; consequential; and experiential. Within the contextual dimension much still needs to be done to make both staff and student bodies 'multicultural'. Programmes, activities and experiences to help staff 'to analyse, clarify and, as appropriate, change their racial, sex and class values, attitudes and behaviour within a liberal democratic tradition' are emphasized within the moral and affective dimension. With regard to the cognitive dimension further progress needs to be made in clarifying and defining content for teacher education, 'through which we can perceive the implications for teacher educators.' Lynch argues that this content includes a knowledge of the microcultures of society, alertness to prejudice and racism, awareness of educability and achievement as social constructs deriving from specific cultural assumptions and the implications of cultural diversity for the curriculum and teaching methods of schools. Pedagogical modes are needed that 'positively and manifestly value diversity and democratic discourse' involving behavioural change in professional action. Concerning the experiential dimension of the typology, teacher education staff release needs to be continued to allow for experience in multiracial schools and community organizations leading to the development of intercultural competence. 'One may expect teacher education to move through a number of stages from its present predominantly ethnocentric emphasis to a future state where institutionally and systematically, philosophically and practically, it would manifest an explicit and active commitment to multicultural education as one of its central core of values.'

(iv) Curriculum

Watson (*op.cit.*) claims that teachers cannot be blamed entirely for taking a cynical approach to the issue of a multicultural curriculum: 'There has been so much heated discussion about the need for a multicultural curriculum that there is a considerable degree of confusion (Mullard, 1981; Stone, 1981; Hastie, 1981)'. (See also, Verma, 1984.)

Education in Schools: A Consultative Document (DES, 1977) states: 'Our society is a multicultural, multiracial one and the curriculum should reflect a sympathetic understanding of the different cultures and races that now make up our society ... the curriculum of schools ... must reflect the needs of this new Britain' (para. 10, 11).

The Rampton Report (DES, 1981c) stated '... that the curriculum in all schools should reflect the fact that Britain is both multiracial and culturally diverse ... the intention of multicultural education is simply to provide all children with a balanced education which reflects the nature of our society . . . all heads should be prepared to develop a multicultural approach towards the curriculum.'

Critics have argued that the ethnocentric nature of much of what is taught in the classrooms has an adverse effect on both black and white children. Further, the development of self-respect is restricted and reproduces prejudice: '. . . it has become an article of faith in multicultural education that the curriculum is biased, yet how often is that assertion the product of a careful analysis of curriculum content and its images?' (Editorial, *Multiracial Education*, 1982).

Leaving aside the comment expressed by some that Britain cannot truly be called a multicultural society (Bullivant, 1981), others view multicultural education as needing recognition at certain points within the curriculum rather than permeating the curriculum. As has been emphasized in an earlier section (in this volume) some believe that racial issues have to be fervently approached. Bullivant (in the section entitled 'Multiculturalism') considers that selections for the curriculum that encourage children from ethnic backgrounds to learn about their cultural heritage, languages, histories, customs and other aspects of their life-styles have little bearing on their equality of educational opportunity and life-chances. These are influenced more by structural, social-class, economic, political and racist factors operating in the wider pluralist society and by the control exercised by dominant groups over access to social rewards and economic resources. Further, the argument can be promoted that teaching *all* children about cultural differences in their societies may reinforce and not reduce the sense of distinctiveness. 'In essence, culture is a form of ever-evolving "survival device" based on adaptive change that enables social groups to cope with the problems of living in a particular habitat. It is *this* kind of culture that children from ethno-cultural groups have to master, rather than a romanticised, fossil-culture based on utopian views of pluralism.' (Bullivant, *op.cit.*).

In similar vein Rex (in this volume) states that his goal or end-state in terms of which to judge multicultural education and the treatment of the minority child is that of 'equality of opportunity within a very competitive credentialling system of education and social selection . . . the introduction of the notion of equality of opportunity effectively ruled out those practices which acknowledged cultural differences but allowed for an inferior role for minority groups in British society' — cultural difference implies not 'being given a fair chance to compete.'

Watson (*op.cit.*) concludes, in line with his general stress on teacher education, that without reform taking place in teacher education institutions there is unlikely to be any real change in classrooms and the curriculum.

Homan, in this volume, presents an empirical study of fifteen educational agencies sponsored within ethnic minority communities. He surveys the genesis and rationale of the 'supplementary school' and its related forms, and the implications of these for state education. Not all forms of supplementary schooling imply by their existence a fundamental discontent with state provision: language classes are organized in recognition that no national system can provide for adequate tuition in all mother-tongues represented by its students. In other institutions, however, dissatisfaction with the form and style of state provision is fundamental; the discontent having academic and moral themes. Teachers have been trained in the view that there exists a stable deterministic relationship between class and educability and that working-class children may therefore be expected to perform badly or to fail because of their home background. The deterministic principle has in recent years been transferred from the working class to women and blacks, and the predispositions of low expectations have been projected upon them: 'on all the evidence of morale, behaviour and achievements, the minority day school has the potential of greater efficiency.'

(v) Educational Achievement

Summarizing from an analysis of the vast literature pertaining to the 'underachievement' of minority pupils, Figueroa (1984) concludes that although some Asians and some Caribbeans are doing well within the British educational system, overall they appear (and particularly the Caribbeans) to be in an unequal position in the system. 'It seems to be failing them insofar as it does not seem to be very successful in fulfilling its educational task in their respect. This state of affairs is often conceptualised in terms of ethnic minority, especially Caribbean "underachievement". Explanations are produced in terms of the supposed individual and group characteristics of these pupils. In particular, supposed deficiencies in or problems with the character, personality, self-concept, ability, language, culture, family organisation, social background and the like in the case of the Caribbean pupils are blamed.'

Figueroa points instead to the need to investigate 'the structures, forces and processes within the educational system which result in or at least do not seem so far to have been able to change this state of affairs. There is still a lack of valid research into how the structures and processes of the educational system and of individual schools might be failing to promote the full potential of Caribbean pupils.' The school and the educational system as a whole could be expected to adjust to the needs of the pupils. The effects of the total educational system in relation to Caribbean pupils need to be assessed: the policies of the DES, LEAs, professional associations, examination boards, the staffing, organization and ethos of the schools, curriculum, teaching materials, attitudes of the teachers and pupils together with the lack of training the teachers. Although adequate research evidence is not available, there are some pointers.

According to Figueroa, more Caribbean pupils than their peers transfer beyond the fifth form to further education than remain in school (Craft and Craft, 1983); reading scores of Caribbean pupils become worse over the years of schooling (Payne, 1974; Little, 1975; Mabey, 1981); there is a significant incidence of misplacement of Caribbean pupils into ESN schools (Coard, 1971); West Indian pupils are overrepresented in school sports teams (Carrington, 1983); there is stereotyping of Caribbean pupils (Tomlinson, 1982); there are negative reactions to Creole (Edwards, 1978, 1979); and the ethos and curriculum of schools are covertly racist or culturally biased (Figueroa and Swart, 1982).

Jeffcoate (1984) in similar vein comments that the discussion of the causes of West Indian underachievement has certainly been a replication in miniature of the discussion of the causes of working-class underachievement — ' "nature" versus "nurture"; "deficit" versus "difference"; "inadequate" homes versus "inadequate" schools.' Radicals have stressed ' "the racialist attitudes and the racist practices in the larger society and in the educational system itself" — as the decisive factor; with particular stress being laid upon prejudices and stereotypes harboured by the teaching profession.' Jeffcoate focuses on data which contradict the above, thereby increasing the momentum of the debate.

Tomlinson comments that the debate on the educational achievement of ethnic minority pupils seems likely to continue for some time. She argues that one reason for this is that the factors responsible for educational achievement are still held to be largely psychogenic — 'underachievement' is seen as an individual failure. Tomlinson contends that achievement must be systematically related to the structure and processes of the education system and the wider social structure. Additional to the issue of the measures used to assess ability is the question of whether the theory of 'underachievement' has become a more acceptable replacement for older theories of cultural deprivation and disadvantage — 'underachievement' has become an acceptable theory to imply that some measure of achievement has occurred but not all that an individual is capable of striving for. She maintains that educators may continue to feel absolved from scrutinizing their own practices and the structures and processes of education if the 'underachievement' of black pupils continues to be such a powerful commonsense belief. Further, there are the 'disturbing and empirically untrue connections' between educational failure, high unemployment and participation in social disorder. There is now evidence that in some inner-city areas black youths leave school as well or better qualified than whites at the lower educational levels, being more anxious to achieve more qualifications than white youths. Their failure to acquire employment does not necessarily depend on their educational qualifications. 'To construct elaborate explanations for any lower achievement of black children in societies which have built practices which disadvantage minorities . . . into their social institutions . . . could be held to be a pointless activity.' The relationship of educational structures and processes to the wider society, as they affect minorities, must be examined, otherwise there will continue to be misleading associations made between 'achievement' and the social behaviours of minority groups.

Berry focuses on the cognitive variation across cultures and the sources of this variation. This analysis is not concerned with the quantitative approach in relation to 'general intelligence' but a more qualitative notion of 'cognitive styles'. The effects of ecological and cultural factors on the development of cognitive styles are examined, using the Field Dependent-Field Independent cognitive style of Witkin and the ecocultural model of Berry. Individuals are different from one another in cognitive style. Berry argues that to the extent that ecological and cultural factors play a communal role, it can also be said that *groups* are likely to differ in cognitive style as well. Acculturational influences may work, both before and after immigration, to reduce these large cultural variations; however, cultural groups do tend to persist in traditional patterns of behaviour in their new home. Host societies are thus likely to encounter nearly the full range of these cross-cultural differences among immigrant peoples. Cultural diversity needs to be recognized as a resource rather than a problem. 'To ignore these stylistic differences is to court the incorrect (and unjust) interpretations which have stemmed from the unilinear "general intelligence" position — that differences are deficits, rather than qualitative variations which can enrich a school, a community and a nation.'

(vi)   Equality of Opportunity

'The new stage in multicultural thinking prioritises the demand for equality rather than integration or the recognition of cultural diversity.' Hatcher and Shallice (1983) expand on this statement with the proviso: 'This is a positive advance, provided that the notion of equality is not divorced from racial oppression and used to subsume black children into some general category of disadvantage. However, the way that equality is often posed, even by radical multiculturalists, as a free-floating notion, not rooted in the realities of class society, means that it remains within the traditional and utopian perspective of liberal social-democratic conceptions of educational egalitarianism' (p. 11).

It is pertinent to recall the equality of opportunity debate that reached its climax in the late 1960s and early 1970s in relation to the Educational Priority Areas emphasis. Hatcher and Shallice comment that the Halsey Report, *Educational Priority*, was perhaps the most radical point reached by social policy. Halsey argued that all previous attempts to overcome working-class educational disadvantage had failed and that even the EPAs would fail unless they were part of a 'comprehensive social movement towards community development'. Hatcher and Shallice consider that Halsey's proposals proved too radical and were never really taken up because the proposed reforms were not related to the social forces that were capable of carrying them out. They relied solely on the state for implementation. Multiculturalists need to base their objectives on the social forces of the black communities themselves and the wider working class of which teachers are 'in the overwhelming majority a part. Only they have the social weight to begin to impose their educational interests on the State and disown reactionary teachers. And their activity around educational demands will be the most powerful factor in winning liberal teachers to serious anti-racial education' (p. 16).

Rex's goal or the end-state in terms of which he proposes to judge multicultural education and the treatment of the minority child in school is that of equality of opportunity within a very competitive credentialling system of education and social selection. Rex argues that the introduction of the notion of equality of opportunity effectively rules out those practices which acknowledge cultural difference but allow for an inferior role for minority groups in British society — cultural difference implies not being given a fair chance to compete. Rex sets out the kind of specific policies which would be relevant to the attainment of equality of opportunity within the educational system and which do not currently form a normal part of the agenda of the multicultural education debate. They include the allocation of school places, particularly in secondary schools, the medium of instruction at the moment of entry to school, the teaching of mother tongue, the teaching of English as a second language at basic levels, the maintenance of minority cultures, the teaching of English as a second language at more sophisticated levels, the provision of courses at examination levels in minority languages, history and culture, specific teaching to combat racism and the modificaton of the curriculum as a whole and for all children in ways that give recognition to minority cultures. When examining educational failure it is important to realise that crude racial and ethnic statistics are always misleading . . . exploration of third variables, on the other hand, would include such factors as parents' occupation, parents' education, membership of one-parent families, housing conditions, children's experience of not only teachers but also other white professionals (including the police), the selective processes as they actually operate in schools and other similar factors . . . . In such a statistical analysis both school system factors and extra-school factors would have to be sharply defined and considered . . . neither existing practice nor the attempt to improve that practice by the sorts of inquiry which have been conducted measures up to our critical standards.'

Multicultural Education: The Interminable Debate

James Banks, in this volume, reviews the various orientations to the multicultural debate and discusses the arguments. He forecasts a 'rough road' ahead in both Britain and the United States. While multicultural education 'is being harshly criticized by both left and right, it is searching for its soul and *raison d'être.*'

Multicultural education is not about exotica but about *all* the people in a plural society and about the interdependent nature of the world. A rational debate on the issues outlined should continue, without premature specialization at a trivial level, and without a degeneration of the debate into political rhetoric or dogma.

References

BULLIVANT, B. (1981) *The Pluralist Dilemma in Education*, Sydney, Allen and Unwin.
CARBY, H. (1980) 'Multi-Culture', *Screen Education*, Spring.
CARRINGTON, B. (1983) 'Sport as a side-track: An analysis of West Indian involvement in extra-curricular sport', in BARTON, L. and WALKER, S. (Eds), *Race, Class and Education*, London, Croom Helm.
COARD, B. (1971) *How the West Indian Child is Made Educationally Sub-Normal in the British School System*, London, New Beacon Books.
CRAFT, M. (Ed.) (1981) *Teaching in a Multicultural Society: The Task for Teacher Education*, Lewes, Falmer Press.
CRAFT, M. (Ed.) (1984) *Education and Cultural Pluralism*, Lewes, Falmer Press.
CRAFT, M. and ATKINS, M.J. (1983) *Training Teachers of Ethnic Minority Community Languages*, University of Nottingham.
CRAFT, M. and CRAFT, A. (1983) 'The participation of ethnic minority pupils in further and higher education', *Educational Research*, 25, 1, pp. 10–19.
CROZIER, G (1983) 'Reviews', *Multiracial Education*, 11, 2, pp. 53–4.

DES (1971) *Educational Survey 13. The Education of Immigrants*, London, HMSO.
DES (1972) *Educational Priority: EPA Problems and Policies ('Halsey Report')*, London, HMSO.
DES (1975) *A Language for Life ('Bullock Report')*, London, HMSO.
DES (1977) *Education in Schools: A Consultative Document*, London, HMSO.
DES (1978) *Special Educational Needs ('Warnock Report')*, London, HMSO.
DES (1979) *Aspects of Secondary Education in England*, London, HMSO.
DES (1980) *Towards a Core Curriculum*, London, HMSO.
DES (1981a) *Primary Education in England*, London, HMSO.
DES (1981b) *The School Curriculum*, London, HMSO.
DES (1981c) *West Indian Children in Our Schools ('Rampton Report')*, London, HMSO.
DES (1983) *Teaching Quality*, London, HMSO.
DHONDY, F. (1978) 'The black explosion in schools', *Race Today*, May.
EDWARDS, V.K. (1978) 'Language, attitudes and underperformance in West Indian children', *Educational Review*, 30, 1, pp. 51–8.
EDWARDS, V.K. (1979) *The West Indian Language Issue in British Schools*, London, Routledge and Kegan Paul.
FIGUEROA, P.M.E. (1984) 'Minority pupil progress', in CRAFT, M. (Ed.), *Education and Cultural Pluralism*, Lewes, Falmer Press, pp. 117–42.
FIGUEROA, P.M.E. and SWART, L.T. (1982) *Poor Achievers and High Achievers among Ethnic Minority Pupils*, Report to the Commission for Racial Equality.
GILL, D. (1982) 'The contribution of secondary school geography to multicultural education: A critical review of some materials', *Multiracial Education*, 10, 3, pp. 13–26.
GREEN, A. (1982) 'In defence of anti-racist teaching: A reply to recent critiques of multicultural education', *Multiracial Education*, 10, 2, pp. 19–35.
HASTIE, T. (1981) 'Why pay for an "industry" that grows fat on social discord?' *Daily Telegraph*, 30 March.
HATCHER, R. and SHALLICE, J. (1983) 'The politics of anti-racist education', *Multiracial Education*, 12, 1, pp. 3–21.
HMSO (1969) *The Problems of Coloured School Leavers*. A Report by the House of Commons Select Committee on Race Relations and Immigration. London.
HMSO (1972) *Teacher Education and Training. ('James Report')*, London.
HMSO (1973) *Education*. A Report by the House of Commons Select Committee on Race Relations and Immigration. Sessions 1972–73, 3 vols. London.
HMSO (1975) *A Language for Life ('Bullock Report')*, London.
HOME OFFICE (1981) *The Brixton Disorders ('Scarman Report')*, London, HMSO.
HOUSE OF COMMONS (1981) *Racial Disadvantage*, 5th Report of the Home Affairs Committee, London, HMSO.
JEFFCOATE, R. (1984) 'Ideologies and multicultural education', in CRAFT, M. (Ed.), *Education and Cultural Pluralism*, Lewes, Falmer Press.
KATZ, J. (1982) 'Multicultural education: Games educators play', *Multiracial Education*, 10, 2, pp. 11–18.
LITTLE, A. (1975) 'The educational achievement of ethnic minority children in London schools', in VERMA, G.K. and BAGLEY, C. (Eds), *Race and Education across Cultures*, London, Heinemann.
LITTLE, A. and WILLEY, R. (1981) *Multi-ethnic Education: The Way Forward*, London, Schools Council.
LITTLE, A. and WILLEY, R. (1983) *Studies in the Multi-Ethnic Curriculum*, London, Schools Council.
MABEY, C. (1981) 'Black British literacy: A study of reading attainment of London black children from 8 to 15 years', *Educational Research*, 23, 2, pp. 83–95.
MULLARD, C. (1981) 'Black kids in white schools: Multiracial education in Britain', *Plural Societies*, 12, 1/2.
MULLARD, C. (1982) *Racism, Society, Schools: History, Policy and Practices*, Occasional Paper No. 1, Centre for Multicultural Education, University of London Institute of Education.

Multiracial Education (1982) Journal, National Association for Multiracial Education, 10, 2, pp. 1–4.

Multiracial Education (1983) Journal, National Association for Multiracial Education, 11, 3, pp. 1–4.

PAYNE, J. (1974) *Educational Priority: EPA Surveys and Statistics*, Vol. 2, London, HMSO.

RILEY, K. (1982) 'Policing the police, teaching the teachers: Scarman, Rampton and MPs read the riot lessons', *Multiracial Education*, 10, 2, pp. 3–11.

SCHOOLS COUNCIL (1970) *Immigrant Children in Infant Schools*, London: Evans.

STONE, M. (1981) *The Education of the Black Child in Britain: The Myth of Multiracial Education*, Glasgow, Fontana.

TOMLINSON, S. (1982) *A Sociology of Special Education*, London, Routledge and Kegan Paul.

TOWNSEND, H.E.R. and BRITTAN, E. (1972) *Organisation in Multiracial Schools*, Windsor, National Foundation for Educational Research.

VERMA, G.K. (1984) 'Multiculturalism and education: Prelude to practice' in VERMA, G.K. and BAGLEY, C. (Eds) *Race Relations and Cultural Differences*. London, Croom Helm.

VERMA, G.K. and ASHWORTH, B. (1985) *Ethnicity and Educational Achievement*, London, Macmillan.

VERMA, G.K. and BAGLEY, C. (1984) (Eds) *Race Relations and Cultural Differences*. London, Croom Helm.

WATSON, K. (1984) 'Training teachers in the United Kingdom for a multicultural society: The rhetoric and the reality', *Journal of Multilingual and Multicultural Development*, 5, 5, pp. 385–400.

2   The Concept of Multi-Cultural Education

Bhikhu Parekh

The idea of multi-cultural education has gained considerable currency in Britain during the last ten years, and has become a subject of acute controversy. For the conservative critics, it represents an attempt to politicize education in order to pander to minority demands, whereas for some radicals it is the familiar ideological device of perpetuating the reality of racist exploitation of ethnic minorities by pampering their cultural sensitivities. In this paper I propose to do three things: first, to elucidate the meaning and implications of the concept of multi-cultural education; second, to show why it is desirable; and third, to assess the validity of the criticisms made of it.

I

According to the traditional and widely accepted view of education, it seeks to achieve the following objectives. First, it aims to cultivate such basic human capacities as critical reflection, imagination, self-criticism, the ability to reason, argue, weigh up evidence and to form an independent judgment of one's own. It is hoped that as a result of acquiring these and other related capacities, the pupil will one day become capable of self-determination and live a free man's life, that is, a life free from ignorance, prejudices, superstitions and dogmas and one in which he freely chooses his beliefs and plans his pattern of life. Second, it aims to foster such intellectual and moral qualities as the love of truth, openness to the world, objectivity, intellectual curiosity, humility, healthy scepticism about all claims to finality and respect and concern for others. Third, it aims to familiarize the pupil with the great intellectual, moral, religious, literary and other achievements of the human spirit. It is concerned to initiate him not merely into the cultural capital of his own community but of the entire mankind in so far as this is possible, and thus to humanize rather than merely socialize him. He is to be taught the languages, history, geography, culture, social structures, religions and so on of other communities in order that his sympathies and affections are enlarged and he learns to appreciate the unity and diversity of mankind.

While this view of education is intellectually persuasive and more coherent than its rivals, it suffers from a serious defect. It is sociologically naive and does not take account of the way in which its realization in practice is constantly frustrated by the social context in which every educational system exists and functions. As a result its advocates do not generally appreciate the extent to which their practice falls short of it, nor explore how the practice can be improved.

An educational system does not exist in a historical and social vacuum. It is an integral part of a specific social structure by which it is profoundly shaped. A social structure, further, is not a homogeneous whole, but composed of different classes, religions and communities. If it is to endure, it must develop a common public culture, that is, a generally shared body of values, beliefs, attitudes and assumptions about man and society. Of the diverse and even conflicting cultures that obtain in any lively society, one generally acquires dominance. It is presented as *the* culture of that society and is embodied in its legal, moral, political, economic, educational and other institutions and becomes its official or dominant public culture. The educational system disseminates the dominant culture among the young and ensures its preservation and reproduction across the generations. Its structure, organization, ethos, pedagogical techniques, its view of what constitutes knowledge and what is worth teaching are all profoundly shaped by the dominant culture. What is more, it does not merely disseminate but also legitimizes the dominant culture. The school is an authoritarian institution in the sense that the teachers wield both intellectual and legal authority; they know the subject whereas their pupils do not, and they have the power to punish and discipline their pupils. By deciding to teach X rather than Y, they proclaim that X is *worth* studying and Y is not, and throw the full weight of their intellectual and legal authority behind it. Similarly by teaching X in a certain manner, they imply that this is the only correct way of looking at it.

Education then is not culturally neutral. Its intellectual content and orientation is permeated by the world-view characteristic of the dominant culture. Further education is not apolitical either. It cultivates specific attitudes and values. In so far as these assist and conduce to the maintenance of a particular type of social and political order, it is also a political activity and cannot be politically neutral. All this means that although an educational system may avow the ideals of freedom, objectivity, independent thought, universality of knowledge, intellectual curiosity, and so on, in actual practice it often does little more than initiate and even indoctrinate its pupils into the dominant culture. To put it differently, it claims to provide *liberating* or liberal education, that is, education in and for freedom; in reality it only provides *Liberal* education, that is, education into the kind of culture that has become dominant in the West since the eighteenth century. The point can be illustrated by taking the example of the English educational system.

II

Although perhaps less so than the educational systems of many other Western countries, the English educational system has a deep mono-cultural orientation. And although the orientation has diminished during the last few decades, it is still pervasive. This is evident in the organization, personnel, the structure of authority, the curriculum, the pedagogical techniques, the competitive ethos, and so on, of our schools. Our schools have a fair number of Jewish, Indian, Pakistani, Chinese, West Indian, and other ethnic minority children. One would naturally expect, even require, them to adjust to the long-established structure and rules of their schools. Equally it would not be unreasonable to expect the schools to respect their children's sensitivities in areas that matter to them deeply and do not defeat the basic objectives of the school. The school's response, however, has been largely negative.

A large number of Hindu children are vegetarians, and Muslim children do not eat pork. Muslim girls and even some Hindu girls hold certain norms of modesty and are deeply averse to undressing in a common room, or wearing swimming costumes, or wearing shorts in a gymnasium. The Asian and West Indian children spontaneously tend to speak to each other in their own languages on school premises. Nearly all Asian children are non-Christian and find the traditional religious assembly a perplexing and pointless exercise. Many of their parents have poor English and occasionally need their children's help when visiting a hospital or a doctor's surgery. There is no reason why schools cannot accommodate minority sensitivities and needs in these areas by making small adjustments in their rules and organization. In fact, however, many school authorities have shown little willingness to alter the school menu, admit alternative dresses in gymnasiums, offer freedom of choice of sport, condone occasional absence of their pupils or exempt them from their daily assembly or give it a multi-faith orientation. And some even forbid them to speak their own languages on the school premises. In their view, a request for a small adjustment is really a plea for a privileged treatment and poses a mortal threat to their very identity. They cannot understand why anyone should be different, why everyone cannot eat the same food, dress the same way, hold the same ideas of propriety and modesty, speak the same language and profess the same religion as their white children do.

The mono-cultural orientation is evident also in what the schools teach and the way they teach. Our curriculum on religious studies largely concentrates on Christianity, and either ignores other religions or goes over them in a confused and cursory manner. Christianity is presented as the greatest or even the only true religion, and others are dismissed as 'primitive' and 'quaint' or of inferior quality. Islam is said to be 'fanatical' and 'dogmatic', whereas the Pope or the Anglican church affirming similar traditional dogmas is held up as a champion of 'eternal verities'. Little attempt is made to raise the pupil above his own religious beliefs and to get him to enter into the spirit of other religions, appreciate their visions of human predicament, understand their complex symbols and imagery, and respect and enjoy them as diverse and fascinating achievements of the human spirit.

Our history curriculum is little better. It concentrates on the history of Britain and, to some extent, parts of Europe and America, and ignores the great non-Western civilizations. Africa is dismissed as a dark continent whose inhabitants never really rose above animal life, and the Asian societies are all supposed to have been governed by despots who lived by plunder and hardly allowed the development of culture and civilization. There are history textbooks still in use which proclaim the glory of Europe and present other societies as if they had neither history nor culture before the Europeans 'discovered' them. Professor Hugh Trevor-Roper writes:

> Perhaps in the future there will be some African history to teach, but at present there is none, or very little; there is only the history of Europeans in Africa, the rest is largely darkness, like the history of pre-European, pre-Columbian America, and darkness is not a subject for history.

Trevor-Roper, who only reiterates here views articulated by Hegel, Marx, J.S. Mill and others, does not care to explain what he means by history, why he defines only certain types of events as historic or even historical, why *his* ignorance of the African history should be taken to imply that the latter does not exist, nor why we should accept his impertinent assumption that what does not exist for *him* does not exist *at all*. A child raised on such a narcissistic diet can hardly be expected to develop sympathetic imagination and acquire much respect for, or even curiosity about, non-European cultures. Mercifully we are becoming increasingly sensitive to the narrow nationalistic bias of our history books. We need to combat Eurocentric and racist bias as well.

Like history, our geography curriculum also heavily concentrates on Britain and some parts of Europe and America, and ignores the rest of the world. When other countries than Britain are discussed, the emphasis is on the locations of towns, cities, rivers, mountains, climate, crops, resources and topography of different parts of the world, and so on. We pay little attention to their people, their culture, their modes of dress, habits of food, arts, and forms of social organization, and explain how their different ways of walking, talking, dressing, eating, treating animals and worshipping mountains and rivers make eminent sense within the context of their climate and natural habitat. We do not locate other societies against their natural background, bring them alive to our pupils, lift the latter out of their prejudices and conventional stereotypes, and stimulate them to participate imaginatively in the vastly diverse forms of life created by intelligent men in other parts of the world.

Other parts of the curriculum are equally narrow in their content and treated in an equally biased manner. The curriculum on social studies rarely steps outside Britain. Home economics includes little more than British and to some extent European styles of food. English literature does not generally include literary works in English by non-Western writers. Art and music taught in our schools are almost wholly European, and those of other cultures are not only not taught but treated as primitive and clumsy. The importance of learning foreign languages has yet to be fully appreciated in our schools. An attitude to a language reflects an attitude to the people who speak it. If one valued and took sympathetic interest in other societies, one would wish to know more about them by learning their languages. Not to encourage a pupil to master another language is not only to shut him off from a different way of understanding and experiencing the world, but also to suggest that he is unlikely to derive much benefit from it.

III

Let us now briefly explore the impact of this type of mono-cultural education (whether in Britain or elsewhere) on the child and how it measures up to the objectives the school claims to achieve.

First, it is unlikely to awaken his curiosity about other societies and cultures either because he is not exposed to them at all or because they are presented in uncomplimentary terms, or both. Thus our curriculum on religious studies is hardly likely to inspire him to enquire how some non-Christian religions manage to do without the idea of God as the creator of the universe, or have very different views of prophets, or conceive human destiny and come to terms with death and suffering in very different ways. A child exposed to no other religion but his own grows up asking only those questions that it encourages him to ask. And since he asks only those questions that his religion answers, he finds its answers satisfactory. In other words, he never gets out of its framework, and never feels disturbed or perplexed enough to explore other religions. What is true of religious studies in equally true of history, geography, literature, social studies and so on, none of which is likely to stimulate his curiosity about other civilizations and societies.

Second, mono-cultural education is unlikely to develop the faculty of imagination. Imagination represents the ability to conceive alternatives; that is, it is the capacity to recognize that things can be done, societies can be organized and activities can be performed in several different ways, of which the most familiar is but one and not necessarily the best. Imagination does not develop in a vacuum. It is only when one is exposed to different societies and cultures that one's imagination is stimulated and the consciousness of alternatives becomes an inseparable part of one's ways of thinking. One cannot then think of anything, be it an activity, a form of enquiry, a culture or a society without at the same time realizing that it can be conceptualized or thought about or conducted in several different ways. And this awareness of alternatives radically alters one's perspective to the way it is organized in one's own environment. One cannot avoid asking *why* it is organized in a particular manner in one's society, and *if* this way of organizing it is better than others. Mono-cultural education blots out the awareness of alternatives and restricts imagination. It cannot avoid encouraging the illusion that the limits of one's world are the limits of the world itself, and that the conventional way of doing things is the only natural way.

Third, mono-cultural education stunts the growth of the critical faculty. A child taught to look at the world from the narrow perspective of his own culture and not exposed to any other is bound to reject all that cannot be accommodated within the narrow categories of his own way of looking at the world. He judges other cultures and societies by the norms and standards derived from his own, and predictably finds them odd and even worthless. And since he judges his society in terms of its own norms, he can never take a genuinely critical attitude to it. Further, as we saw, mono-cultural education blunts imagination, and therefore the child lacks the sharp awareness of alternatives that alone can give a cutting edge to his critical faculties. Unable to criticize his society and unable to appreciate alternatives, he can hardly avoid admiring its 'glory' and the 'genius' and greatness of his 'race', and remains vulnerable to the deadly vice of narcissism.

Fourth, mono-cultural education tends to breed arrogance and insensitivity. The child who is not encouraged to study other cultures and societies or to study them with sympathy and imagination cannot develop a respect for them. Imprisoned within the framework of his own culture, he cannot understand and appreciate differences nor accept diversity of values, beliefs, dress, food, ways of life and views of the world as an integral part of the human condition. He does not welcome, let alone rejoice in, diversity. Naturally he feels threatened by it and does not know how to cope with it. He approaches the world on his own terms, expecting it to adjust to him and seeing no reason why he should adjust to it. This leads to arrogance and double standards and, what is but a converse of it, an attitude of hypocrisy. When he visits other countries, he sees no need to learn their languages and adjust to their customs, whereas he expects others visiting his own to speak his language and accept its customs. If an outsider makes a mistake in speaking his language or pronouncing his name, he is quietly corrected and even mocked. If, on the other hand, he makes similar mistakes, this is 'only to be expected' and, indeed, he even expects to be complimented for attempting to learn a foreign language or pronounce a foreign name. In short, he makes demands on others that they are not allowed to make on him, and he judges others by standards they are not supposed to apply to him.

Fifth, mono-cultural education provides a fertile ground for racism. Since a pupil knows very little about other societies and cultures, he can only respond to them in terms of superficial generalizations and stereotypes. These, in turn, are not haphazard products of individual imagination but culturally derived. A culture not informed by a sensitive appreciation of others cannot but judge them in terms of its own norms. It sets itself up as an absolute, that is, as the only universally valid point of reference, and evaluates others in terms of their approximation to it. The greater the degree to which they resemble it, the more civilized or developed they are supposed to be. And conversely the more they diverge from it, the more uncivilized they are judged to be. This is indeed how the Victorians built up a hierarchy of human societies. They placed the African societies at the bottom, the Asians a little higher, the Mediterranean still higher, and so on until they got to the English whom they regarded as representing the highest stage of human development. When asked why other societies should have remained backward and one's own should be so advanced, the usual tendency was, and is, to give a racist explanation. It is the 'genius' of the English 'race' that has enabled it to achieve such great heights, and conversely the misfortunes of other societies are due to the inferiority of their 'race'. Such an attitude, albeit in an attenuated form, is still discernible in our text-books and in the attitudes of some of our teachers. It should hardly surprise us that white children grow up thinking of non-whites as racially and inherently inferior.

We have so far considered the impact of mono-cultural education on white children. We may now briefly consider its impact on their black peers. The latter obviously suffer from the same consequences as the former. In addition they also suffer from other sets of consequences.

The white children raised on a mono-cultural diet look at their black peers through the prism of the stereotypes they have acquired from their education. They find it difficult to accept them as equals, relax in their presence, appreciate their desire to retain their distinct cultural identity, and generally treat them with a mixture of contempt and pity. For their part, the black children either reciprocate the hostility, or bend over backwards to conform to their white peers' expectations and in so doing alienate their parents and less conformist peers. Like the white children, some white teachers have grown up on a mono-cultural diet and share their cultural arrogance and insensitivity. Consciously or unconsciously they approach their black pupils with the familiar stereotypes; they expect little of them, tend not to stretch them to their fullest, and fail to provide them with necessary educational and emotional support and encouragement. Not surprisingly many black children tend to under-achieve, rarely feel relaxed at school, lack trust in their teachers and go through the school with a cartload of frustrations and resentment.

When constantly fed on an ethnocentric curriculum that presents their communities and cultures in a highly biased and unflattering manner, black children can hardly avoid developing a deep sense of inferiority and worthlessness. They feel that they belong to a 'race' which is culturally deficient and scarred by grave defects of character and intelligence; and that their ancestors have contributed 'nothing' to the growth of human civilization, invented nothing of which others should take note, composed nothing which others could read with profit, built no empires, left behind nothing that is worth preserving or even cherishing, and indeed had lived such a fragile and primitive life that, but for the white colonizers, they would have by now become extinct. The impact of all this on the self-respect and identity of a black child and on his relations with his parents, brothers, elders and indeed with the members of his community in general is shattering. Lacking a sense of worth, he develops self-pity and self-hatred. He resents his parents for what they are and what they have done to him. He feels they have nothing worthwhile to teach or transmit to him; and that diminishes his respect for them, and consequently their authority over him. With their authority diminished, the parents feel compelled to rely on physical force to maintain a modicum of order in the family.

Like his relation with his parents, the black child's relations with other members of his family and community suffer a deep distortion. At one level he feels that he is one of them; at another level he feels like a total stranger. When he is with them, he recalls all that he has read and heard about them and cannot help thinking what his white friends would think and feel if they were there. He knows that they would find his compatriots noisy, loud, talking in funny ways, doing strange things, eating weird food, and so on; and he finds himself saying all this to himself silently and without any outward sign lest he should hurt those he loves and cares for . At times he gets caught thinking thoughts the others had often suspected him of harbouring and which they had themselves often half-thought. He denies it all or makes a self-righteous confession; in either case, he is full of rage and soon of tears. He wonders how he will cope with it the next time round.

The black child raised on a mono-cultural diet in an English school experiences profound self-alienation. His colour and his affections bind him to his people; the culture he is in the process of acquiring distances him from them. His birth and his destiny, his past and his future, point in wholly different and incompatible directions. His present is nothing but a battleground between his present and his future, and he is not quite sure which will eventually win. He feels suspended between two worlds; he half-wishes to leave one but he cannot, and it would not let go of him either; he half-wishes to embrace the other, but fears that he cannot and that it will not accept him either.

IV

If what we have said so far is not wholly mistaken, the consequences of mono-cultural education are disturbing. It damages and impoverishes all children, black or white. So far as white children are concerned, it restricts the growth of imagination, curiosity and critical self-reflection, and encourages narcissism, moral insensitivity and arrogance. It prevents them from appreciating the great ingenuity with which the human spirit copes with problems of human existence and develops so many different types of culture, religion, morality, social structure, systems of belief, and so on. It restricts their range of moral sympathy and denies them access to several finer feelings and sentiments that their own culture ignores or underemphasizes. What happens to white children also happens to the black. In addition they suffer from a sense of worthlessness, self-pity, confusion of identity, self-alienation, a self-divided and schizophrenic consciousness and a haunting fear of losing their roots.

If we are worried about these consequences, we should explore ways of releasing our educational system from its mono-cultural prison and opening it up to the liberating influences of other cultural perspectives. No educational system can, of course, be wholly detached from its specific cultural milieu. If it is a lively and self-critical system, it can, however, become receptive to other cultures and endeavour to broaden its perimeters. Instead of resenting and ignoring diversity, it can welcome it and encourage its children to enter into the spirit of and appreciate other cultures, religions, ways of life, civilizations and societies. It can help them to look at the world the way others do and to realize that almost everything in experience can be construed in several different ways, some more partial than others but none wholly impartial, and that partiality can only be reduced by entering into a sympathetic and critical dialogue with others.

What is, perhaps clumsily, called multi-cultural education is ultimately nothing more than this. It is essentially an attempt to release a child from the confines of the ethnocentric straitjacket and to awaken him to the existence of other cultures, societies and ways of life and thought. It is intended to de-condition the child as much as possible in order that he can go out into the world as free from biases and prejudices as possible and able and willing to explore its rich diversity. Multi-cultural education is therefore an education in freedom — freedom *from* inherited biases and narrow feelings and sentiments, as well as freedom *to* explore other cultures and perspectives and make one's own choices in full awareness of available and practicable alternatives. Multi-cultural education is therefore not a departure from, nor incompatible with, but a further refinement of, the liberal idea of education. It does not cut off a child from his own culture; rather it enables him to enrich, refine and take a broader view of it without losing his roots in it.

The inspiring principle of multi-cultural education then is to sensitize the child to the inherent plurality of the world — the plurality of systems, belief, ways of life, cultures, modes of analyzing familiar experiences, ways of looking at historical events and so on. How it can be realized in practice is a difficult question about which a few remarks would be in order.

A school is almost like a little world with its own distinct ethos, form of organization, schedule of work, modes of interpersonal relationship, curriculum and pedagogical methods. Although the principle of multi-cultural education is more directly relevant to some of these than to the others, it has important implications for all of them. For example, the structure of the school could be so broadened as to reflect the different cultures of its pupils. The school could provide a multi-faith assembly, accommodate different dietary requirements, permit variation in dress or choice of sport, celebrate major holidays of its constituent religious communities, and so on, and thereby build plurality and diversity into its day-to-day practice. Similarly its ethos could become multi-cultural if it were to encourage its pupils to speak their languages, talk about their ways of life and customs, come to school in their conventional dress or play their music or decorate their classrooms the way they like on certain days, and so on. In these and other ways the school celebrates diversity and becomes a home for all its pupils, be they white or black, Christian or Muslim.

The area where the principle of multi-cultural education is most relevant is obviously that of the curriculum. A curriculum conceived in a multi-cultural perspective has two features. First, it is not unduly narrow. No curriculum can cover everything in the world and must of necessity be selective. However, selection can be made on various grounds, some more justified than others. Selection based on a multi-cultural perspective would aim to ensure that the child acquires some familiarity with the major representative forms of the subject in question and that, while he would concentrate on some, his curiosity would be sufficiently stimulated to lead him to follow up the rest on his own. Thus the curriculum on religious studies would include the major religions of the world and aim to enable the child to appreciate the different ways in which they conceptualize and respond to basic perplexities of human existence. Similarly the history curriculum would include the major civilizations of the world, including not only the Greco-Roman but also those such as the Chinese, Hindu and the Arab which he is unlikely to encounter in the normal course and were constituted very differently from ones with which he is already familiar.

Second, the curriculum should be taught in a manner that is as little biased and dogmatic as possible. Slavery, for example, can be seen in several different ways and is viewed very differently by the slave-owning and slave-supplying societies. Similarly, colonial rule looks very different, depending on whether one studies it from the standpoint of a metropolitan power or its colony. In other words, the so-called facts are always and necessarily impregnated with interpretations, and although some are more plausible than others, all interpretations are partial and corrigible. The curriculum should therefore be taught in a manner that alerts the pupil to this fact and leaves him free, even encourages him to examine the various interpretations and arrive at a view of his own.

The teacher needs to be equally cautious in teaching other societies, cultures, religions, moral systems and so on. He should elucidate their beliefs and practices with sympathy and sensitivity, and give an account of them as close as possible to one that would be given by someone belonging to them; ideally he should let another culture, religion or society speak for itself. It is only when this is done that evaluation of it has a meaning. However, evaluating another society in terms of the norms of one's own inevitably leads to distortion and is intellectually illegitimate. Instead, a teacher should encourage his pupils to set up a dialogue between their own and another society, exploring each in terms of the other, asking questions about another society that arise from their own and asking questions about the latter that someone from another society would wish to ask. Beyond this a teacher cannot go. He is not an arbiter between different societies; and it is not his business to deliver the final judgment. He owes it to his pupils to let them arrive at their own judgments.

Contrary to what some writers have said, the principle of multi-cultural education does not imply that other cultures *cannot* be judged. Rather that the judgment must be based on the fullest understanding of their character and complexity, and a child is hardly capable of this degree of understanding. Further, if they can be judged, so can one's own, and therefore the latter cannot be treated as sacrosanct. Again, judging a culture is a highly intricate enterprise and one must avoid the mistake of judging it on the basis of the norms and values of one's own culture. Finally, the judgment of a culture cannot be equated with the judgment of the human beings involved in the sense that, if a culture is judged to be defective, it does not follow that the human beings involved are defective and inferior.

Nor does the principle of multi-cultural education imply that different cultures, societies and religions are all *equally* good. Such a judgment presupposes a trans-cultural standard, and that is simply not available. Even as respect for all men does not commit one to the view that they are all equally good or possess an equal potential; respect for all cultures as implied in the principle of multi-cultural education does not mean that they are all equally good. Rather it means that they make sense in their own contexts, have a right to be understood in their own terms, and need to be explored with sensitivity and sympathy. Respect for a culture is not a *reward* for its achievements. Rather a culture itself is an achievement, and to respect it is to recognize it as the expression of the efforts and aspirations of a group of intelligent fellow human beings.

V

In the light of our discussion, the case for multi-cultural education can easily be made. If education is concerned to develop such basic human capacities as curiosity, self-criticism, capacity for reflection, ability to form an independent judgment, sensitivity, intellectual humility and respect for others, and to open the pupil's mind to the great achievements of mankind, then it *must* be multi-cultural in orientation. Mono-cultural education not only does not fully develop these qualities and capacities, but tends to encourage their opposites. It is simply *not* good education. That it tends to inflict grave psychological and moral damage on the ethnic minority child is a further argument against it.

The case for multi-cultural education does not in any way depend on the presence of ethnic minority children in our schools. Their presence has, no doubt, brought into sharp relief the mono-cultural orientation of our education and highlighted its consequences. However, their presence is *not* the reason for accepting multi-cultural education. As we saw, multi-cultural education is good education, whereas mono-cultural education is not. It is good for *all* children, white or black, and the case for it would be just as strong even if there were to be no ethnic minority children in our schools. Indeed the case for it would then be even stronger for, lacking the physical presence of people of different cultural backgrounds and outlooks, the educational system would have to make a special effort to awaken the white pupil to the diversity and plurality of the world.

VI

As we have outlined it, multi-cultural education is not open to the criticisms of its conservative and radical critics. The conservatives object to it on three grounds. First, it damages a good educational system by subordinating it to the demands of ethnic minorities. Second, it militates against the basic purpose of education, namely to initiate future citizens into a common public culture without which a society cannot be held together. And third, multi-cultural education is socially divisive as it accentuates the cultural self-consciousness of the ethnic minorities, and prevents their integration into British society.

The first criticism is obviously mistaken. As we saw, the case for multi-cultural education does not depend on the presence of ethnic minority children in our schools. It is desirable for no other reason than that it is *good* education for all children, white or black. Further, to argue for multi-cultural education is not to imply that the English educational system is not good, rather that it can be made even better. As for the second criticism, education is concerned with a much wider objective than initiating a pupil into a common public culture. Indeed, if this were its sole purpose, it would be difficult to distinguish it from indoctrination. Further, to advocate multi-cultural education is not to deny the need for a common public culture, but only to argue that the common culture could be less rigid and biased. As for the third criticism, there is no reason why the heightened self-consciousness of the ethnic minority should militate against their integration. The Polish-Americans or the Irish-Americans are no less American for being Polish or Irish. Further, the conservative model of social integration is likely to be even more divisive as it is intolerant of differences and requires the ethnic minorities to obliterate their cultural identity as a price for social integration. The price is bound to be resented, and is in any case too high. Finally, multi-cultural education does not subvert social integration, rather it offers a different model of it. It asks for a loosening of the cultural rigidity of British society so that a social space is created for the ethnic minorities to grow without endangering its unity.

The writers on the Left criticize multi-cultural education on very different grounds. In their view education should aim, among other things, to remove racism, and multi-cultural education cannot do this as the roots of racism lie too deep to be affected by cosmetic tinkering with curriculum, school assemblies, and so on. They would replace multi-cultural education with anti-racist education. Second, multi-cultural education not only leaves racism untouched but strengthens it. It lulls the ethnic minorities into a false sense of self-complacency by encouraging them to think that multi-cultural education will give their children a positive self-image and make their white peers more hospitable. Third, multi-cultural education defuses black resistance by diverting it into harmless channels. Like the rest of the 'race relations industry' of which it is an important part, it 'pacifies' ethnic minorities and coopts them into British society. Fourth, in viewing racism as a simple matter of attitudes, multi-cultural education depoliticizes it and ignores its social and economic roots. It fails to appreciate the fundamental fact that racism is an ideological rationalization of the exploitation and domination of the blacks by the whites and will continue unabated until such time as the inequality and domination are ended.

Although they highlight the limits of multi-cultural education, these and other similar criticisms are not persuasive. The so-called anti-racist education is likely to be either not education at all but anti-racist propaganda, or is in substance little different from multi-cultural education as we have outlined it. Racism cannot be eliminated by reiterating a million times that all races are equal. White children do not think so, and have to be confronted patiently with facts and arguments. Even this is hardly enough for they may accept that all races are equal, and yet avoid blacks. One therefore needs to awaken their curiosity, get them to take an interest in black students' culture, appreciate their tragic historical treatment by the whites, and so on. In short, one needs to embark on multi-cultural education. Indeed, a careful examination of the curriculum developed by the advocates of anti-racist education would show that it is not very different from the multi-cultural curriculum as we have suggested it. Further, the impact of the ethos of the school and especially of the curriculum on its pupils is so deep that it makes little sense to describe changes in them as merely cosmetic. It makes little sense either to say that a minority child who has, as a result of multi-cultural education, learnt to respect himself lacks the will to fight racism in society at large. In fact the opposite is generally the case. Again, it is true that multi-cultural education concentrates on changing attitudes. However, it is a *non-sequitur* to conclude that it therefore regards racism as *merely* a matter of attitude. Its advocates recognize that racism is closely tied up with the inequality of economic and political power, but believe that the school *qua* school can do little about it.

Racism is obviously an evil and must be fought. The question, however, is how, and what role the school can play. Racism is sustained by both social attitudes and the vast economic and political inequality between the races. It cannot be eliminated unless one attacks both. So far as the latter is concerned, the school has little direct role to play. It cannot spearhead a political movement, and if it ever tried to do so, it would lose its educational character and become an arena of struggle between large social and political forces over which it can exercise no control. Its energies must be primarily concentrated on combating racist attitudes. It can do this in several ways. It must take a stern view of racist insults and attacks in the school, forbid racist propaganda and ensure that racism is outlawed within its premises. It must create an environment in which minority children are able to relax, grow, develop their full potential, acquire pride and self-respect and build up easy social relations with their white peers. Without becoming aggressive and artificial, it should explain to its pupils how racist ideas developed in the context of the colonial encounter, how the blacks were systematically exploited and degraded, and why racism is an incoherent and self-contradictory doctrine. Above all, the school should aim to cultivate in its white pupils an attitude of respect for ethnic minority cultures, a measure of intellectual and moral humility in their judgment of them, a sensitive understanding of their beliefs and practices, and so on. In these and other ways the school can hope to undercut the intellectual and moral roots of racism and weaken it. It cannot, of course, hope to eliminate it altogether, for education has its limits and the social and political roots of racism lie beyond the control of the school. However, it can make its distinctive contribution by tackling the intellectual and moral basis of racism that is amenable to and indeed falls within its purview. To ask it to do more is perhaps the surest way to ensure that it will not be able to do even this much.

3 Towards Radical Multiculturalism: Resolving Tensions in Curriculum and Educational Planning

Brian Bullivant

A recurring phenomenon of the perennial search for solutions to the problems of educating children from ethno-cultural and racial minorities in English-speaking pluralist societies has been the regular historical evolution of ideologies of pluralism. Each in its turn has been promoted as *the* solution, only to have its weaknesses exposed, and to be superseded by another. Thus, in such countries as the United States, Canada, Britain, Australia and New Zealand we have seen numerous ideologies come and go: assimilation, melting pot, integration, cultural mosaic, biculturalism, multiracialism. Each has influenced educational planning, policy-making and the curriculum, often with wasteful expense and duplication of research and development. For the time being educationists in these pluralist societies have adopted, or are moving into, multicultural education as the claimed panacea to cure the ills that beset their educational systems. This and its legitimating ideology of multiculturalism show all the signs of developing into a bandwagon, if not an educational juggernaut.

A disturbing feature of this approach is that it seems to be based on the same conventional wisdom about pluralist and compensatory education as previous approaches. That is, given sufficient intercultural understanding and goodwill between members of ethnic groups, enough government funding and the kind of democratic liberal idealism that has long characterized Western societies, the problems of achieving intercultural understanding, equality of opportunity and improved educational achievement will be solved: so runs the belief. Spurred on by its underlying assumptions, alternative approaches are denigrated, and more realistic interpretations of the nature and effects of pluralism ignored.

Yet criticisms of multicultural education have been common for at least a decade in all English-speaking countries (see Bullivant, 1981a). Gibson's (1976, p. 16) comment about the situation in the United States is typical of many others:

> . . . multicultural education has become in a few short years one of this decade's fastest growing educational slogans. In reviewing the literature on multicultural education, we find that program proponents have provided no systematic delineation of their views, and that all too frequently program statements are riddled with vague and emotional rhetoric.

Even alternatives to multicultural education do not escape similar criticisms. 'Concepts such as multicultural education, multiculturalism, multi-ethnic education, ethnic education, ethnic studies, cultural pluralism, and ethnic pluralism are often used interchangeably or to convey different but highly ambiguous meanings,' (Banks, 1977, p. 73). In Appleton's (1983, p. 2) opinion, the concept of cultural pluralism (multiculturalism) in particular 'is plagued with ambiguity, generality, and confusion, particularly in educational circles.'

In the racially charged atmosphere of Britain, and most recently the developing situation in Australia, multiculturalism is totally inadequate to deal with problems caused by 'racial' differences unless one does violence to the concept of culture by extending it to include racial, i.e., phenotypical, categories. As Corlett, the recently appointed chairman of the Royal Anthropological Institute's Education Committee, has pointed out (Corlett, 1983a, p. 18):

> More recently it has been argued that the 'cultural pluralist' approach is inadequate and even misleading, since it ignores the element of power. Education for a multicultural society must confront the inequalities in British society: it must be not just multicultural or multi-ethnic but positively anti-racist.

Benthall, a British anthropologist, has gone even further, and at a conference organized by RAI and the Minority Rights Group in February 1983 systematically demolished the terms 'multi-racial', 'multi-cultural', 'multi-ethnic', and 'even the prefix "multi-"' (Corlett, 1983b, p. 24). His conclusion that 'no-one has been able to formulate a defensible philosophy' about such pluralist approaches should be warning enough that they are sufficiently suspect to make their adoption as social theories problematic.

However, we face more than mere theorizing about society. In Canada with its policy of multiculturalism within a bilingual framework, Australia, New Zealand and, to a lesser extent, Britain, each with an official government or semi-government policy of multiculturalism, the intervention of the state has played the major role in creating and subsequently promoting this variant of an ideology of pluralism. Many educationists and even some social scientists have been content to accept the state's definition of the pluralist situation: testament, if one were needed, to the seductive power of an official ideology (Bullivant, 1981a, pp. 218–44). The ready acquiescence of social scientists is surprising. They at least should know that an ideology 'work[s] most effectively when we are not aware that how we formulate and construct a statement about the world is underpinned by ideological premises; when our formulations seem to be simply descriptive statements about how things are (i.e. must be), or of what we can "take-for-granted"' (Hall, cited in Centre for Contemporary Cultural Studies, 1982, p. 47).

However, some social scientists are waking up to this in Canada where, as Peter (1983, p. 46) has commented:

> . . . there is also some evidence that suggests that the leading role which the Federal Government has played in the invention of conceptual frameworks, theories and symbols regarding ethnicity and multiculturalism is slowly coming to an end, at least among Canada's social scientists. Through a process of critical inquiry regarding the basic assumptions, and by investigating the stated and unstated goals of established theories and models, Canada's social scientists seem to indicate their willingness to shake off the tutelage of political interests and begin to apply themselves to the problem of ethnicity and culture from other than the state's point of view.

Similar revisionist thinking can be found among social scientists in the other English-speaking countries, but a surprising number still prefer to remain seduced. Many more educationists are similarly afflicted. When one considers this, it is difficult not to be cynical about the degree of genuine commitment such knowledge managers have to promoting a constructive form of pluralist education that will benefit children from ethno-cultural and racial minorities. One wonders whether this might not be unrelated to the healthy research and development growth industry this bandwagon has generated.

Tensions between Interpretations of Pluralism

An alternative explanation can be found from the past. To anyone familiar with the history of socio-political thought since the time of Plato, the current debate over the merits and demerits of multiculturalism has all the hallmarks of the 'eternal dispute between those [utopians] who imagine the world to suit their policy, and those [realists] who arrange their policy to suit the realities of the live world' (Sorel, in Carr, 1946, p. 11). In education the 'eternal dispute' has been waged with varying degrees of acrimony in the form of what can be termed a debate with the ghost of Rousseau's *Emile*. This has taken us through the progressive school movement via A.S. Neill and 'Summerhill' *et al.*, through deschooling, open classrooms, various kinds of compensatory education to the present day and multicultural education. Like their counterparts in the political arena, all have suffered from an excess of utopian enthusiasm 'in which wishing prevails over thinking, generalisation over observation, and in which little attempt is made at a critical analysis of existing facts or available means' (Carr, 1946, p. 8).

In opposition, there have been periodic phases when more hard-headed, realistic views of education have been taken. The reassessment of American schooling and curriculum in the immediate post-Sputnik period was one such phase; recurrent 'back-to-basics' movements have been others. In 1983-84 a rigorous assessment of the work of bilingual schemes and research and development centres in the United States was being conducted, partly as a counter to the utopian idealism on which many have been based, and partly as a result of financial cuts and

'Reaganomics' — political realism par excellence! At the classroom level, Skinnerian behaviourism has been a long-running endeavour to inject more empirical realism into the instructional process.

Perhaps the most telling indictment of egalitarian utopianism has come from one who has played a major research role in Britain, trying to find out if it had succeeded, through 'political arithmetic' studies common in the sixties and seventies. As Halsey (1972, p. 6) has admitted: 'the essential fact of twentieth century educational history is that egalitarian policies have failed.' In a more recent study (Halsey, Heath and Ridge, 1980) this opinion is slightly qualified, but only to the extent that its findings show how slowly the attainment of greater educational opportunity for lower working-class children has been since the 1944 Education Act in Britain. The expansion of educational provisions has had some effect, but the optimism of continued reduction of inequality is tempered by the realization that the cultural reproduction thesis or its variants (e.g., Boudon, 1973; Bourdieu and Passeron, 1977; Bowles and Gintis, 1976) still holds. Halsey *et al.* (1980, p. 217) point out:

> The evidence from capitalist and communist countries alike is overwhelmingly that stratification along class, ethnic, status, or cultural lines heavily conditions both what knowledge is regarded as socially valuable and the eagerness and capacity of the children of the different strata to receive it . . . There are [in Britain] educational, demographic, economic, and even class forces which in future might favour high educational standards more equally spread. Even though inequality survived the 1944 Education Act and may find accommodation in a comprehensive system, we cannot yet conclude that class differences are immutable.

The tension between utopian and realist views of a pluralist society can show up even in official statements. Australia is one such example. Its official policy of multiculturalism arose out of a review of migrant services and programs (Galbally, 1978), and was promulgated by Act of Parliament by the Prime Minister in November 1978, for what many observers saw as blatant political opportunism. Even before this, in 1973, multiculturalism had been officially endorsed by the then Minister for Immigration and Ethnic Affairs, the Hon. A.J. (Al) Grassby, a utopian of some eminence, in the publication, *A Multicultural Society for the Future* (Grassby, 1973). He was followed in 1977 by the Australian Ethnic Affairs Council's (AEAC) publication, *Australia as a Multicultural Society*. In these and subsequent publications some of the metaphorical language is explicitly utopian. Australia should become 'a Family of the Nation'; it possesses 'a national fabric' woven from 'rather ill-assorted strands'. Other metaphors echo those employed overseas: 'cultural mosaic', 'unity in diversity'. In the opinion of the Australian Ethnic Affairs Commission, chaired by the Australian sociologist Professor Jerzy Zubrzycki, *'Multiculturalism means ethnic communities getting "into the act"'* (AEAC, 1977, p. 17; italics in original).

Spurred on by such lofty sentiments, some school programs teaching about community cultures, ethnic heritages and languages have been developed, and ethnic

(Saturday) schools have proliferated, financed by federal funds through legislation initiated by the Galbally Committee in 1978. Quite obvious development of other ethno-specific institutions has led to some concern in the national press that social cohesion is being threatened (Warneke, 1981). However, prior to this, a more official, realistic caution had appeared in the position statement, *Multiculturalism and Its Implications for Immigration Policy*, prepared by the joint Australian Population and Immigration and Australian Ethnic Affairs Councils (1979, p. 14).

> A major cause for concern is whether the creation of a network of ethnic organisations and the formalisation of group differences will adversely affect national unity . . .
> This is a delicate subject, but also a crucial one. It would certainly be legitimate for Government in a multicultural society to prevent the formation of divisive institutions that threatened national security.

A similar warning was issued by the newly constituted Australian Council on Population and Ethnic Affairs (1982) in its publication, *Multiculturalism for All Australians: Our Developing Nationhood*. Despite the somewhat utopian title and nature of much of its contents, realism reasserts itself in the injunction (pp. 26, 30):

> Groups should not separate themselves from the rest of the community in a way that denies either the validity of Australian institutions or their own shared identity as Australians . . .
> Inevitably, there will be clashes between the core culture and elements of the minority cultures making up our society . . . where clashes occur, the core culture must prevail until it is modified by consensus or by appropriate authoritative action.

Tensions in the Curriculum

(a)   The Nature of the Pluralist Society

In the light of the tensions between utopian and realist views of pluralism that exist in such social and political spheres, it is not surprising to find similar tensions influencing the decision-making in schooling and curriculum. To analyze them we propose a definition of the curriculum, which, like that of culture proposed below, has been evolved over a number of years. It comprises that set of knowledge, ideas and experiences resulting from ideologically influenced and value-laden processes of *selection* from a social group's public stock of traditional and current knowledge, ideas and experiences, their *organization* into sub-sets (syllabuses and units), *transmission* to clients (students, pupils) in teaching-learning interface situations, and periodic *evaluation* which provides feedback into previous processes.

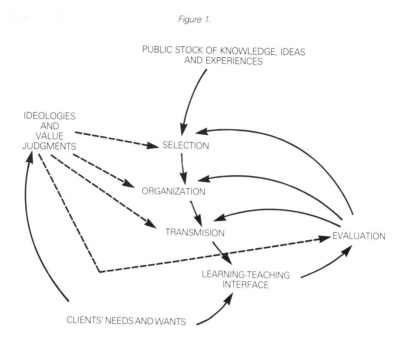

Figure 1.

PUBLIC STOCK OF KNOWLEDGE, IDEAS
AND EXPERIENCES

IDEOLOGIES
AND
VALUE
JUDGMENTS

SELECTION

ORGANIZATION

TRANSMISION

EVALUATION

LEARNING-TEACHING
INTERFACE

CLIENTS' NEEDS AND WANTS

Source: Bullivant, B.M. (1983) *The Pluralist Dilemma in Education,*
Sydney: George Allen & Unwin.

As Figure 1 illustrates, the three processes of selection, organization and transmission of the public stock of knowledge, ideas and experiences are integrated through the fourth process of evaluation, in a continuous feedback loop. Clients' needs and wants also provide feedback influencing value judgments and to some extent ideologies. However, the major influences on values and ideologies come from individuals, organizations and institutions in the supra-system and from individuals within the open system of the school itself, in interaction with the supra-system. They involve sociological, philosophical, psychological and even economic considerations. Of these the first two are of most relevance for our discussion.

Sociological value judgments concern the nature of the society which the school system serves, and are basically of two types — substantive and normative. Substantive value judgments are descriptive and attempt to state preferences for the kind of society that exists in the present. Such preferences are truth-claims and can be verified by empirical, reality tests, the hallmark of the realists' approach to the world. Thus, the statement, 'Britain is a multicultural society', stands or falls by the empirical test of establishing how many (multi-) cultures it comprises. The figure is only about $4\frac{1}{2}$ per cent of the population at most, originating mainly from three parts of the world with different cultures — Asia, Africa, Caribbean — and even these numbers need to be reduced by the considerable number born in Britain. Thus on empirical evidence we should be quite sceptical about the claim that Britain *is* a *multi*cultural society. Tricultural might be nearer the mark.

Even the assertion, 'Australia *is* a multicultural society', has to be treated with caution. It is frequently claimed, especially by the government's propaganda machine or 'ideological state apparatus' (Althusser, 1971) that up to 40 per cent of the population are culturally different from the remaining largely Anglo-Celtic-Saxon majority. This kind of claim has been repeated so often, by so many eminent ideologues, that one is almost seduced into believing that it is fact, and that Australia *is* a multicultural society. However, when the realistic empirical test is applied a different picture emerges. According to the 1981 Census, approximately 78 per cent of the population were born in Australia. Of them $88\frac{1}{2}$ per cent had both parents who were also born in Australia. When one adds another 5 per cent of the population who were born in the United Kingdom and Ireland, plus another 2 per cent born in English-speaking countries such as New Zealand, America and parts of Africa, the proportion of the Australian population that is markedly different culturally drops to a much lower percentage than the 30–40 per cent commonly cited. In other words, the picture of the Australian population as being composed of many recently arrived non-English-speaking migrants is no longer tenable, and other models relating to ethnicity, class and, in recent years, race, are needed to fully describe Australian society.

The second kind of sociological value judgment about society, relating to the curriculum selection process, is normative and prescriptive. That is, it predicts the kind of society to be attained in the future, and usually specifies the strategies to be adopted to achieve this goal. Normative value judgments of this type easily become utopian flights of fancy, backed by the quite banal claims and mythical statements one associates with an ideology (Barthes, 1973; Edelman, 1977). Rarely is the time span needed to achieve utopia specified. Instead, considerable imprecision and vagueness characterize normative statements, as in the claim that Australia will become multicultural 'in a matter of years, decades, if not generations' — from a professor of sociology, yet probably the leading utopian ideologue in Australia.

Examples of such thinking can be found from all of the English-speaking countries. As Carr (1946, p. 5) has noted, it is typical of an initial stage in socio-political theorizing.

> During this stage, the investigators will pay little attention to existing 'facts' or to the analysis of cause and effect, but will devote themselves whole-heartedly to the elaboration of visionary projects for the attainment of the ends which they have in view — projects whose simplicity and perfection give them an easy and universal appeal.

(b)   Conceptions of Culture in the Curriculum

Philosophical value judgments and ideologies relating to the selection process in the curriculum, that are of relevance to pluralist education, concern the types and worth of knowledge, ideas and experiences. The public stock from which these are selected is closely related to the culture of a society, and the way educationists define this concept largely determines the content of the selection they will make. The utopian-realist opposition is as influential here as in conceptualizing the nature of pluralism.

Utopian definitions of culture tend to follow the classic but dated view of Tylor (1871) — 'that complex whole which includes knowledge, belief, art, morals, law, custom, and any other capabilities and habits acquired by man as a member of society' — or similar enumeratively descriptive definitions. Following the Galbally Committee's lead, the Schools Commission's Committee on Multicultural Education (1979, p. 68), for example, adopted the 'most common, popular usage in education which equates culture with a social group's heritage, i.e. traditions, history, language, arts and other aesthetic achievements, religion, customs and values.' One of Australia's most influential utopian theorists, George Smolicz, has followed the dated, classic views of Znaniecki and other Polish theorists for a number of years, with the result that his concepts of culture and curriculum content have tended to emphasize European, neo-idealist aspects such as literary 'high culture', values, works of literary criticism and so on (Smolicz, 1979, 1981).

Content analysis of the regular publication, *Education Journal*, from the Commission for Racial Equality in Britain appears to indicate that a great deal of multicultural education there stresses such cultural aspects as heritage and history, language, literature, foods and customs. Similar emphases can be found in New Zealand, where much of the bicultural (rather than multicultural) approach to teaching Maori studies in primary schools concentrates on the aesthetic aspects of Maoridom: Maori myths, ceremonies and customs, some language and songs.

There is nothing intrinsically wrong with such approaches to selecting these aspects of knowledge, ideas and experiences from the public cultural stock every society possesses, as long as one recognizes that it is a simplistic and one-sided view of culture, and has several limitations. Firstly, it emphasizes the expressive rather than instrumental aspects of the cultural programme. Secondly, it emphasizes the historical life-styles of ethno-cultural groups in society, but has little to say about their *current* strategies for adapting to present circumstances and gaining rewarding life-chances in their new homeland.

For example, teaching the current generation of children in New Zealand about the great canoe fleets of the original Maoris who set up tribal structures and fortified rural villages (*pas*) may have a certain glamorous fascination for them. However, unless it is used also to tell children how important Maori institutions, values and customs have been adapted to have an instrumental function to help Maoris cope with living in big-city areas, to which the majority have migrated, such knowledge remains unrelated to the present. A similar case can be made about the limitations of teaching Ashanti legends and myths in British schools, the glories of ancient Greece and Rome in Australian schools (as one Minister of Education once advocated), or the historical structure of Navaho Indian culture in state schools in Arizona.

Thus, thirdly, what is being stressed in such selection of historically dated knowledge about customs, heritage and traditions is conservative. It can easily lead to the preservation of a *fossilized culture* in the minds of children and adults from ethno-cultural groups. This phenomenon is well-recognized in Australia where romanticized versions of 'home' and the 'old culture' are assiduously nurtured through ethnic 'Saturday schools', clubs and associations. Meanwhile, the countries concerned have experienced such rapid social and cultural change that visitors from them to Australia are often amazed and even shocked to see such fossilized versions of culture existing in Australia.

Fourthly, the teaching of the historical, expressive side of ethnic groups' cultures will do little to inform children from such backgrounds, let alone all children, about the real nature of the society in which they live. The assumption that teaching them about ethnic heritages, customs, languages and so on will lead to greater 'self-esteem' for ethnic children and, for all, 'understanding' cultural differences, and thus lead to tolerance, reduced prejudice, harmony and 'social cohesion', has been a major element of Australian thinking about multicultural education, as it has in other countries. The Australian Ethnic Affairs Council (1977, pp. 11–13) established this trend by endorsing a view 'that policies and programs concerned with education for a multicultural society apply to *all* children, not just children of non-English-speaking background, and have ramifications throughout the curriculum.' Five out of six concrete proposals cover English language teaching (TESL), bilingual education, community language education and support for ethnic schools. The sixth recommended that:

> Schools should be given incentives to develop ethnic studies programs and to infuse the curriculum in general with the reality of the pluralist nature of Australian society, with the object both of enhancing the self-esteem of students of ethnic origin and giving *all* children a more authentic view of the nature of the society.

The Galbally Committee (1978, p. 104) continued the trend and it was rapidly followed in 1979 by the Schools Commission's Committee on Multicultural Education (1979) which made a number of recommendations in *Education for a Multicultural Society* (1979, pp. 11–12). Again, the stress is placed on 'understanding' the various cultural aspects of ethnic groups resident in Australia, particularly through 'programs or studies which aim at presenting to all our students an opportunity to study [their] historical, social, aesthetic, literary and cultural backgrounds and traditions.' International and intercultural studies are recommended on the same principle and, for all children, it is suggested that community language programs be provided to give them an opportunity to study an 'Australian language other than English'.

In a more recent statement the Australian Council on Population and Ethnic Affairs (ACPEA) is still wedded to a utopian view of culture, to judge from its endorsement of three 'educational ideals' (ACPEA, 1982, p. 18):

- inter-cultural understanding, tolerance of and respect for cultural patterns other than one's own;
- improved communication between members of one cultural group and those of others;
- maintaining and nurturing the cultural and linguistic heritages within society.

In similar vein, the Australian Schools Commission's *Report for the Triennium 1982–84* stresses (1981, pp. 14–16) that: 'The essential challenge is to promote diversity and choice while maintaining social cohesion.' However, it restricts the meaning of 'diversity and choice' to encouraging ethnic groups 'to pursue a plurality of lifestyles and to foster their own values and customs.'

The Commission has at least tacitly accepted one of the major criticisms of current approaches to teaching about multiculturalism by warning against educational programs and 'lessons devoted to ethnic food, dance, festive clothing or national days'. These the Commission suggests, 'while possibly providing useful connecting points, are relatively superficial aspects of cultural difference and may moreover reinforce the notion that multiculturalism is merely acceptance of some exotic strangeness.' This is a much-needed warning as a great deal of multicultural education has tended to concentrate on the exotic or strange, through programs that deal with 'spaghetti-eating-and-basket-weaving' aspects of ethnic cultures, thus diverting attention away from the key dilemma in educating children from ethnic backgrounds. Only a realistic view of society that stresses other dimensions of culture will redress the imbalance.

(c) The Pluralist Dilemma in Education

The dilemma can be stated in a nutshell: selections for the curriculum that encourage children from ethnic backgrounds to learn about their cultural heritage, languages, histories, customs and other aspects of their life-styles have little bearing on their equality of educational opportunity and life-chances. These are influenced more by structural, social class, economic, political and racist factors operating in the wider pluralist society, and by the control exercised by its dominant groups over access to social rewards and economic resources. Thus, to claim, as many romantic utopian multicultural advocates do, that teaching an ethnic child about his or her cultural heritage will lead to greater ethnic self-esteem and therefore better educational attainments and ultimately a better job is simplistic in the extreme, as Stone's (1981) research in Britain suggests. It is more likely that such multicultural programs would, if over-emphasized, divert ethnic children's energies and attention away from mastering the dominant language of English, which is necessary for 'getting on' in the socio-economic system.

The supporters of multicultural education attempt to counter this type of criticism by reiterating that the aim is to teach *all* children about cultural differences in their societies. In theory this is a laudable, but again naive, idea, as it too conceals a subtle danger. Connor (1972, pp. 343–4) has pointed out that ethnic consciousness — the sense of 'us' or 'we' — depends on obtaining information about other ethnic groups who are in some ways different. These constitute the 'them' which gives a basis or referent for appreciating the uniqueness and significance of 'us'. Thus giving, say, Anglo-Celtic children information about other ethnic groups in their societies may reinforce and not reduce their sense of distinctiveness. 'Minimally, it may be asserted that increasing awareness of a second group is not certain to produce harmony, and is at least likely to produce, on balance, a negative response' (*ibid.*, p. 344).

As comprehensive research by Le Vine and Campbell (1972) has established, understanding prejudice is best achieved through realistic-group-conflict theory. They reject psychological explanations of ethno-centrism, prejudice and discrimination, including racism. Their preferred theory 'assumes that group conflicts are rational in the sense that groups do have incompatible goals and are in competition for scarce resources' (*ibid.*, p. 29). Schermerhorn (1970, p. 6) similarly supports a view of prejudice that is anti-psychologistic. 'If research has confirmed anything in this area, it is that prejudice is a product of *situations*, historical situations, economic situations, political situations; it is not a little demon that emerges in people simply because they are depraved.' Informed by such views, one can maintain that programmes of multicultural education are misguided if they attempt to improve children's understanding of cultural and even racial differences on the assumption that this will reduce their prejudice and possible discrimination. This kind of psychological, reductionist thinking, based on what has become known as the 'contact hypothesis', has been shown by Amir's (1969) extensive review of the literature to have many shortcomings.

We are more likely to gain a realistic view of the causes of prejudice and appreciate the logic of Connor's view, thereby exposing the overall weakness of much multicultural thinking, by taking a modern definition of culture as the basis for planning educational programmes. At least this would avoid being diverted away from considering issues such as migrants' access to a fairer share of social rewards and economic resources, which are obscured by using outmoded definitions of culture, or those like Tylor's associated with a particular historical period, or neo-idealist European scholarly traditions.

Following the lead given by Kroeber and Kluckhohn (1952, p. 181) and more recently the definitions suggested by Goodenough (1964, p. 36), Geertz (1973), Keesing (1976), Redfield (1962) and others (discussed in Bullivant, 1984), we define culture in a way that is much less utopian than more dated definitions. It is the generalized composite of interdependent and valued traditional and current public knowledge and conceptions, embodied in behaviours and artefacts, and transmitted to present and new members, both symbolically and non-symbolically, which a society has evolved historically and progressively modifies and augments, to give meaning to and cope with its definitions of present and future existential problems.

In essence culture is a form of ever-evolving 'survival device' based on adaptive change that enables social groups to cope with the problems of living in a particular habitat. It is *this* kind of culture that children from ethno-cultural groups have to master, rather than a romanticized, fossil-culture based on utopian views of pluralism.

However, the definition opens up other considerations. Culture in this sense has instrumental value, but it is also important to recognize the expressive function of parts of a social group's survival programme. In other words, social groups maintain parts of the culture to give quality to life or to express important values, in addition to the basic task of survival. This gives us one explanation of why such apparently anachronistic inherited features as classical ballet, art, literature (the works of Shakespeare, for example) and other aesthetic interests are retained in the culture programme and passed on from generation to generation. They too are an important part of culture and should not be neglected, but not overemphasized.

Another component in a culture programme concerns a group's religious beliefs and values. It is difficult to see these as having instrumental survival value if one concentrates solely on their use in relation to the natural or geographical environment. Many societies believe in what might be termed a 'metaphysical' environment, and religious knowledge concerns their relationships with its 'inhabitants'. Such knowledge and beliefs in a culture programme also have an expressive function in enabling important values and attitudes to be periodically rehearsed and reaffirmed (Bullivant, 1978, pp. 65–89). Religion also provides valuable instrumental ways of coping with emotional and psychological problems posed by environments in cases where technological coping mechanisms are unavailable.

(d)   Multifaceted Pluralism and Group Survival

By throwing the emphasis on group survival, the definition enables us to conceptualize the mechanisms by which the majority ethnic group in a pluralist society controls the life-chances of minority-status individuals and groups, in terms of their access to economic resources, power and social rewards. Such mechanisms operate through processes of exclusion and inclusion. These use status-position, ethnicity, cultural, phenotypical ('racial') and even gender differences as boundary markers or cultural symbols to include those of the dominant in-group who control power, and exclude those different from them who are in minority out-groups, but want a greater share of power. To achieve it, they attempt to use their own methods of inclusion and exclusion in a process of usurpation, which will improve their life-chances (see more detailed discussion in Banton, 1983; Bullivant, 1984; Parkin, 1974).

Moreover, the saliency of any one, or combination, of boundary markers will vary historically and according to the dynamics of the socio-economic, political situation at any given time. Thus, in periods of economic downturn, exclusion strategies employed by dominant individuals and groups to maintain their vested interests are likely to become more apparent. When the economic situation improves, such strategies can be relaxed, boundaries may become weaker and more minorities may be included in a share of socio-economic resources and social rewards.

Towards Radical Multiculturalism

Such a multifaceted model of pluralism is a far cry from simplistic, utopian multicultural thinking. The strength of the latter's seductive powers should not be underestimated, and we cannot expect that our version of a realistic-group-conflict/competition theory of culture and survival will lead to multiculturalism being abandoned, at least in the short term. However, it must become more radical. Multicultural education must be politicized and made more power-sensitive, because it is through the curriculum and schooling that children from ethno-cultural backgrounds are being deprived of their much-needed share of survival knowledge, if the selection process only stresses aspects of fossilized culture.

Hopefully, the multifaceted model of pluralism will also make policy-makers aware of the limitations and theoretical oversimplifications of seeing ethnicity solely in cultural terms. This is only one component of an ethnic group's bases for collective identity, according to theorists who have specialized in studying ethnicity (e.g., Barth, 1969; Schermerhorn, 1970; Despres, 1975; Hoetink, 1975; van den Berghe, 1975), *but* they also point to the equal and often greater importance of taking account of other features such as racial characteristics, national sentiment and memories, and the self-ascription and social- (other-) ascription of ethnicity. As van den Berghe (1975, p. 72) stresses, 'Ethnic groups are defined BOTH by the objective cultural modalities of their behavior (including most importantly their linguistic behavior), and by their subjective view of themselves and each other.' To ignore the latter by concentrating the argument on culture is a weakness that has beset much of the thinking about ethnicity.

The possession of a distinctive culture is neither a necessary nor a sufficient condition for the existence of an ethnic group. However, the situation is much more complex because it is possible to take issue with both the subjectivist conception of ethnicity, and the exclusively objectivist or cultural conception, and regard both as equally unserviceable. 'This makes theoretically problematic not only the relationship between cultural distributions and categorical ethnic ascriptions but also the role and overall significance of the subjective element in respect to such ascriptions' (Despres, 1975, p. 191).

Radical multiculturalism and multicultural education are essentially a compromise that can be drawn between utopian wish-dreams and the critical cynicism that extremes of realism can produce (Carr, 1946, p. 10). Such an approach is a deliberate departure from what has been attempted hitherto in all English-speaking countries. Lynch's (1983) suggested models and programmes for a multicultural curriculum in Britain follow somewhat similar lines. Bullivant's (1981b) development of a 'poly-ethnic survival curriculum' for Australian conditions is explicitly power-sensitive, especially in the suggested social studies syllabus. Various approaches in the United States described by Gibson (1976) have attempted without great success to inject 'education for cultural pluralism' into the curriculum, even to the extent of politicizing multicultural classroom and school processes so as to mirror what occurs in the wider world. Canadian researchers are becoming more conscious of the need for similar reappraisal of curricula that hitherto have favoured British-Canadian points of view (D'Oyley, 1978). Here, however, Lupul (1978, p. 15) has noted pessimistically that the dominance of second and third language provisions has meant that 'in terms of other aspects of the school curriculum, Canada's multi-ethnic or multicultural reality has as yet hardly made a dent.'

Even by using a power-sensitive definition of culture, radical multiculturalism may have difficulty in providing a framework that adequately takes into account all the boundary markers that are used as bases of inclusion and exclusion in multifaceted pluralist societies. True, knowledge and conceptions about them and how such processes operate are part of the wider public stock of knowledge and conceptions concerning inter- and intra-group relations that every society possesses. But 'race', gender and social class possess extra properties that make even anthropological cultural analysis barely adequate. Full solutions to them will have to wait for the evolution of another ideology of pluralism in education in the long line of those we have seen since Rousseau's *Emile*.

References

ALTHUSSER, L. (1971) 'Ideology and ideological state apparatuses', in *Lenin and Philosophy and Other Essays*, London, New Left Books.

AMIR, Y. (1969) 'Contact hypothesis in ethnic relations', *Psychological Bulletin*, 71, 5, pp. 319–42.

APPLETON, N. (1983) *Cultural Pluralism in Education Theoretical Foundations*, New York, Longmans.

AUSTRALIAN COUNCIL ON POPULATION AND ETHNIC AFFAIRS (1982) *Multiculturalism for All Australians: Our Developing Nationhood*, Canberra, AGPS.

AUSTRALIAN ETHNIC AFFAIRS COUNCIL (1977) *Australia as a Multicultural Society*, Canberra, AGPS.

AUSTRALIAN POPULATION AND IMMIGRATION COUNCIL AND AUSTRALIAN ETHNIC AFFAIRS COUNCIL (1979) *Multiculturalism and Its Implications for Immigration Policy*, Canberra, AGPS.

AUSTRALIAN SCHOOLS COMMISSION (1981) *Report for the Triennium 1982–84*, Canberra, AGPS.

BANKS, J.A. (1977) 'Pluralism and educational concepts: A clarification', *Peabody Journal of Education*, 54, pp. 73–8.

BANTON, M. (1983) *Racial and Ethnic Competition*, Cambridge, Cambridge University Press.

BARTH, F. (Ed.) (1969) *Ethnic Groups and Boundaries*, Boston, Mass. Little, Brown.

BARTHES, R. (1973) *Mythologies*, selected and translated from the French by Annette Lavers, St Albans, Herts, Paladin.

BOUDON, R. (1973) *Education, Opportunity and Social Inequality*, New York, John Wiley.

BOURDIEU, P. and PASSERON, J.-C. (1977) *Reproduction: In Education, Society and Culture*, translated by R. Nice, London, Sage Publications.

BOWLES, S. and GINTIS, H. (1976) *Schooling in Capitalist America*, New York, Basic Books.

BULLIVANT, B.M. (1978) *The Way of Tradition: Life in an Orthodox Jewish School*, Melbourne, Australian Council for Educational Research.

BULLIVANT, B.M. (1981a) *The Pluralist Dilemma in Education: Six Case Studies*, Sydney, George Allen and Unwin.

BULLIVANT, B.M. (1981b) *Race, Ethnicity and Curriculum*, Melbourne, Macmillan.

BULLIVANT, B.M. (1984) *Pluralism: Cultural Maintenance and Evolution*, Clevedon (Avon), Multilingual Matters.

CARR, E.H. (1946) *The Twenty Years' Crisis 1919–39: An Introduction to the Study of International Relations*, London, Macmillan.

CENTRE FOR CONTEMPORARY CULTURAL STUDIES (1982) *The Empire Strikes Back: Race and Racism in 70s Britain*, London, Hutchinson/CCCS.

CONNOR, W. (1972) 'Nation-building or nation-destroying?' *World Politics: A Quarterly Journal of International Relations*, 24, pp. 319–55.

CORLETT, J. (1983a) 'Anthropology in British education', *Royal Anthropological Institute News*, 59, pp. 16–19.

CORLETT, J. (1983b) 'Review of Ben Whitaker (editor) *Teaching about Prejudice*', *Royal Anthropological Institute News*, 59, p. 14.

DESPRES, L.A. (Ed.) (1975) *Ethnicity and Resource Competition in Plural Societies*, The Hague, Mouton.

D'OYLEY, V. (Ed.) (1978) *Black Presence in Multi-Ethnic Canada*, Vancouver, Centre for the Study of Curriculum and Instruction, Faculty of Education, University of British Columbia; Toronto, Ontario Institute for Studies in Education.

EDELMAN, M. (1977) *Political Language: Words That Succeed and Policies That Fail*, New York, Academic Press.

GALBALLY, F. (1978) *Migrant Services and Programs*, Report of the Review of Post-Arrival Programs and Services for Migrants (The Galbally Report), Canberra, AGPS.

GEERTZ, C. (1973) *The Interpretation of Culture: Selected Essays*, New York, Basic Books.

GIBSON, M.A. (1976) 'Approaches to multicultural education in the United States: Some concepts and assumptions', *Anthropology and Education Quarterly*, 7, 4, pp. 7–18.

GOODENOUGH, W.H. (1964) 'Cultural anthropology and linguistics', in HYMES, D. (Ed.), *Language in Culture and Society*, New York, Harper and Row, pp. 36–9.

GRASSBY, A.J. (1973) *A Multicultural Society for the Future*, Canberra, AGPS.

HALSEY, A.H. (1972) *Educational Priority: E.P.A. Problems ad Policies*, London, HMSO.

HALSEY, A.H., HEATH, A.F. and RIDGE, J.M. (1980) *Origins and Destinations: Family, Class, and Education in Modern Britain*, Oxford, Clarendon Press.

HOETINK, H. (1975) 'Resource competition, monoploy, and socioracial diversity', in DESPRES, L. (Ed.), *Ethnicity and Resource Competition in Plural Societies*, The Hague, Mouton.

KEESING, R. (1976) *Cultural Anthropology: A Contemporary Perspective*, New York, Holt, Rinehart and Winston.

KROEBER, A.L. and KLUCKHOHN, C. (1952) 'Culture: A critical review of concepts and definitions', *Papers of the Peabody Museum of American Archaeology and Ethnology*, 47, 1.

LE VINE, R.A. and CAMPBELL, D.T. (1972) *Ethnocentrism: Theories of Conflict, Ethnic Attitudes and Group Behavior*, New York, Wiley.

LUPUL, M.R. (1978) 'Multiculturalism and educational policies in Canada', *Multiculturalism*, 1, 4, pp. 13–16.

LYNCH, J. (1983) *The Multicultural Curriculum*, London, Batsford Academic.

PARKIN, F. (Ed.) (1974) *The Social Analysis of Class Structure*, London, Tavistock.

PETER, K. (1983) 'The semantics of multiculturalism: Ethnic bureaucracy, social control, and ethnic research in Canada', in MANNING, F. (Ed.), *Consciousness and Inquiry: Ethnology and Canadian Realities*, Ottawa, National Museums of Canada, pp. 42–6.

REDFIELD, M.P. (Ed.) (1962) *Human Nature and the Study of Society*, The Papers of Robert Redfield, Volume 1, Chicago, University of Chicago Press.

SCHERMERHORN, R.A. (1970) *Comparative Ethnic Relations: A Framework for Theory and Research*, New York, Random House.

SCHOOLS COMMISSION COMMITTEE ON MULTICULTURAL EDUCATION (1979) *Education for a Multicultural Society*, Report to the Schools Commission, Canberra, Schools Commission.

SMOLICZ, J.J. (1979) *Culture and Education in a Plural Society*, Canberra, Curriculum Development Centre.

SMOLICZ, J.J. (1981) 'Cultural pluralism and educational policy: In search of stable multiculturalism', *The Australian Journal of Education*, 25, 2, pp. 121–45.

STONE, M. (1981) *The Education of the Black Child in Britain: The Myth of Multiracial Education*, Glasgow, Fontana.

TYLOR, E.B. (1871) *Primitive Culture*, London, John Murray.

VAN DEN BERGHE, P.L. (1975) 'Ethnicity and class in highland Peru', in DESPRES, L. (Ed.), *Ethnicity and Resource Competition in Plural Societies*, The Hague, Mouton.

WARNEKE, R. (1981) 'Do we really want a multi-culture?' *The Age*, Melbourne, 2 October.

4   Multiculturalism, Class and Ideology: A European-Canadian comparison

Christopher Bagley

Introduction

The assumption of this paper is that racism in Western societies is a sub-system of societies whose basis is the exploitation of human beings through capitalism. A society based on the accumulation of capital through profitable entrepreneurship needs a stable and largely acquiescent work force, as well as a reserve army of labour which can be laid off in slack times without problems of social unrest. This latter role is usefully filled by assimilated migrant workers, women, and degraded ethnic minorities such as aboriginal people in North America.[1]

We have argued that in Britain racism has been highly functional for capitalism, drawing in particular on Lenin's (1934) analysis of European capitalism (Bagley and Verma, 1979). Lenin, developing commentaries by Marx and Engels, had argued that for certain countries such as Britain, the proletariat had a 'false consciousness' rooted in the social chauvinism of an exploiting, colonial society. The true proletariat for Britain were the exploited workers of the colonies, an exploitation that had enabled the lower class in Britain to enjoy a falsely high standard of living. The infection of the British working class with the values of social chauvinism was reflected in their traditional racism. Working class they may have been, but they were not black or brown, and they worked with their leaders to maintain the values of the Empire. Capitalism too had similar cooperation from the British workers, and the infection of the British working class with the values of racism proved to be highly functional for the exploiting class.

Only since 1945 did Britain's 'true proletariat' — from Africa, India, the Caribbean and Hong Kong — appear in Britain. Now the despised ethnic groups competed with sectors of the British working class for jobs, housing and services. It is not surprising, given this analysis, that all post-war surveys of racism in Britian have shown racist attitudes and behaviour to be most highly prevalent in the working class (Bagley and Verma, 1979).

In schools, white working class youth have been the most racist, and their attitudes and behaviour have been most resistant to change (Bagley and Verma,

1983). Since black immigrants have perforce had to settle in the city's most decayed areas, they have been confonted with the most racist sectors of the white working class. The result is the broth and boil of urban race relations of Britain today. What may emerge is a synthesis of human relations, a purified but not a fixated identity (to employ Sennett's model of city change), in which not only is racism unmasked, but the humanness of black and white interaction will create a new people neither black nor white whose identity transcends the notion of mastery over material resources and transcends today the 'bourgeois' Marxist ideal of mastery over nature (Bookchin, 1980).

As Bookchin asserts,

> The development of a revolutary project must *begin* by shedding the Marxian categories from the very beginning, to fix on more basic categories created by hierarchical society from its inception, all the more to place the economic ones in their proper context. It is no longer simply capitalism we wish to demolish; it is an older and more archaic world that lives on in the present one — the domination of human by human, the rationale of hierarchy as such. (p. 210)[2]

Cultural Uniqueness in Patterns of Race and Ethnic Relations

Though Weber (1948) has argued, from his historical investigations, that 'status' and 'ethnicity' are frequently the salient bases of social differentiation and the allocation of life chances, in times of economic stress it is material interests which transcend:

> Every technological repercussion and economic transformation threatens stratification by status and pushes the class situation into the foreground. Epochs and countries in which the naked class situation is of predominant significance are regularly the periods of technical and economic transformations. And every slowing down of the shifting of economic stratification leads, in due course, to the growth of status structures and makes for a resuscitation of the important role of social honor. (p. 194)

The three societies addressed in this chapter — Britain, Canada and the Netherlands — are all in states of technological and economic change, and in each of these societies culturally specific reactions to problems of ethnicity have emerged. One of the implications is that 'multicultural policy' for education and social services has markedly different form and meaning in the contrasted cultures. The interminable debate surrounding multi-cultural education relates in part to the fact that multi-cultural education itself has plural forms, and in part to the fact that the debate itself is part of the dialectic of change.

In the Netherlands, a society had evolved in which influences of external change were resisted, and a complex system of vertical stratification based on religious groupings obscured class divisions. Ethnic and racial groups were easily absorbed into these 'pillars' of society, and it mattered less that a man was black than whether he was a Catholic or a Protestant (Bagley, 1973). Yet, in a decade, this unique and seemingly stable pattern of race relations crumbled because of the thrust of prosperity and change brought about largely through the Netherlands' participation in the European Economic Community. In a rapidly secularizing society economic conflicts asserted themselves, and traditional methods of accommodating diverse ethnic minorities could no longer be applied (Amersfoort, 1982). The result has been chaos and confusion in policies for ethnic minorities, and the profound alienation of a sector of the young black population (Bagley, 1983a). Ironically, this retreat into drug subcultures had no parallel in British society, where the traditional treatment of black minorities had been much worse than in the Netherlands (Bagley and Verma, 1979).

The recent history of Britain has seen a polarization between class interests, and a sharpening of class lines. Black and white have united on the barricades, and there is some evidence that traditional class correlates of racism are changing, with an alliance between a brutal section of the white working class and traditional middle class reactionary forces set against a more unified working class: a curious echo of the conflicts which ended in the Nazi ascent to power in the 1930s.

A remarkable and pleasing feature of the new alliance between black and white in Britain has been the large increase in racially mixed marriages: some 20 per cent of marriages involving a black person are black-white marriages, a far higher rate than in the United States (Bagley, 1979a). Moreover, such marriages produce children neither black nor white, with a clear identity and sense of purpose in life (Bagley and Young, 1984). The debate on multi-cultural education in Britain has not taken proper account of this phenomenon; but groupings of pupils into 'black' and 'white' or 'West Indian' and 'British' for purposes of comparison are becoming increasingly meaningless. The majority of children of Britain's future will be neither black nor white.[3]

The most dramatic change in race relations policy in the West is that experienced in Canada. Canada was founded by Empire Loyalists reacting to the movement for independence in the United States, and for many decades embodied the most conservative principles of empire, within a rigid, white, Anglophone culture. Asian immigrants were admitted only as cheap labour under highly discriminatory conditions, and were subject to arbitrary programs culminating in the arrest, confiscation of property and confinement in remote camps of Japanese Canadians in the early 1940s (Buchignani, 1984). Both political factors (the surgence of Francophone nationalism) and economic factors (the discovery of huge oil and gas reserves, and an integration with US manufacturing sectors) have led to profound changes in Canadian society, including the development of an official policy of multi-culturalism in the early 1970s, which identified some eighty different ethnic or cultural groups who could apply for financial support to the Minister of Multiculturalism for programs to support linguistic and cultural identity. To the extent that many ethnic groups seem to have had little interest in such cultural retention, the program has been financially cheap and ideologically successful.

The recent multi-cultural programs in Canada have been framed so as to exclude aboriginal people, who angrily resist a policy which would treat them as just another immigrant group, assimilating into the main body of Canadian society. Aboriginal people see themselves as a group of independent nations, struggling for autonomy and return of their original lands. Such claims are vigorously resisted by Canadian authorities, especially when large oil and natural gas reserves are discovered on lands claimed by native people.

The European–Canadian Comparison

Only in the 1950s did Canada develop an ideology of race and ethnic relations which was distinctly different from that of the white, Protestant English-speaking group which had dominated the Empire for a century (Palmer, 1982). Change reflected new patterns of migration; the assertion of power by migrant groups from Southern and Eastern Europe and Ireland; and the assertion of Francophone consciousness. Today Canada in its multi-cultural policies is a dramatically changed society, unique in its policies which coincide with (but which have not created) a society in which racism's impact seems, on the face of things, less dramatic than in many other ethnically mixed societies.

European comparisons make these Canadian developments seem even more interesting. For example, at one time Dutch race relations were regarded as the prime example of good practice: a very large number of ethnically different refugees from Indonesia had been successfully absorbed in the Dutch plural society, as were other minorities (Bagley, 1973). Yet in only a decade, race and ethnic relations in the Netherlands deteriorated dramatically as large numbers of black Dutch people arrived from Surinam and the Antilles, and the bonds of pluralism, coincidentally, began to crumble. The result has been the development of an alienated, despairing and rebellious black youth culture which could not be accommodated in Dutch society (Bagley, 1983b).

The Dutch situation and its deterioration is worth stressing for it illustrates how a racist culture (as in the Canadian case) or a seemingly non-racist culture (as in the Dutch case) can change rapidly in relation to structural factors independently of policy formation and action by governments. Hubert Campfens illustrates this in his important comparative study of the 'integration of ethno-cultural minorities' in Canada and the Netherlands (Campfens, 1980). In his conclusion, Campfens points to an interesting paradox. Despite a strong tradition of central and local government involvement in everyday affairs, Dutch public policy has played a relatively small part in assisting the integration of minorities. Yet in Canada, which lacks a tradition of strong government involvement, both federal and provincial levels of government have taken significant initiatives to foster elements of cultural autonomy through both policy and fiscal support.

The reasons for Dutch inaction are related to moral confusion in a declining capitalist society in which the structural cement provided by religious bonds has decayed. The ground for Canadian action can be traced to self-interest — a desire to palliate potentially disruptive minorities following radical accommodations to Francophone interest, and the desire to incorporate minorities into a healthy capitalist economy. Canadian multi-cultural policy has developed in ways which obscure the lines of class and economic exploitation within a complex and seemingly attractive mosaic of vertical rather than horizontal stratification (Moodley, 1981). Paradoxically too the accommodation of the cultural aspirations of diverse ethnic groups in Canada seems to be paralleled by a decline in ethnic commitment.

In truth, Canadian ethnic policies work because the population has been highly selected in terms of its commitment to the social relations required by capitalism. Canada is generally liberal in its treatment of the aspirations of ethnic and cultural minorities, but is fascist in its policies towards 'illegal' citizens.[4] Moreover, one ethnic group — the aboriginal peoples — are rigidly excluded from this multi-cultural policy, since Native cultural aspirations are fundamentally threatening to the capitalist aspirations of the white settlers, and those they have chosen to assist them in the exploitation of Canada's resources (Bagley, 1983c).

For legal immigrants to Canada, committed to economic advancement within a capitalist framework, Canadian social structure offers many advantages. In this Canada differs profoundly from Britain, where ethnic minorities are treated with discrimination rather than accommodation, despite their assimilationist aspirations.

In Britain, and to some extent in the Netherlands, the frustration of legitimate aspirations of ethnic minority groups by a racist social structure has led to profound states of *alienation* (Bagley, 1976). We can best illustrate this by the comparative study by the Jamaican social geographer, Elizabeth Thomas-Hope (1983). Thomas-Hope compared the adjustment and satisfaction with achieving the goals of migration of similar groups of Caribbean migrants to Britain, Canada and the United States. She interviewed several hundred Caribbean respondents in London and other centres in the UK; in New York, Hartford and Boston in the US; and in Toronto and Hamilton in Canada. The highest levels of satisfaction with achieving the goals of migration were reported by West Indians in the US centres, closely followed by those in Canada; but levels of satisfaction were dramatically lower in respondents in the UK.

The goals of migration were quite simple: to advance occupationally and materially, and to achieve both for themselves and their children. These goals were most easily met in Canada and the US which are 'open' capitalist societies, used to accommodating the upwardly mobile aspirations of legal migrants in largely non-racist ways. Britain has no such tradition, and continues to discriminate against black people in jobs, housing, schools and colleges. The racism of the blue collar and many white collar segments in Britain is profound and deep-rooted, and many British people have still not accepted the reality that a significant minority of the British population consists of the previously-exploited colonial peoples, who now have the affrontery to compete directly with the indigenous population in the job and housing market (Bagley *et al.*, 1979). This discrimination extends to the second and third generation of Caribbean settlers in Britain, in profound contrast to the United States (and to some extent Canada) where second generation Caribbean migrants are largely absorbed into the black middle class, from whom they are indistinguishable.

In Britain, alienation and the knowledge that educational achievement is unlikely to bring success has led to two contrasted outcomes for minority youth. On the one hand, significant sectors of black youth have retreated from educational goals, and are labelled as 'deviant' by teachers and the educational system (Bagley, 1975). On the other hand, significant numbers of Asian youth have become ritualistically attached to education and enrol in yet further courses to postpone the ultimate (and usually unsuccessful) job search (Verma *et al.*, 1983).

At an official level, British policy has passed through a variety of phases. The first phase (beginning around 1960) involved an unsuccessful assimilationist policy coupled with harsh immigration restrictions which specifically discriminated against people of colour and kept families divided, through a rigid immigration system. The second phase (since 1970) made the immigration system still harsher, but began to develop a 'multi-cultural' policy which involved a limited and largely ineffective palliative directed to the accommodation of minority aspirations. But the central problems of racism and racial discrimination have not been addressed in British society, and with the advent of massive structural unemployment problems of racism have become significantly worse (Verma, 1983; Brown, 1984). The facile use of the terms 'multi-culturalism' and 'pluralism' have ignored the gross imbalances of power between ethnic groups. A description of the separateness of ethnic groups as a plural condition without reference to imbalances of power is to mask the racism inherent in such a situation: the most extreme example of this is the South African case (Bagley, 1972), but the separation and gross equality of aboriginal people in Canada comes uncomfortably close in similarity.

We have become profoundly dissatisfied with the trivialization of the idea of multi-culturalism by many British educational writers and practitioners (Verma and Bagley, 1984): 'multi-cultural education' has become for many a masking ideology, and a synonym for minor curriculum accommodations to the needs of some ethnic groups, without beginning to address the problems of racism, and the need to educate all ethnic groups (including whites) for inter-cultural living in a non-exploitive world.

The Canadian Experience

We have argued that particular features in the emerging social structure of Canada have meant that problems of race and ethnic relations are generally not so profound (or rather are different) from those observed in a number of European countries.

Canada, as a successful capitalist economy, has an openness in its accommodation of immigrants (including ethnic minorities) who have been specially selected for their combinaton of professional experience, education, youth, linguistic ability, and their willingness to fit in with a social structure based on individuality and individual enterprise.

Educational institutions in Canada, as the servants of the economy, generally socialize ethnic minorities without overt discrimination, to undertake successful roles in a free enterprise system. Such a process of selection through careful immigration, control, education, socialization, and training for successful participation in a capitalist society has served the needs of the selected immigrants well, but it is not in an absolute sense fair or unbiased. The Canadian system leaves unchallenged the world's most profound system of stratification, that between rich and poor countries (Bagley, 1979b). Recruiting certain of the educated class from countries of Asia and the Caribbean is, for Canada, a policy of self-interest, not of enlightenment. The recruitment of Vietnamese refugees is a case in point. Canada smartly entered the camps, and recruited younger, healthy, educated people who spoke French or English. Canada's 'generous' quota of immigrants was rapidly filled.

The ideologies of Canadian social structure are implicit rather than explicit. The ruthless self-interest of Canadian capitalism is rarely discussed, and multi-cultural and immigration policies are either rarely analyzed, or are seen as autonomous and even enlightened aspects of policy development, without reference to the wider economic and social policy connections. Coy phrases such as 'visible minorities' replace the harsher British emphasis on 'racial minorities'. Yet the question of who is a 'visible minority' remains undefined and undiscussed in Canada.

Other issues fail to reach the multi-cultural agenda in Canada. We have little data on the educational achievement of ethnic minority students in Canada. The nature, extent and social and psychological correlates of prejudiced beliefs in young people, and the extent to which these might be changed by curriculum methods of school organization is largely unexplored in Canada.[5] And we have few studies on discrimination against ethnic minorities in metropolitan Canada.[6]

The most perplexing issue which is not on the agenda of Canadian ethnic relations is the massive exploitation of the conquered aboriginal nations, the denigration and suppression of their culture, and an oppressive educational system which fails to address the cultural, affective or cognitive needs of Indian and Metis children (Morse, 1984; Bagley, 1984b).

In sum, Canada has apparently been relatively successful in absorbing certain higly selected immigrant groups whose aspirations fit in with the goals of a capitalist society, oriented to the fulfillment of individual needs for material advancement. However, full evidence to evaluate this proposition is lacking, largely because fundamental research and policy questions have not been posed. Such radical questions, about Canadian ideologies on ethnicity, the exclusion of poor and radical people from Canada, and the continued colonial exploitation of a dominated and excluded people within Canada, are not asked. The failure to ask these questions, we suggest, is an ideological matter, and relates to the presently unmasked nature of Canada's capitalist institutions. This silent ideological agenda may account too for the imprecise nature of multi-cultural policy in Canada, and the vagueness of official terms used to describe minority groups (Buchignani, 1980; and Moodley, 1983).

The aggressive and exploitive nature of settlement in Canada has been to the profound advantage of the white settlers, and the non-white minorities absorbed, through 'multi-culturalism', into the exploiting class. The exploitation of the land and natural resources has been to the profound disadvantage of the original inhabitants: their exclusion from both prosperity and autonomy, the denial of their land claims, and a continuation both directly and indirectly of a policy of cultural genocide against the aboriginal people is in our view the major but unaddressed issue in Canadian 'race relations'.

Conclusions

We have argued, using a Marxist-Weberian model, that ethnicity becomes a salient basis for social differentiation in times of economic quiescence; or when the proletariat itself is an identifiable ethnic group (as in some colonial situations, and in the 'plural' situation of South Africa). The ideologies and forms of 'multi-cultural' education will reflect the transitional state of any society, and the degree to which the ideological interests of dominant economic groups (who may, coincidentally, be ethnic groups) are manifest or latent. Current economic crises and the difficulties of capitalism in some countries, particular in Europe, has meant a sharply focused polarization of class interests which have implied a changed focus on the implications of ethnicity: nowhere is this better illustrated than in current Dutch society.

In many European countries the constrictions on capitalism seem analogous to the constrictions of narrow city streets: capitalism has little room to expand, and land and resources are used up. Accumulated capital, like many of the population, has migrated to the Second World, there to begin new forms of the liberal economy where capital and its human counterparts are protected by constitutional guarantees.

The trifling difficulty and embarrassment in this process in North America has been the objection of the land's original inhabitants. Solutions to the aboriginal problem have been only partially effective: in Newfoundland an island ecology meant that the natives could not escape, and they were efficiently hunted down and completely exterminated.[8] On the mainland only the buffalo were completely exterminated, and starving native people were rounded up and concentrated in camps or reservations, where they died in large numbers. Subsequent policy, still only partially successful, has been to remove children from parents as a deliberate instrument of educational policy (Morse, 1984) or latterly as an instrument of child welfare policy (Johnston, 1983).

Yet there is irony and hope in this process. In terms of the Post-Marxian, ecological society envisaged by Murray Bookchin (1980) there is, in counteraction to the ruthless violation of the land and its original people, a movement to abandon or at least temper the traditional Judao-Christian view of man's domination of nature. This movement seeks to acknowledge and indeed adapt the harmony-with-nature approach of North America's first peoples.

If we need multi-cultural texts for Canada there are works like Charles Eastman's *Indian Boyhood* (1902 and 1971) and Hugh Brody's *Maps and Dreams* (1981). The existing 'multi-cultural' texts, reflecting the ideologies of Canada's ruling class, simply stress an education for limited cultural autonomy within a dominant capitalist economy. That culture within the multi-cultural framework which stresses harmony of the people with the land, rather than its capitalist exploitation, is both deviant and unacceptable.

The interminable debate about multi-cultural education is a debate, fundamentally, about the values which inform the working of society itself. The superficial multiculturalism of Canada, Britain and the Netherlands not only fails to address the basic problem of class exploitation (of which racism is but a part); it also actively assists class exploitation by putting stress on what are in fact superficial differences between people. Multi-culturalism in its present form is little more than a masking ideology with which an artful and ruthless capitalism protects itself.

Notes

1 The aboriginal people of the British Isles are the despised 'Celtic fringe', ruthlessly suppressed and exploited by the Anglo-Saxon and Norman ascendancy for many centuries. The struggles of Celtic people for autonomy and justice are continuing. This struggle is totally ignored in the multi-cultural curriculum in Britain. Schools have accepted without question the ideology that the Irish struggle reflects the aspirations of contemptible and evil man who shall not be admitted to the halls of civilization. The Celtic fringe have occupied a 'reserve army' status for the British economy and share many of the material disadvantages of the migrant groups from the New Commonwealth (Bagley, 1983c). In Canada, migrant labour is shipped in from Asia and Central America for the growing season, and shipped out again in the Fall. No such nonsense as union organization is encountered with these groups. As Theunis (1979) observed in another context, 'Ze zien liever mijn handen dan mijn gezicht'.
2 There is an interesting parallel here with Philip Mason's idea of 'dominance' (Mason, 1970).
3 Given the present numbers of 'black' and 'brown' children in British schools (up to a quarter of all children in most urban areas) and the high rate of ethnic intermarriage (Bagley, 1979a) it is literally possible that in a hundred years' time all children in Britain will be neither white nor black, but 'mixed race'.
4 This thesis is expanded in more detail in Bagley (1984a), an article from which the present chapter is a revision.
5 The extent of Canadian knowledge in this field is ably summarized in the chapters by Berry, Kalin, Ijaz, Kehoe and Pratt in Samuda, Berry and Laferriere (1983).
6 Buchignani, N. (1983) 'Social science research on South Asians in Canada', paper given to the State of the Art Symposium, Center for South Asian Studies, University of Toronto, January and published in the proceedings of that symposium. Note that an earlier study has pointed to 'considerable discrimination' against blacks in Hamilton, Ontario — Henry, F. (1969) 'The measurement of perceived discrimination: A Canadian case study', *Race*, 10, pp. 449–61. The continued extent of that discrimination is largely unmeasured. See, Reitz, G. (1981) *Ethnic Inequality and Segregation in Jobs*, Toronto, Center for Urban and Community Studies, and Henry F. (1985) *Who Gets the Work?* Toronto, Social Planning Council. Henry's study reveals discrimination in employment of ethnic minorities in competition for law status occupations which are in short supply. The degree to which this finding can be generalized to the broader fields of employment, and to other areas than Toronto is unclear.
7 We have argued that, in general, the coincidence of cognitive style and ethnicity is not strong enough to justify special programs addressed to the cognitive needs of minorities — Bagley, C. (1984) 'Cultural diversity migration and cognitive styles: A study of British, Japanese, Jamaican and Indian children', in Samuda R. *et al.* (Eds) *Multiculturalism in Canada*, Toronto, Allyn and Bacon. However, more recent work on cognitive styles with children of the Blackfoot Nation in Southern Alberta leads us to propose that a culturally and cognitively relevant educational system, under the control of Blackfoot people themselves, is needed — Bagley C. and Verma G. (Eds) (1985) *The Cross-Cultural Imperative: Studies of Personality, Social Behaviour and Cognition*, London, Macmillan.
8 For an account of the extermination of the Beothuk Nation see Buchignani (1984).

References

AMERSFOORT, H. (1982) *Immigration and the Formation of Minority Groups: The Dutch Experience 1945–1975*, Cambridge, Cambridge University Press.

BAGLEY, C. (1972) 'Pluralism, development and social conflict in Africa', *Plural Societies*, 3, pp. 13–32.

BAGLEY, C. (1973) *The Dutch Plural Society: A Comparative Study in Race Relations*, London, Oxford University Press.

BAGLEY, C. (1975) 'The background of deviance in black children in London', in VERMA, G. and BAGLEY, C. (Eds) *Race and Education Across Cultures*, London, Heinemann.

BAGLEY, C. (1976) 'Sequels of alienation: A social psychological view of the adaptation of West Indian migrants to Britain', in GLASER, K. (Ed.) *Case Studies in Human Rights and Fundamental Freedoms*, Vol II, The Hague, Nijhoft.

BAGLEY, C. (1979a) 'Inter-ethnic marriage in Britain and America', *Sage Race Relations Abstracts*, 3, pp. 1–21.

BAGLEY, C. (1979b) 'Social policy and development: The case of child welfare, health and nutritional services in India', *Plural Societies*, 10, pp. 3–26.

BAGLEY, C. (1983a) 'Achievement, behaviour disorder and social circumstances in West Indian children and other ethnic groups', in VERMA, G. and BAGLEY, C. (Eds) *Self-Concept, Achievement and Multicultural Education*, London, Macmillan.

BAGLEY, C. (1983b) 'Dutch social structure and the alienation of black youth', in BAGLEY, C. and VERMA, G. (Eds) *Multicultural Childhood*, Aldershot, Gower.

BAGLEY, C. (1983c) 'Social policy in the Prairies to 2003: The future of the family, the plight of Native children, and the Universal social wage', paper given to Canadian Institute of Planners Conference, Life in the Canadian Prairies to the Year 2003, Regina, Saskatchewan, October.

BAGLEY, C. (1984a) 'Education, ethnicity and racism: A European-Canadian perspective', *Currents: Readings in Race Relations*, 2, pp. 8–12.

BAGLEY, C. (1984b): 'State of the world's children', *Canadian Children*, 9, pp. 1–4.

BAGLEY, C. and VERMA, G. (1979) *Racial Prejudice, the Individual and Society*, Farnborough, Saxon House.

BAGLEY, C. and VERMA, G. (1983) 'Self-concept and long-term effects of teaching about race relations in British schools', in VERMA, G. and BAGLEY, C. (Eds) *Self-Concept, Achievement and Multicultural Education*, London, Macmillan.

BAGLEY, C. and YOUNG, L. (1984): 'The welfare and identity of children from intercultural marriage', in VERMA, G. and BAGLEY, C. (Eds) *Race Relations and Cultural Differences*, London, Croom Helm.

BAGLEY, C., VERMA, G., MALLICK, K. and YOUNG, L. (1979) *Personality, Self-Esteem and Prejudice*, Farnborough, Saxon House.

BOOKCHIN, M. (1980) *Toward an Ecological Society*, Montreal, Black Rose Books.

BRODY, H. (1981) *Maps and Dreams: Indians and the British Columbia Frontier*, London, Pelican.

BROWN, C. (1984) *Black and White in Britain: The Third PSI Survey*, London, Heinemann for the Policy Studies Institute.

BUCHIGNANI, N. (1980) 'Culture or identity? Addressing ethnicity in Canadian education', *McGill Journal of Education*, 15.

BUCHIGNANI, N. (1984) *Cultures in Canada: Strength in Adversity*, Edmonton, Weigl.

CAMPFENS, H. (1980) *The Integration of Ethno-Cultural Minorities in the Netherlands and Canada: A Comparative Analysis of Policy and Programme*, The Hague, Government Publishing Office for the Ministry of Cultural Affairs.

EASTMAN, C. (1971) *Indian Boyhood*, New York, Dover Books (originally published by McLure of New York in 1902).

JOHNSTON, P. (1983) *Native Children and the Child Welfare System*, Toronto, Lorimer.

LENIN, V. (1934) *Lenin on Britain*, London, Lawrence and Wishart.

MASON, P. (1970) *Patterns of Dominance*, London, Oxford University Press.

MOODLEY, K. (1981) 'Canadian ethnicity in comparative perspective', in DAHLIE, J. and FERNANDO, T. (Eds) *Ethnicity, Power and Politics in Canada*, Toronto, Methuen.

MOODLEY, K. (1983) 'Canadian multiculturalism as ideology', *Ethnic and Racial Studies*, 6, pp. 1–12.

MORSE, B. (1984) 'Native Indian and Metis children in Canada: Victims of the child welfare system', in VERMA, G. and BAGLEY, C. (Eds) *Race Relations and Cultural Differences*, London, Croom Helm.

PALMER, H. (1982) *Patterns of Prejudice: A History of Nativism in Alberta*, Toronto, McLelland and Stewart.

SAMUDA, R., BERRY, J. and LAFARRIERE, P. (1983) *Multicultural Education in Canada*, Toronto, Allyn and Bacon.

SENNETT, R. (1970) *The Uses of Disorder: Personal Identity and City Life*, New York, Knopf.

THEUNIS, S. (1979) *Ze zien Liever mijn Handen dan mijn Gezicht: Buitenlandse Arbeiders in ons Land*, Amsterdam, Het Wereldvenster Baarn.

THOMAS-HOPE, E. (1983) 'Identity and adaptation of migrants from the English-speaking Caribbean in Britain and North America', in VERMA, G. and BAGLEY, C. (Eds) *Self-Concept, Achievement and Multicultural Education*, London, Macmillan.

VERMA, G. (1983) 'Consciousness, disadvantage and opportunity: The struggle for South Asians in British society', in BAGLEY, C. and VERMA, G. (Eds) *Multicultural Childhood: Education, Ethnicity and Cognitive Styles*, Aldershot, Gower Press.

VERMA, G. and BAGLEY, C. (1984) *Race Relations and Cultural Differences*, London, Croom Helm.

VERMA, G., MALLICK, K. and ASHWORTH, B. (1983): 'The role of attitude and experience in the transition from school to work in young South Asians in Britain', in BAGLEY, C. and VERMA, G. (Eds). *Multicultural Childhood: Education, Ethnicity and Cognitive Styles*, Aldershot, Gower Press.

WEBER, M. (1948) *Essays in Sociology*. (trans by H. GERTH and C. WRIGHT MILLS), London, Routledge.

5 Figure and Section: Ethnography and Education in the Multicultural State

Paul David Yates

As an uneven mirror distorts the rays of objects according to its own figure and section, so the mind in forming its notions mixes up its own nature with the nature of things.

Francis Bacon (1620)

There are two objects I hope to achieve in what follows. First, and this is my major task, I shall describe the nature and methodology of ethnography in educational research. Secondly, I suggest a possible shift in emphasis which might bring the ethnography of education more firmly into the ambit of multiculturalism.

I shall begin with a discussion of what sort of thing ethnography is. This will be followed by a review of some of the methods and methodologies associated with it. An analysis of some recent work on the perennial epistemological problems associated with the production and validation of ethnographies provides the final part of the first section. This latter discussion focuses on the question of how the ethnographer stands in relation to the potential field of knowledge.

The second section is more speculative and begins by noting the dominance of sociology in educational ethnography in the UK compared to the vigorous anthropology of education in America. This may partly explain the relative lack of interest amongst UK ethnographers in the description and analysis of cultural groups within the educational sphere. Finally, I suggest the role an ethnography of cultural groups might assume in providing necessary knowledge of ways of life and thought, and crucially, of contributing to an adequate theory of culture on which our multicultural education can be based.

What Is Ethnography?

Ethnography is the study of the world of a people. In the introduction to a recent book on ethnography and education, Woods suggests, ' "teaching" and "learning" may be "fronts" — dramatic activities designed to cover more significant ones, or merely one kind of activity, and not necessarily the most important, among many,'

(Woods, 1980, p. 9). Similarly, Williamson in a text on the comparative sociology of education suggests that

> 'In fact, the classroom and the lessons are perhaps the least significant aspects of school learning, of far greater importance are the great public routines of the school, the ceremonies, symbols and rituals of the school's corporate life.' (Williamson, 1979, p. 6)

Both of these quotations point to the signal feature of the ethnographic perspective, that is, a willingness to look again at existing categories and emphases which explain educational phenomena, and to recategorize and reconceptualize the field of study. This broadens our understanding of our own position in the process of education, and increases our facility for productive action. This is the value of ethnography.

The ethnographic perspective is difficult to reduce to a formula. Rather like the traditional image of liberal education, its acquisition results in a particular orientation to reality (what Goodman inelegantly called 'crap-detecting') and the propensity to a social analytic mode of thought, rather than the mastery of a set of techniques and the absorption of a specific body of theory. The goals of ethnography are rarely understood as the production of science or truth, but more pertinently understanding, and the personal development of sympathetic imagination free from sentiment.

What the ethnographer attempts is the reconstruction of an observed reality. This requires selection, translation and interpretation. However, an emphasis on the interpretive is not an invitation to idiosyncrasy. Data must be reliable, the product of systematic investigation using methods compatible with the problem, and the constraints of the field. These qualifications are vital, for interpretation by its nature is the product of usually individual, although sometimes collaborative, attempts to redefine, to make new orders from old conceptual categories. This activity is itself social and must have rules, but the rules are to facilitate maximum understanding, and not simply to ensure conformity to any particular model of social science. That would be to put the cart before the horse.

The necessary inclusion of the interpretive intellect in the act of translating social experience into ethnographic accounts may be seen as a weakness from a positivist viewpoint, but it remains a prerequisite of ethnographic methodology. Thus from the hard science perspective in sociology Spindler's quoted remark of a state department of education official might seem justified. 'Anything anyone wants to do that has no clear problem, no methodology, and no theory is likely to be called "ethnography" round here' (Spindler, 1982, p. 1). The point of ethnography is that it can, 'as the field arm of anthropology, give fresh insights into perplexing educational problems,' (*ibid.*, iii). This may sound rather unspecific and indeed it is, but it is precisely in the recognition and formulation of general cultural propositions regarding education that ethnography can provide a developed and informed context for discussion and a valuable critique of practice. In North America and in many countries in Europe the problem of how to adjust a monocultural educational tradition to a multicultural society is a constant political problem. It is also a complex one.

There is, as Cropley suggests, agreement that immigrant children in general, 'have lower average marks, obtain lower scores on standardised tests of achievement, are concentrated in the lower ability streams' (Cropley, 1983, p. 34). The Swann Committee's Interim Report called the expectation of low achievement in West Indian pupils by their teachers 'unintentional racism' (HMSO, 1981). Cohen and Manion argue that it is best understood by the notion of stereotyping, that teachers respond to individuals as members of a generic class with generalizable attributes, and in the case of West Indian children these stereotypes are negative (Cohen and Manion, 1983, p. 59). They also quote Tomlinson's report that Asians 'were felt to be supportive of school, keen on education, and their children were viewed as likely to persevere in acquiring some kind of school or work qualifications' (*ibid.*, p. 60). If teachers have a high expectation of Asians and a low expectation of West Indians, why does 'unintentional racism' only operate against one non-white group and not the other? Why are Asians and West Indians differently perceived by teachers? As both can be represented stereotypically, can we then go on to ask, is stereotyping morally obnoxious by nature or only when it is negative? And most importantly, upon what assumptions, information and habits of perception are teachers' expectations based, and how far can we attribute pupil performance to teachers' control of the outcomes of schooling, and how far to the demands of the pupils' own culture? Asians may be more likely to be well perceived by teachers than West Indian pupils, but they are also more likely to be victims of racial violence outside school. Why does race seem to have different meanings in different contexts? These are the sorts of questions where ethnography can provide the necessary context, not only in offering cultural descriptions of groups, but in developing reasoned frameworks which may challenge existing categories and ways of thinking, especially in the areas of race and culture.

Methods and Methodologies

Einstein regarded the whole of science as 'nothing more than refinement of everyday thinking.' Social scientific research in education or elsewhere does not produce especially true or more real accounts by virtue of simply being called research. The accounts of researchers are records of events that have been made within the constraints of a set of rules. These rules are not arbitrary but are the application of principles or assumptions to concrete purposes. Methodology is the study of these principles and assumptions. It is logically prior to the problem of methods. The questions addressed by methodology are about the nature of the phenomenon to be studied, and dependent upon the answers arrived at; criteria can be derived by which we can recognize an adequate account. Methodology has regard to the necessary *a priori* assumptions that the researcher makes about the nature of the world. Methods are the devices by which the data, that is, those elements in the events studied which are relevant to the conscious purposes of the researcher, are recognized, apprehended and recorded. For example, Spindler develops eleven criteria by which we can recognize 'a good ethnography of schooling' (Spindler, 1982, p. 7). These criteria cover the assumptions which validate ethnography as a methodology and include reference to ways of obtaining data consistent with the ethnographer's view of the world.

The things which are seen as significant to the educational psychologist, interested in cognitive development, may not be the same as those which are significant for the ethnographer interested in the culture of schooling. They may be observing in the same school or classroom but their accounts of the same events could be radically different.

Some methods can be appropriate to more than one methodological perspective. While participant observation is normally associated with anthropology, and more latterly the sociology of education, the interview can be a tool used from several different perspectives and can vary its form in each. For example, a formal interview schedule with set questions, and limited opportunity for divergent response, may be used by a sociologist on a structured sample, to determine teachers' understanding of particular set areas of Asian cultural practice, say kinship and marriage or diet and commensality. This would involve setting the parameters of relevant data quite tightly. The researcher might ask specific questions with factual rather than interpretive answers, such as those related to the geographical distribution of kin, or to intergenerational educational achievement. Resultant data might be processed and represented both qualitatively and quantitatively. On the other hand, if, for example, information were sought on the comparison of the articulation of education with other institutions among different cultural groups, then quite open-ended interviews might be required. These might elicit the range and nature of possible relationships between education and the marriage market, or education and employment and how recession had affected these conceptions among different cultural groups. More generally the perception of education as a social status could be investigated. In this case the respondant might be encouraged to determine much of the content of the encounter in order for the ethnographer to discover the emic, or folk view, and to provide data for the generation and testing of broad hypotheses about the significance of education to different cultural groups. Turning data into an account in this case would require an emphasis on interpretation rather than quantification.

Ethnography in education takes many forms, micro-studies of classrooms, studies of pupils and of teachers, of institutions and of communities and their schooling (Stubbs and Delamont, 1976; Delamont, 1981; Hammersley, 1980; Woods, 1980; Barton and Walker, 1983; Burgess, 1983; Willis, 1977). These different works are written from a range of perspectives focusing on fields of different natures, sizes and complexities. There is no ideological uniformity within them and they employ the full range of ethnographic methods. What unites them is that they provide, in Pelto and Pelto's terms, 'true and useful information' (Pelto and Pelto, 1978, p. 1). The quotation marks indicated that the truth was not thought absolute, but that truth and utility were interdependent, 'the truth value of our information is best measured by criteria of usefulness — in predicting and explaining our experience in the natural world' (*ibid.*). I think the confusion of veracity with utility is mistaken. The first is a methodological problem about the status of accounts, and the second a concern with their subsequent employment. Nonetheless it points to something important. Ethnography need not be whimsical and provide accounts of the world simply because it is there. It can be adapted to precise purposes, the description of an institution or the investigation of relationships, and can form a part of larger research strategies and problems, for example, what should a multicultural education be premised upon?

Subject and Object in Ethnography

A perennial problem for all scientists, both natural and social, is what is the proper relationship between the knower and the object of knowledge, and what is the epistemological status of the result? In two recent works Hammersley has brought his considerable experience in the field of educational ethnography to bear on the matter (Hammersley, 1983; Hammersley and Atkinson, 1983.) What Hammersley provides is a critique of naturalism, and in its place he advocates what he refers to as reflexivity.

Positivism and naturalism are the two poles of empiricism. Both see knowledge residing in the object and its extraction as the task of the scientist or ethnographer. Positivism is normally recognized in social science by the attempt to treat the social world in much the same way as inductive empiricist scientists are believed to treat the natural world. Thus the characteristic procedures are the development of hypotheses, and the design of tests, within the experimental model. Survey techniques and quantification may be employed in achieving the desired result, a generalizable proposition having something of the quality of a universal law. This image of social science depends centrally on the logic of the experimental method and the neutrality of the hypothesizing scientist in the face of the real external facts.

Naturalism

What has come to be known as naturalism is equally insistent on the pristine quality of external reality as the source of knowledge, but differs radically from positivism in assumptions about the nature of that reality and how it is to be apprehended. Naturalism 'implies commitment to the observation and description of social phenomena in much the manner that naturalists in biology have studied flora and fauna, and their geographical distribution' (Hammersley, 1983, p. 5). That is to say the stress is on perceiving and representing the social field in a manner which takes account of its special nature, not as with positivism, through the intermediary of an adapted natural scientific method. 'Rather than imparting methods from the physical sciences, naturalism argues, we must adopt an approach that respects the nature of the social world, which allows it to reveal its nature to us' (Hammersley and Atkinson, 1983, p. 12). The ethnographer's or participant observer's task here is to reflect, chameleon-like, the cultural world under observation with as little prejudice and artifice as possible. Arguably, however, prejudgment is not only inevitable but forms a major part of the equation.

When we come to understand events, or represent them to ourselves, we necessarily select from all possible interpretations that which satisfies the particular criteria we are operating with. All humans, including ethnographers, symbolize their experience in language. Experience acquires form through subjection to a mediating theory of culture, implicit or explicit. Perhaps the notion that the social world will reveal itself as long as we do not attempt to distort it with our own theories should be seen as a dogma within naturalism. That is to say, it is a core axiom, held to be true but not susceptible of testing, and upon which the whole enterprise is dependent.

The emphasis on the natural implies the possibility of the artificial, and naturalism is in some sense an antithetical response to the laboratory techniques of some psychology and the standardization of unique events through questionnaire surveys. Nonetheless, 'artificial settings set up by researchers are still part of society . . . they are social occasions subject to all those processes of symbolic interpretation and social interaction to be found elsewhere in society' (Hammersley and Atkinson, 1983, p. 11). The attempt to separate the natural from the artificial in society violates the unity of the social and suggests that some activities and occasions are in a sense supra-social.

If the task of ethnography is to produce a facsimile of what is observed, then the role of social theory seems largely redundant, if not positively pernicious. Also, the intellectual processes of interpretation and representation appear natural themselves, or at least potentially atheoretical. To apply a Marxist or structuralist framework to the reconstruction of events and experiences would thus be illegitimate, an unwarranted imposition on the real nature of things.

Reflexivity

Reflexivity is the term Hammersley has given to his working out of the effective relationship between the researcher, the objects of research, and any subsequent accounts. Essentially his ideas are based on the unity of subject and object. The researcher is social, and 'this is not a matter of methodological commitment, it is an existential [sic] fact' (Hammersley and Atkinson, 1983, p. 14). We are also reminded that methods themselves are part of society: 'However distinctive the purposes of social science may be, the methods it employs are merely refinements or developments of those used in everyday life' (*ibid.*, p. 15). For example, we all have conversations with high levels of specificity, with the milkman or our solicitor, which closely resemble the interview. We hypothesize about the nature of society in pubs and on trains, and use comparative method to test experimentally our ideas against reality.

The notion that ethnography is social activity also 'suggests that the researcher's own actions are open to analysis *in the same terms* as those of other participants' (Hammersley, 1983, p. 3). This is an important point: not only does it domesticate and demystify ethnographic research, it also makes it clear that the strategies and tactics of the researcher in the field are governed by her own sociability expressed through the aim of constructing ethnography. However, this notion might sail close to naturalism without the necessary caveat, that although ethnography is social activity, it is specific and conscious in a way that overlays the participation in the field. Thus, I was aware that having to sit on the platform with the President of the Hindu Union, the local priest and other community leaders during the Diwali celebrations not only dignified me, but more important for the ethnographer, it cut me off from the action. There is a distance between the researcher and the social setting which might be called the ethnographic agenda, which entails the constant awareness of the effect of self as actor, on the field, in the light of the goals of ethnography. Decisions taken in the field close, as well as open, options. The biography and theoretical orientation of the ethnographer will influence decisions and determine what are to be recognized as data, and this in turn constrains the possibilities of any resultant account.

Hammersley and Atkinson are rather dismissive of cultural description as an aim of ethnography and assert:

> In our view the development and testing of theory is the distinctive function of social theory [sic] ... the idea of relationships between variables that, given certain conditions, hold across all circumstances seems essential to the very idea of theory. (Hammersley and Atkinson, 1983, p. 19)

I fear these last strictures rule most social science atheoretical, and their satisfaction would be likely to require of the ethnographer a total access to, and control over, the field. However, the criteria for *pukka* theory are further elaborated.

> A theory must include reference to mechanisms or processes by which the relationship among the variables identified is generated. Moreover, such reference must be more than mere speculation, the existence and operation of these 'intervening variables' must be described. (Hammersley and Atkinson, 1983, p. 20)

The goal of ethnography thus becomes 'formalized theory'. While this highly refined view is later qualified with some ethnographies being simply 'way stations on the road to theory', this particular description of ethnography bears comment (*ibid.*, p. 201).

I think it possible and desirable that ethnography should go beyond the attempt to describe, and to develop and test hypotheses; I think some of the other aims, while admirably rigorous, go beyond the normal possibilities of field-based ethnography. The ethnographer can be thought of as an organizing focal consciousness within any particular cultural setting. Although there are ways of maximizing information through the use of informants and the collection of documents, the eventual data can represent only a very partial penetration into the complex reality of the field, comprising, as it does, constantly interacting and developing systems of meanings. Naturalism may rightly be taken to task for employing unrealistic notions of unalloyed transference of the reality under study, in order to preserve its integrity. An over-laborate machinery for analysis may run the opposite risk of satisfying the demands of theoretical propriety at the expense of authenticity, and incidentally artificially limiting the possible fields of study. It may be the case that the extreme variability of variables in the domain of meaning makes such a view of science incompatible with the practice of ethnography.

The development and testing of hypotheses, however, is an entirely plausible aim of ethnography in education. For example, the literature on differential educational performance between ethnic groups prompts the question: why should this be so? A reasonable hypothesis from available evidence is that educational performance is a function of culture. This can be broken down into specific areas of investigation around definite questions. Do different ethnic groups hold different images of education? How do these articulate with other aspects of culture? How is education ranked with alternative sources of status and prestige? Such an investigation is possible using participant observation, documentation and perhaps structured interview in the collection of data, which could subsequently provide both qualitative and quantitative accounts which could be compared along significant variables and relationships. Such research would not necessarily qualify as social theory in Hammersley and Atkinson's terms but may be of great value to policy-makers and classroom teachers.

Similarly in vexed and complex local issues, such as the introduction of halal meat in state schools, ethnographic data may provide a counter-balance to implacable moral assertion. Again this may not necessarily be productive of much in the way of social theory, but may aspire in Pelto and Pelto's terms to be 'true and useful'.

The Necessity of Culture

As Burgess reminds us, there was a period in Manchester, under Max Gluckman, when anthropology and sociology came together in a joint ethnographic venture, which produced the first generation of school studies (Burgess, 1983; Hargreaves, 1967; Lacey, 1970; Lambert, 1970). After this initial joint impetus most indigenous ethnography, and certainly the ethnography of education, has been largely taken up and developed by sociologists, both in the small-scale setting of the classroom and the larger settings of institutions and localities (Woods and Hammersley, 1977; Stubbs and Delamont, 1976; Delamont, 1983, 1984; Willis, 1977; Ball, 1981; Burgess, 1983). The two traditions in ethnography are fully discussed by Delamont and Atkinson (1980).

In America, however, especially through the work of Spindler, an anthropology of education has been developing, in some ways independent of the sociology of education and naturally focused on problems of ethnography (Spindler, 1977, 1974a, 1982a). On both sides of the Atlantic there has been a move towards a broadening of ethnographic methodology to embrace quantitative method (Hammersley and Atkinson, 1983; Pelto and Pelto, 1978; Wilcox, 1982). A significant distinction has been the focus of American anthropologists on the concepts of culture and transmission in education (Singleton, 1974; Spindler, 1974, 1982; Leacock, 1973; Bruner, 1972; Cohen 1971).

It is important to note that the accent has been on relatively small-scale studies of aspects of transmission and culture, and is not commensurate with reproduction theory (Bowles and Gintis, 1976; Bourdieu, 1977). The former is mainly concerned with how the younger and elder generations renegotiate the nature and content of culture within a generally conservative social structure. The negotiation refers to the nature of social transactions rather than to radical change (Wallace, 1973). The latter are attempts to explain the persistence of class structures through generations. For Bowles and Gintis this is achieved through correspondence, the notion that school is organized on a class basis as anticipatory socialization for the workplace (Bowles and Gintis, 1976). Bourdieu uses the concept of cultural capital, which is access to the experience of those elements of French culture on which the schooling system draws, and the consequent ability to discourse upon and within it, which is the means of achieving academic success (Bourdieu, 1977).

Apart from the interest in transmission in the American anthropology of education, which is not absent from UK sociology of education, there is a commitment to cross-cultural research and comparative analysis which does not typify British educational ethnography. As Williamson reminds us, the development of comparative analysis was seen as a necessary element in the new sociology of education but 'as a strategy to develop further the theoretical framework of the subject these suggestions have not, however, been taken seriously' (Williamson, 1979, p. 3). Currently, comparative analysis is more likely to be a part of social psychology in the study of plural society than of ethnography (Verma and Bagley, 1975, 1979; Cropley, 1983).

The importance of comparative studies of cultural transmission is that the very idea itself demonstrates something of the nature of cultural reality; it is diffuse and differentiated. It is constantly in the process of being maintained and renewed with each human transaction. As with language it can be analyzed and recognized on different levels, idiolect, dialect, vernacular, each one a sub-system of culture or language. Neither cultures nor languages are discrete, but are permeable and constantly permeated. Hindi and Punjabi are separate languages but have common antecedents and shared aspects. Hinduism and Sikhism again have the dual quality of similarity and difference, perhaps standing in a similar relation to each other as English Catholics and non-conformists. Hindus and Sikhs share what might be broadly termed Asian cultural characteristics, but conceive of themselves, and are so conceived of by others, as separate communities. Unity and diversity are the bases of comparative analysis.

I want now to suggest briefly something of the possibilities and potential for ethnographic research within the comparative analysis of culture. Since the publication of the interim report of the Swann Committee the curriculum has become an area of renewed interest (HMSO, 1981; Hicks, 1981; Lynch, 1981; James and Jeffcoate, 1981; Cohen and Manion, 1983). Much of this work is premised on the notion that the curriculum should in some way reflect the cultures of its participants, rather than academic culture, which is argued to be closer to the culture of middle-class whites than other groups.

Although an area of some confusion, it can no longer be thought of as an area of neglect. Both urban and suburban schools have recently employed a variety of strategies and methods in devising curricula thought appropriate for a multicultural society (Twitchen and Demuth, 1981). The image of culture, which is very rarely theorized, is often exotic and Eurocentric. That is to say, there is culture (white British) which is unproblematic and taken for granted, and there are other cultures recognizable solely through their difference, or exotic quality compared to indigenous white culture.

Two problems occur immediately which can have only essentially arbitrary answers. First, whose cultures qualify for inclusion and by what criteria? Secondly, to what precisely in the organization and content of school life should the culture of its participants relate?

The confusion of culture and race is endemic, which goes some way to explain the popular association of West Indians and Asians as solely constituting the other cultures within the UK. This simple typology is unrealistic and unreliable. It is true that West Indian and Asian cultures are those most frequently discussed in the literature. Is this because they are non-whites, or because some are immigrants? Should either of these conditions be the basis for rethinking the curriculum? The first leads us into the cul-de-sac of anti-teaching, and the second cannot provide any sensible cultural information. We cannot say that the school should take account of the cultures of immigrants, for the UK has such a highly variegated immigrant population, most of whom are rarely considered. Are the Poles and the Irish immigrant populations constituting cultural groups with a right to inclusion? If we agree that West Indian and Asian cultures are definitely candidates, what account is to be taken of diversity within those groups? Are language groups to be considered as distinct culture groups, and if so what levels of linguistic differentiation are to be employed within the complex of contemporary British language types (Stubbs and Hillier, 1983)? For example, a pupil may speak French-based St Lucian *patois* and an indigenous dialect, or Jamaican creole, London Jamaican and standard English, as do many West Indian students in higher education. The West Indian archipelago is not culturally homogeneous, indeed 'the term West Indian is itself culturally precarious. The nearest to a factor of cultural homogeneity among the British West Indies has been their love for cricket' (Lashley, 1981, p. 229).

Asian culture is no less complex, divided by religion, caste and class. The erstwhile East African, Gujarati-speaking, Patidar family, with financial and domestic outposts in Germany or Canada, and a land base in Kaira district, may be considered as culturally distinct from the more passive and proletarian Sikh family in Huddersfield (Tambs-Lyche, 1980; James, 1974). These two groups have different histories and patterns of migration and different conceptions of what it means to be immigrant.

If we begin to recognize the complexity of cultural identity, then the problem of how culture relates to curriculum becomes more acute. Indeed, the cultural identity of particular groups and individuals may be difficult to distinguish in itself.

For example, as Cropley (1983) points out, West Indian and Asian pupils may be born in Britain and have no first-hand knowledge of a homeland which formed their parents' cultural identity, and thus in some ways determined their own early socialization. Also, in what he describes as 'the double bind', children are encouraged to succeed in school, which means taking on British norms and values, while simultaneously living in the shadow morality of the homeland which is antagonistic to British mores (*ibid.*, p. 115).

If a particular identified culture is to be recognized in school, what levels and aspects of culture can be included? School is renowned for excluding the cultural lives of most of its participants, the working class. The notion that school alienates minorities is not uncommon, but how is school to authentically include the culture of its participants? Can, or should, the school system include male, working-class, West Indian, urban street culture? If the answer is yes, should it then be extended to say female, home counties, suburban youth culture? This would imply that school should reflect local cultures, but how this might be done and how the content might be turned into school knowledge is not clear. We do know that some cultural groups do not value being schooled, and it is difficult to see a reciprocal relationship between the cultures of school and that of Willis's working-class 'lads' (Willis, 1977).

School can also be seen as jealous of its own cultural territory. The incursion of non-indigenous cultural behaviour is not automatically welcomed. Allowing Muslim girls to wear trousers or opt out of games is sometimes seen as a concession rather than a right, and the proposed introduction of halal meat into Bradford school meals has caused something of a furore. Thus it may be that school is capable in some ways, perhaps restricted to the curriculum, of symbolizing the integration of different cultures into its organization, but there is little evidence of the accommodation of actual cultural diversity.

Putting high culture on the curriculum is a possible means of symbolizing inclusion, but Basham's exquisite account of classical India is as remote from the life of modern Asian youth as Harvey and Bather's account of the British constitution was from political reality for indigenous pupils of a previous generation. This is not to argue that idealized versions of cultural reality have no place in school, but that they require a sympathetic and supportive context if they are to be valued by pupils.

The teaching of comparative religion is now commonplace in secondary school, but on what basis can the comparison be made? For example, is being Hindu in any sense comparable to being Christian? The UK is a secular society and its established church has a Protestant bias. Thus, religion may be generally thought of by the indigenous white population as being primarily a matter of the individual's voluntary belief. Christians can both apostatize and renounce their religion because they have first to ascribe to it as a set of intellectual propositions, found in their most basic forms in creeds. Protestantism is Christian individualism. It is because religion is seen to have this abstracted and external form that we can conceive of religious education as compatible with the notion of a subject on the school curriculum.

The basic categories of caste are communal not individual, and Hinduism is the eschatology of a communal caste society (Dumont, 1980). Verma and Mallick (1981) quote Pandit Nehru on Hinduism, 'It is hardly possible to define it, or indeed to say precisely whether it is religion or not, in the usual sense of the word.' Individuals are born into a caste and are definitionally Hindu. They do not have to subscribe actively intellectually to any particular articles of faith, they simply are the personification of Hinduism. Because being Hindu is not a voluntary condition, it cannot sensibly be renounced. The final complication is that because it is not identified with a specific historical revelation, as is Christianity, it has come to comprise an amorphous and contradictory set of teachings, and to identify it solely with the Bhagavad-Gita and the Upanishads is to distort it on two counts. It is to suggest that it is a religion of the book like Islam and Judaism, and it blurs a central characteristic, that there is a definite distinction between its theology, the Brahmanical tradition, and the local and domestic practices of Hindus, Redfield and Singer's great and little traditions (Marriott, 1972). It is reasonable to include courses in Hindu philosophy and eschatology in a curriculum because these represent the abstracted intellectual elements of Hinduism. But arguably it is a distortion of the nature of Hindu culture to represent it as items of knowledge on particular propositions. These transformations are nonetheless required if it is to be suitable for inclusion, as school knowledge, on the curriculum.

Rastafarianism as an aspect of West Indian culture presents even greater problems. It has no formal organization, it is raw and overtly millenarian and has many of the characteristics of a youth subculture as well as those of a religion. Whatever its significance for West Indian youth, as a complex of cultural knowledge it is incompatible with formal schooling.

These two short examples are intended to illustrate the following points. First, the cultural lives of groups are complex meaning-making systems which may have a limited potential for inclusion in schooling. Secondly, a minimal elaboration of the concept of culture provides a tool for the critique of current practice.

Conclusion

I have tried, albeit briefly, to indicate something of the possible nature of the areas within which an ethnography of schooling might work. I hope at least to have indicated that multiculturalism requires an adequate theory of culture, that can plausibly be generated through the accumulation of ethnographic accounts and comparative analysis. This would require a programme of small- and larger-scale studies of classrooms, institutions and the communities they serve, and of the people, organizations and networks of those who control and direct the education system.

School is the central state agency of cultural transmission, but we have no clear idea of how culture should relate to schooling. To focus upon the curriculum is in some sense an automatic response of the internal or practitioner view of what school is, especially given its current importance, along with managerial skills, in in-service training. However, it is not at all clear that a multicultural curriculum is what is needed, nor if it is, then what it should be. It may be the case that the social needs of at least minorities would be better served by concentrating on raising levels of certification (Stone, 1981). If, on the other hand, school is to reflect the lives of its participants, then prevailing notions of culture need to be submitted to more rigorous analysis than has been the case, and also require a proper empirical grounding. Without this prior basis to innovation, there can be no clear logical connections between the analysis of the problem, the strategy for meeting it and the criteria for evaluation. How are we to decide in what ways schools should be trying to symbolize cultural diversity? What analytic framework do we currently have for deciding between the exotic view of the otherness of other cultures, which makes Diwali extracurricular and Christmas intra, and the Bullock-like notion of culture across the curriculum which tends to founder outside the humanities and religious education?

An ethnography of cultural diversity, which would include indigenous white culture as equally problematic as any other, would provide the necessary context within which hitherto unheard debates could provide us with answers to these most pressing problems, and with them a reliable guide to action.

References

BALL, S.J. (1981) *Beachside Comprehensive: A Case Study of Secondary Schooling*, Cambridge University Press.

BARTON, L. and WALKER, S. (Eds) (1983) *Race, Class and Education*, London, Croom Helm.

BASHAM, A.L. (1967) *The Wonder That Was India*, London, Fontana.

BOURDIEU, P. (1977) 'Cultural capital and pedagogic communication', in BOURDIEU, P. and PASSERON, J.-C. (trans R. NICE) *Reproduction in Education, Society and Culture*, Beverley Hills, Calif., Sage, pp. 71–106.

BOWLES, S. and GINTIS, H. (1976) *Schooling in Capitalist America*. London, Routledge and Kegan Paul.

BRUNER, J. (1972) *Relevance of Education*. Harmondsworth, Penguin.

BURGESS, R.G. (1983) *Experiencing Comprehensive Education: A Study of Bishop McGregor School*, London, Methuen.

COHEN, Y.A. (1971) 'The shaping of men's minds: Adaptations to the imperatives of culture', in WAX, K.L., DIAMOND, S. and GEARING, F.E. (Eds), *Anthropological Perspectives on Education*, New York, Basic Books, pp. 19–50.

COHEN, L. and MANION, L. (1983) *Multicultural Classrooms*, London, Croom Helm.

CROPLEY, A.J. (1983) *The Education of Immigrant Children: A Social Psychological Introduction*, London, Croom Helm.

DELAMONT, S. (1981) 'All too familiar? A decade of classroom research', *Educational Analysis*, 3, 1, pp. 69–83.

DELAMONT, S. (1983) *Interaction in the Classroom*, 2nd ed., London, Methuen.

DELAMONT, S. (Ed.) (1984) *Readings on Interaction in the Classroom*, London, Methuen.

DELAMONT, S. and ATKINSON, P. (1980) 'The two traditions in educational ethnography: Sociology and anthropology compared', *British Journal of Sociology of Education*, 1, 2, pp. 139–52.

DUMONT, L. trans SAINSBURY, M., DUMONT, L. and GULATI, B. (1980) *Homo Hierarchicus: The Caste System and Its Implications*, University of Chicago Press.

HAMMERSLEY, M. (1980) 'Classroom ethnography', *Educational Analysis*, 2, 2, pp. 47–74.

HAMMERSLEY, M. (Ed.) (1983) *The Ethnography of Schooling: Methodological Issues*, Driffield, Nafferton.

HAMMERSLEY, M. and ATKINSON, P. (1983) *Ethnography, Principles in Practice*, London, Tavistock.

HARGREAVES, D.H. (1967) *Social Relations in a Secondary School*, London, Routledge and Kegan Paul.

HARVEY, J. and BATHER, L. (1968) *The British Constitution*, 2nd ed., London, Macmillan.

HICKS, D.W. (1981) *Minorities: A Teacher's Resource Book for the Multi-Ethnic Curriculum*, London, Heinemann Educational Books.

HMSO (1981) *West Indian Children in Our Schools*, Cmnd 8273, London, HMSO.

JAMES, A.G. (1974) *Sikh Children in Britain*, Oxford University Press for Institute of Race Relations.

JAMES, H. and JEFFCOATE, R. (Eds) (1981) *The School in the Multicultural Society*, London, Harper and Row.

LACEY, C. (1970) *Hightown Grammar: The School as a Social System*, Manchester University Press.

LAMBERT, A.M. (1970) 'The sociology of an unstreamed urban grammar school for girls', unpublished MA thesis, University of Manchester.

LAMBERT, A.M. (1976) 'The Sisterhood', in HAMMERSLEY, M. and WOODS, P. (Eds), *The Process of Schooling*, London, Routledge and Kegan Paul/Open University Press.

LASHLEY, H. (1981) 'Culture, education and children of West Indian background', in LYNCH, J. (Ed.) *Teaching the Multi-Cultural School*, London, Ward Lock Educational, pp. 227–50.

LEACOCK, E. (1973) 'The concept of culture and its significance for school counsellors', in IANNI, F.A.J. and STOREY, E. (Eds), *Cultural Relevance and Educational Issues: Readings in Anthropology and Education*, Boston, Mass., Little, Brown and Co., pp. 189–200.

LYNCH, J. (Ed.) (1981) *Teaching in the Multi-Cultural School*, London, Ward Lock Educational.

MARRIOTT, M. (Ed.) (1972) *Village India: Studies in The Little Community*, University of Chicago Press.

PELTO, P.J. and PELTO, G.H. (1978) *Anthropological Research: The Structure of Inquiry*, 2nd ed., Cambridge University Press.

SINGLETON, J. (1974) 'Implications of education as cultural transmission', in SPINDLER, G.D. (Ed.) (1974) *Education and Cultural Process*, New York, Holt, Rinehart and Winston.

SPINDLER, G.D. (1955) *Education and Anthropology*, Stanford University Press.

SPINDLER, G.D. (1963) *Education and Culture*, New York, Holt, Rinehart and Winston.

SPINDLER, G.D. (1974a) *Education and Cultural Process*, New York, Holt, Rinehart and Winston.

SPINDLER, G.D. (1974b) 'Schooling in Schönhausen: A study of cultural transmission and instrumental adaptation in an urbanizing German village', in SPINDLER, G.D. (Ed.) *Education and Cultural Process*, New York, Holt, Rinehart and Winston, pp. 230–72.

SPINDLER, G.D. (Ed.) (1982a) *Doing the Ethnography of Schooling: Educational Anthropology in Action*, New York, CBS College Publishing/Holt, Rinehart and Winston.

SPINDLER, G.D. (1982b) 'General introduction' in SPINDLER, G.D. (Ed.) *Doing the Ethnography of Schooling: Educational Anthropology in Action*, New York, Holt, Rinehart and Winston, pp. 1–14.

STONE, M. (1981) *The Education of the Black Child in Britain*, Glasgow, Fontana.

STUBBS, M. (1983) 'Understanding language and language diversity': What teachers should know about educational linguists', in STUBBS, M. and HILLIER, H. (Eds), *Reading on Language, Schools and Classrooms*, London, Methuen, pp. 11–38.

STUBBS, M. and DELAMONT, S. (Eds) (1976) *Explorations in Classroom Observation*, Chichester, Wiley.

STUBBS, M. and HILLIER, H. (Eds) (1983) *Readings on Language, Schools and Classrooms*, London, Methuen.

TAMBS-LYCHE, H. (1980) *London Patidars: A Case Study in Urban Ethnicity*, London, Routledge and Kegan Paul.

TOMLINSON, S. (1981) 'Multi-racial schooling: Parents' and teachers' views', *Education 3–13*, 9, 1, pp. 16–21.

Twitchin, J. and Demuth, C. (1981) *Multicultural Education: Views from the Classroom*, London, BBC Publications.

Verma, G.K. and Bagley, C. (Eds) (1975) *Race and Education across Cultures*, London, Heinemann Educational Books.

Verma, G.K. and Bagley, C. (Eds) (1979) *Race, Education and Identity*, London, Macmillan.

Verma, G. and Mallick, K. (1981) 'Hinduism and multi-cultural education', in Lynch, J. (Ed.) *Teaching in the Multi-Cultural School*, London, Ward Lock Educational, pp. 184–201.

Wallace, A.F.C. (1973) 'Schools in revolutionary and conservative societies', in Ianni, F.A.J. and Storey, E. (Eds), *Cultural Relevance and Educational Issues, Readings in Anthropology and Education*, Boston, Mass., Little, Brown and Co., pp. 230–49.

Wilcox, K. (1982) 'Ethnography as a methodology and its application to the study of schooling: A review', in Spindler, G.D. (Ed.), *Doing the Ethnography of Schooling: Educational Anthropology in Action*, New York, Holt, Rinehart and Winston, pp. 456–88.

Williamson, B. (1979) *Education, Social Structure and Development*, London, Macmillan.

Willis, P. (1977) *Learning to Labour: How Working Class Kids Get Working Class Jobs*, Farnborough, London, Saxon House.

Woods, P. (Ed.) (1980) *Pupil Strategies*, London, Croom Helm.

Woods, P. and Hammersley, M. (Eds) (1977) *School Experience, Explorations in the Sociology of Education*, London, Croom Helm.

6   *Toward Pluralism in Education**

Harry C. Triandis

The main thesis of this chapter is that multicultural education should be a regular subject in the educational curriculum of most countries. With the ease of transportation and communication, with the movement of peoples from one country to another, with the increased economic interdependence of the world, ethnocentrism is as detrimental as illiteracy. We now know a lot about intercultural education. For example, Landis and Brislin (1983) have provided a three-volume *Handbook* on this subject. It is time to think of using some of this information, skills and perspectives in our regular educational systems. The purpose of such training is to (a) increase awareness of the extent to which our thoughts, values and behaviors are products of our own culture, and not necessarily functional; (b) increase ability and skill in interaction with poeple who have different norms, values, ways of thinking and perspectives; and (c) increase ability to control our own behavior so as to be optimally effective in relating to those of different cultures.

Definitions

Pluralism, in contrast to *monism*, was first used by philosophers to deal with the questions: 'How many things are there in the world?' and 'How many kinds of things are there in the world?' When translated to societal issues, these questions become: 'How many kinds of cultures can coexist in a given society?'

By 'culture' I mean the man-made part of the environment. This includes not only the material part of the environment, objective culture, but also the way the man-made part of the environment is perceived, subjective culture. As people live in different environments, which provide them with different schedules of reinforcement, they develop distinct points of view about the way the environment is

* This chapter is a modified and updated version of Triandis, H.C., 'The Future of Pluralism', presented as the presidential address to the Society for the Psychological Study of Social Issues, Division 9 of the American Psychological Association, in September 1976. It was published in the *Journal of Social Issues*, 1976, 32, pp. 179–208.

structured. For example, some learn that planning is a useful activity, and others that it is a waste of time.

By 'society' I mean the collective body of persons composing a community as citizens of civil government. Thus within the United States we have more than 200 million persons who are subjects of one government, but these persons may have very different subjective cultures. The environment of the economically depressed ghetto is very different from the environment of the affluent suburb. Furthermore, historical factors and migrations are antecedents of major aspects of the heterogeneity of American society.

Assimilation refers to a policy of making each cultural group adopt the culture of the mainstream. *Integration* refers to the policy of coordinating the goals of each cultural group, but allowing each group to maintain its culture. There is some evidence suggesting that integration is to be preferred. Murphy (1961, 1965) reports fewer breakdowns and psychiatric hospitalizations among immigrant groups, per capita, in countries with an integration policy (e.g., Canada) than in countries with an assimilation (melting pot) policy, such as the US.

This is the place to state my broad biases, which are against assimilation of the melting pot variety and in favor of *additive multiculturalism*, a concept that I will define in detail later in this chapter. My biases come both from personal sources — I am multicultural — and from the reading of history. I value creativity, and history tells us that creativity is maximal when thesis and antithesis are in clear view. A homogeneous society will inevitably become stale, static and unlikely to survive in a fast-changing environment.

The work of Janis (1972) clearly shows that homogeneity in opinion leads to major mistakes in both judgment and behavior. I realize, of course, that heterogeneity has a price: it means interpersonal conflict. But I believe that there are ways to teach people to deal with it, and when this happens one has an exciting, creative, well-adjusted-to-its-environment kind of society, with productive conflict.

Theoretical Analysis

To address the question, 'How are people of different cultural backgrounds to coexist in a given society?', we need to look at a prototypical relationship — a dyad consisting of one individual from culture A and one individual from culture B. What is the meaning of a good relationship within this dyad? Exchange theorists (Thibaut and Kelley, 1959; Homans, 1974) have given us some guidelines: a good relationship is one in which the rewards exceed the costs.

Rewards are transfers of resources from one person to another. Thus, if O *gives* P love or status or a service or a gift or some information or some money, O transfers a reward to P. A cost is incurred when a resource is taken away or denied, or when a person is forced to behave in a way which precludes obtaining the benefits an alternative behavior provides. Thus, if O takes away money, say steals, or denies status, say by insulting P, there is a cost for P.

A complication arises from the fact that it is not so much the absolute size of the resource exchange itself, but the meaning of the exchange that determines if it is a reward or a cost. The meaning of the exchange depends on at least two variables: (a) expectations and (b) the perceived antecedents and consequences of the exchange. For example, if *P* expects to receive a gift worth $10 and instead receives a gift worth $1000, the surprise, embarrassment and activity required to understand the event may make this event more like a cost than a reward, in spite of the fact that the amount of the resource that was transferred is 100 times greater than expected. The second complication concerns the perceived antecedents of the behavior. *P* explains *O*'s behavior to him /herself in terms of perceived antecedents or consequences. For example, *P* may attribute the strange behavior of *O*'s giving a $1000 gift to *O*'s attempt to bribe him/her, or to pressure that *O* received from others to make this gift, or to the intrinsic pleasure that *O* might experience from making a gift, and so on. Each of these perceived causes or antecedents results in a different meaning for the behavior. *P* may feel that the gift is a *cost* if he/she sees it as a bribe. On the other hand, *P* may see it as a reward if he/she sees it as a consequence of *O*'s deriving pleasure from making it.

Expectations in the form of stereotypes, implicit personality theories, attribution habits and strategies for perceptual selectivity provide further complications. A behavior may be perceived very differently when it is associated with a person of a particular race or social class from when it is associated with another person. In short, pre-existing good or bad relationships between two people or two groups tend to engender self-fulfilling prophecies. In other words, a *good relationship* means that the interactions between *P* and *O* are consistent with their expectations, and do not involve antecedents or consequences that are perceived to be costly in the future or implying a negative meaning for the exchange.

Still another complication is that some resources are perceived to be more valuable to the individual than other resources. Generally the economists are correct in considering relationships between prices and supply and demand. When a resource is abundant its value is low; when it is scarce its value is high. Foa and Foa (1974) have assembled much evidence supporting the hypothesis that particularistic exchanges, such as exchanges of love, status and services, are more valuable than universalistic exchanges, such as exchanges of money, information or goods. This is true at least in highly developed, technological societies, where generally there is considerable affluence, stores are full of goods and libraries and the mass media disseminate more information than we really care to have. By contrast, these societies do not have well-developed systems for exchanges of love, status and services. One often gets more of these particularistic exchanges in a traditional society, such as an Indian village, where, with the exception of the lowest castes, the majority have status given to them by virtue of caste membership, the extended families can be sources of much exchange of love (though also of hate), and very complex systems of interdependence result in a lot of services being given — for cooking, shopping, laundry, education, social events, etc. For example, even in today's relatively modern India an important marriage is celebrated over a period of a month or so, with relatives coming from all over the country to participate in the celebration. For American tastes, so much celebrating and the receipt of so much status and service from so many relatives would be overwhelming, but many Indians find it a memorable experience that they would not like to be without. The point of my argument is simple: modern technological society while giving to most people certain kinds of resources (e.g., goods) is depriving them of others (e.g., status). Thus, the values of particularistic exchanges are particularly high in modern technological societies.

Applications to Intergroup Relations

Now let us examine the relationships among different groups within a hetero-geneous society. One of the realities of different subjective cultures is that they result in different expectations and different perceptions of antecedents or consequences of interactions. Thus, the greater the heterogeneity within a given society, the greater the probability that interactions will be costly. As the interactions become more and more costly and less rewarding, as we move from consideration of relatively similar groups interacting with each other, we are seeing an increase in the conditions of alienation. This argument might imply that heterogeneity is undesirable. But this is not the case if we use other criteria to judge the society. For example, creativity has been found to be maximal where there is political fragmentation and instability (Simonton, 1975). The great civilizations of the past have been characterized by heterogeneity (Naroll *et al.*, 1971). Thus, rather than banish heterogeneity we must discover ways to harness it. We must discover how to make optimal use of it.

Much of the discussion which follows focuses on black-white relations. This is because I have limited space. I could provide a parallel discussion for Native Americans, Spanish-speaking Americans, white ethnics, Eskimos and so on. In principle, relationships between old and young, men and women, straights and gays, and numerous other such contrast groups can be analyzed in the same way and the analysis will lead to similar conclusions. The black-white conflict is the most visible and most intensive, and the one whose reduction can serve as a prototype for the reduction of the other conflicts. Thus when I talk about blacks in general, if you want you can add the other 'unmeltable ethnics' (Novak, 1972) to the argument, since a parallel argument can easily be constructed.

Heterogeneity is likely to lead to conflict within a society, particularly when it involves a physically visible division of majority and minority groups, as is the case with racial distinctions in the United States. Historical and cultural antecedents of interracial relationships in this country have resulted in situations in which the rewards received by the white majority from exploitation of the black minority have been constantly greater than the costs. For the blacks there has been enough hope and enough improvement in social standing to place increasingly larger segments of the black community in situations where their rewards exceed their costs; however, this does not imply that all is well. Most blacks probably still feel outside the mainstream of American life and there is a substantial group within the black community whose costs are greater than the rewards. I think this heterogene-ity within the black community has not been emphasized enough. I bring it to your attention in the most emphatic way, since I believe it has major implications for the issues of pluralism, integration and racial harmony.

Our research on black and white subjective cultures (Triandis, 1976) suggests that overall the similarities of black and white subjective cultures are much more overwhelming than the differences. Yet some segments of the black community — namely, the unemployed, male, ghetto dwellers — look at the world around them in a manner that is very different from the way other samples of blacks look at the world. Specifically, our data suggest that the black unemployed see their environment as chaotic; they do not trust other people, institutions and other blacks who 'have made it'. This syndrome, which we called *ecosystem distrust*, is a natural outcome of an environment in which extreme poverty, discrimination, rejection and unpredictability are the defining characteristics. Let us not make the mistake of blaming the victim; the blame must be placed on the environment of this group of people.

One must recognize, however, that in many cases the behavior of people with ecosystem distrust must be changed, because it fails to take advantage of opportunities offered in the environment. After all, environments often change. Ecosystem distrust may develop in one environment as a perfectly natural outgrowth of that environment, and then persist in all sorts of other environments. This is somewhat parallel to Solomon and Wynn's dogs who, once shocked in a particular box after a particular signal, persisted in jumping out of the box as soon as the signal was presented, long after the shock was turned off. Thus, those samples who learn to be helpless in some environments persist in their helplessness (Seligman, 1975) even when the environment has changed. Such situations require intervention.

While our data show that the black ghetto unemployed male is extreme in ecosystem distrust, we find traces of this syndrome in other black groups. Other research (Schuman and Hatchett, 1974) also finds alienation in the black community. Such alienation is a direct outcome of the poor relationships between blacks and the dominant group. It probably also applies to Amerindians, Eskimos in Alaska and other groups that have cultures that are still quite different from those of the majority.

To understand this alienation better, let us look at the social exchanges between minority and majority groups in terms of our theoretical scheme. Take a black, Amerindian, or Eskimo who is very poor and consider his exchanges with the majority culture. Minority members are denied the most valuable particularistic resources of status or services. Rather, they receive mostly money, goods or information. By contrast, the majority receives from the minority some services, in the form of activities of servants, waiters, bus drivers, garbage collectors, etc., and some status, in the form of being elected by them to important positions in society, such as mayor, governor, congressman, senator or president, and in some cases even love — admiration, imitation. In other words, the exchange is definitely in favor of the majority; they receive the valuable resources and they give the less valuable resources.

Homans (1974) has pointed out that when one person (O) receives less from the interaction with another (P) than P does from interaction with O , then P has *power*.

It has long been known that whites have the resources and the power. What we need to know, however, is precisely how much of a difference this difference in power makes. Of course this is very difficult to determine, but estimates do exist. Specifically, Dowdall (1974) has estimated gains and losses by examining family income, unemployment rates and occupational status levels of blacks and whites with equivalent demographic characteristics — age, sex, education and so on. He finds little evidence of a change in the white-gain/black-loss picture over the last few years, and quotes Thurow's (1969) computation that whites gain somewhere between 5 and 15 billion dollars per year (in 1960 dollar values) which are lost by blacks as a result of differential wage structures, job discrimination and so on. Even if we accept Otis Dudley Duncan's analysis (cited in Mosteller and Moynihan, 1972) that the black-white income gap is only 40 per cent due to job discrimination, with 46 per cent due to particular techniques of child rearing in black families and 14 per cent due to poor schooling, still we would conclude that between 2 and 6 billion dollars (in 1960 dollar values, close to 20 billion dollars in today's) constitute losses sustained by blacks or gains obtained by whites. The picture is even more bleak if you consider that these white gains are realized to a large extent by those whites who are most privileged, since employers are among those who gain most from wage differentials.

All this discussion concerns the least valuable resource — money. In the case of the most valuable resources, such as status, the situation is undoubtedly much more unequal, unfair and offensive to the black minority. We cannot estimate the cost of the disrespect by the police, the low self-esteem engendered by our educational system, the relative lack of high status models in the black horizon, and so on. We can only guess that these costs are substantial.

Of course inequality is inconsistent with the dominant American ideology. As Myrdal (1944) pointed out, the *American Dilemma* is that the ideology includes the 'all men are created equal' notion, yet inequality is clear and present. How do humans deal with such cognitive inconsistencies? While we do not have to accept all aspects of cognitive dissonance theory, there is enough support for the notion that Western people strive toward consistency (Abelson *et al.*, 1968) to know that such inconsistencies lead to some form of cognitive work. Abelson (1959) pointed out that there are different ways in which individuals can handle inconsistency. Mechanisms that might be used by the majority include the following:

1 They can stop thinking, and undoubtedly many members of the majority have adopted this way out. Many people are annoyed when somebody brings up these inconsistencies, since that forces them out of their preferred mode of functioning.

2 They can bolster one cognition. 'Why,' they would say, 'all Americans are equal, there is no inequality; exploitation talk is a Communist plot to disgrace this great country.'

3 They can differentiate. Here the subject might say, 'The American creed refers to people like me. People who are very different in skin color, beliefs and so on are not in the set. In fact, they are inferior and must be taken care of, protected, given welfare.' Noblesse oblige!

4   Still another way to deal with the inconsistency is to transcend it. 'It is true that there is inequality, but I am at the bottom of some hierarchies too. It is a fact of life; if you live in a society you are unequal sometime. We are all equally unequal, so we are equal!'

Consider now the effect of exploitation on the minority. Here, too, there is a discrepancy between what one expects to receive from a relationship and what one does receive. In equity theory (Berkowitz and Walster, 1976) the perceiver sees his own inputs and outcomes and compares them to the inputs and outcomes of the other. Inputs include efforts to have a good social relationship, skills, status and other resources a person brings to the relationship. Outcomes include both the costs and the rewards that one experiences from a relationship. Positive outcomes occur when rewards exceed costs. Minority members consider as costs the fact that members of their group have been exploited in the past while contributing to the economic development of this continent, have (as in the case of Amerindians) given up their lands and their way of life and have signed treaties that have not been observed.

What about the rewards? Participation in a modern state can be a reward. But in the case of the minorities this also involves being paid less, being excluded from important jobs, being an underdog in most power relationships. When the minority members compare themselves with the majority they see large costs and small rewards. Hence the relationship is seen as grossly inequitable. How can equity be restored? One can stop thinking, but that is unlikely if one is severely injured by the inequity. One can bolster some element, such as exaggerate the benefits received from the relationship. Undoubtedly many blacks, described as Uncle Toms, do just that. One can differentiate and think of the self as unworthy of comparison with the majority other. Thus, many blacks accept the views of the majority concerning themselves; they think of themselves as inferior. It is interesting to note that in the research of Marx (1967) and of Schuman and Hatchett (1974) the more educated the blacks the more alienated they felt. Being educated makes it much less probable that they will accept the notion that they are inferior. Finally, one can transcend the inequity by believing that inequity is a normal state of affairs.

Cognitive solutions to inequity are likely to occur among people who are introspective. But those who are more pragmatic must *act* to restore equity. How can this be done? Clearly, by decreasing one's costs and/or increasing one's rewards.

Not all minority members are in a state of inequity, and not all who are in a state of inequity will choose the same means to restore equity. But it is useful to explore what people can do in such situations. To decrease costs, minority group members can sometimes give less of value to the majority. This can take many forms, including producing less, cooperating less, revealing less, giving less status and so on. Behaviors that the majority interprets as laziness, irresponsibility, uncooperativeness, hostility and so on might be due to efforts by the minority to reduce costs and to pursue its self-interest. The increasing difficulties of white researchers in getting information from such samples (X[Clark], 1973) provide another example of such cost reduction efforts.

As for increases in rewards, taking away from the majority group status, money, information or services sometimes can be rewarding. Some behavior that the majority considers antisocial or criminal might be seen as an effort to reduce inequity. For example, a black adolescent who snatches away the purse of a white old lady may be viewed as taking away a resource and as restoring equity.

Foa and Donnenwerth (1971) made the important point that for some blacks violence may constitute one of the very few means of obtaining status available to them. A similar point has been made about some sections of the Italian lower class, both here and abroad. Lewis (1966), in his discussion of the culture of poverty, made the distincton between cultural groups who are poor in monetary terms and those who are also poor in their ability to provide social support. It is when both kinds of poverty are present that Lewis described the situation as a 'culture of poverty'. This distinction is important, because it is not poverty in universalistic resources such as money that is really important, but poverty in particularistic resources such as love and status that is important. Many unemployed minority group members have neither. Unemployed majority group members may lack money but they often have institutions that maintain interpersonal support systems; they thus escape from the culture of poverty. In any case, I want to emphasize the rather different situation of the unemployed blacks, and the fact that many undesirable behaviors, such as reliance on drugs and violence, are the outcomes of their particular condition.

The situation of the unemployed blacks is also very different from the situation of other minority groups. The most important difference, it seems to me, is that centuries of slavery altered the social fabric of the black community so that the patterns of interdependence characteristic of traditional societies were severely weakened. A characteristic of many European or Asian groups that migrated to this country was that they had strong norms, imposed sanctions on those who broke them and had a system of interdependence that included both rights and obligations. Slavery broke up the African social systems and created an intrinsically anomic social situation. Thus I see the black case as extremely different and in no sense comparable to the Chinese or Eastern European immigration to this country. Those who dismiss this argument on the grounds that slavery has been dead for more than 100 years simply show their narrow time perspective. One hundred years is an insignificant period on the scale of cultural evolution. Historians find strong connections between events that took place thousands of years ago and the present. We tend to be too impressed by superficial changes in technology and forget the extent to which our fundamental, unquestioned and unchallenged assumptions and our values reflect events that occurred 2000 years ago in the eastern Meditèrranean. For example, the concepts of male superiority, property values, democracy, freedom and so on have a long history.

To judge blacks against the standards created by the Eastern European or Asian migrations is to ignore essential distinctions. Violence and other natural mani-festations of the existing inequitable social relationships are condemned with attributions to dispositional characteristics, forgetting the importance of situational variables. This is a problem that has been clarified by studies of human attribution tendencies (Jones *et al.*, 1972). Humans apparently have a tendency to make dispositional attributions for negative behavior when the actor is disliked, and situational attributions for negative behavior when the actor is liked (Nisbett *et al.*, 1973). This could be deduced from a balance-theoretical perspective as well. In any case, there are numerous studies that show that positive behavior is attributed to internal dispositions of ingroup members and to external influences on outgroup members, while negative behavior is attributed to external influences in the case of ingroup members and to internal dispositions in the case of outgroup members (Taylor and Jaggi, 1974).

There is no doubt that criminal behaviors are undesirable from the point of view of both minority and majority groups. The majority group sometimes suffers directly; the minority group is even more often the target of aggression by frustrated members of its own group and also sustains a loss of status because the behavior of some minority group members is socially undesirable. But the way to stop these unfortunate actions is not to increase the number of police. As Lewin observed long ago, social systems tend to reach quasi-stationary equilibria. An equilibrium which is maintained by large police forces by its very nature involves large forces on the minority group side. Guerrilla warfare is a real possibility if we choose repression rather than reconciliation.

The only way to stop such unfortunate behaviors is to restore equity. To restore equity we need to close the status gap. The status gap is great because there are real differences in education, income and socially desirable behavior between some black subgroups and other blacks.

Illinois Studies of the Economically Disadvantaged

A three-phased study was designed to develop training materials for white supervisors and black hardcore unemployed workers. In Phase I the major variations in the perception of the social environment among blacks and whites were determined (Triandis, 1976). In Phase II we constructed training materials, called 'culture assimilators', to train white supervisors and black hardcore workers. In Phase III we attempted to show that the training has beneficial effects and improves the interaction between blacks and whites (Weldon *et al.*, 1975). For our purposes Phase I is the most relevant.

We selected samples of (a) white, middle-class, college females, (b) white, lower-class, high school males, (c) black, lower-class, high school males, and (d) black, lower-class, hardcore unemployed males. These samples were strategically selected to examine the limits of variation of black and white subjective cultures; the first and last samples differed in age, sex, race and social class, while the two other samples were as similar as possible, except that they differed in race.

We asked these samples to make a large number of judgments, 5600 to be exact, involving different kinds of social stimuli. Specifically, we studied the stereotypes of these groups, using items requiring each person to assign a number between 0 and 9 to reflect the extent to which they saw particular social categories as having particular attributes (e.g., black policemen are intelligent). Subjects assigned a 0 if they thought that the category never had the attribute, a 9 if they thought that the category always had the attribute, and some number in between if they thought the connection between social object and attribute was present sometimes, often, frequently, almost always, etc. We studied role perceptions by presenting more than 100 roles and asking the respondents to indicate the frequency of particular behaviors within each role (e.g., if a mother is interacting with her son, what is the perceived frequency of asking for advice?). We examined conceptions about the characteristics of jobs by asking our respondents to assign a number between 0 and 9 to certain attributes (e.g., are truck drivers well paid? never = 0; always = 9). We inquired about behavioral intentions of the respondents with respect to samples of social categories (e.g., would you ask a black policeman for help? never = 0; always = 9). We also asked about probable causes for certain behaviors and probable effects of the same behaviors (e.g., what are the causes of a person 'doing his own thing'? What are the consequences?). In short, we asked a large number of questions about a variety of topics.

The analysis employed a technique developed by Tucker (1966) called three-mode factor analysis. This technique gives the patterns of consistency revealed by the answers of the respondents across different modes. For example, with respondents reacting to 100 or so roles on twenty or so behaviors, it is possible to obtain patterns of consistency across roles, across behaviors and across respondents. One might find that some roles involving interracial relations and hostile behaviors are used by the subjects quite frequently. But even more interestingly, one looks for patterns of consistency across subjects; some subjects give responses that are quite similar to responses given by other subjects and quite different from the responses given by still other subjects. Using discriminant function analysis it is then possible to find out if the groupings of subjects as selected for study are strongly related to the subject-points-of-view that emerge from the factor analysis.

The results show that for many kinds of questions there is a definite pattern. The answers of one sample are relatively homogeneous and differ from the answers given by the other samples. Thus, we were able to determine which patterns of answers had primarily race or social class or sex correlates. This first study, which explored the limits of variation of subjective culture, provided us with some 500 hypotheses about possible differences in subjective culture between blacks and whites.

The next step was to test these hypotheses. We developed a schedule of questions that included those questions that gave the most striking differences in the previous study. We then studied 240 persons, making sure that half of these respondents were black and half white; one-third middle-class, one-third working-class, and one-third hardcore unemployed; one-half females and the other half males; one-half young (18–25) and the other half older (35–45). With ten persons in each cell of this twenty-four-cell design, we were able to do multivariate analyses of variance to confirm some of the hypotheses of the first study.

What emerges from these studies? First and most striking is the tremendous heterogeneity of the black samples. What emerges is a black majority that is very much like the white majority, looking at the social environment in more or less the same terms as the whites. They have the same beliefs, the same aspirations. But then there is a black minority that may constitute something like 10 per cent of all blacks and that is very different. Consider just one specific finding, as an illustration: we asked people to assign numbers between 0 and 9 to the concept 'I myself' on the attribute *unimportant*. The black hardcore assigned numbers almost two scale points higher than other groups to this idea. This was not the case for the white hardcore unemployed. In fact, they never thought of themselves as unimportant. The only other samples that showed self-devaluation were the working class, white or black, who were old. Apparently, in this society if you reach your forties and are still a member of the working class, you begin to have doubts about being important.

In any case, the black hardcore sample is different from the other samples. As you look at their answers on the various instruments the impression is clear. They see the ecosystem as unreliable and unpredictable, other people as untrustworthy, behavior as haphazardly connected with outcomes, black professionals as exploiters and the establishment as exploitative. If you look at the responses of this sample, you learn that they believe that getting a job requires that one be a paragon of virtue, finishing high school requires high levels of ability, motivation, and lots of money and so on. In short, this sample views events that are considered ordinary in American society as requiring high levels of skill and much good luck. Furthermore, this sample appears to perceive the work situation in terms more appropriate for a family than for a work setting. They see more love and admiration exchanged in work settings and less superordination and subordination than is true for those who have had experience with work settings. This sample also expects less satisfaction from working than do other black samples.

I feel relatively secure that these conclusions are reliable, because they converge with conclusions derived by entirely different methods. Thus, Ley (1974), a social geographer, used a variety of methods, including participant observations, to study a section of the Philadelphia black ghetto. He reports that the environment is of 'unrelieved uncertainty' (p. 159), involving much internal competition, a 'jungle' in the words of some of the residents, with maximum potential hostility needing maximum defensiveness for survival, and characterized by ' exploitative anarchy' (p. 285). I want to stress here once again that this is the environment that has been created by discrimination and prejudice, in which the black community are the victims. Almost anyone placed in such an environment would react with ecosystem distrust, though there are a few unusual individuals — orchids in the jungle, as Ley calls them — who do not exhibit such distrust. Turner and Wilson (1976) have also concluded that the most disaffected blacks are young, urban, low SES males.

Another set of findings reflects differences in the perception of friendship between the deprived hardcore unemployed and the other samples. Here we can think of the consequences of severe deprivation of resources as a cause of competition with everybody — friend or foe — and hence higher levels of distrust, cynicism and even aggression. For example, our data indicate that many blacks believe that unless they have money they cannot have friends. Whites see other factors determining whether one has friends, such as being honest and listening to other people's ideas. A consequence of having friends, for the white sample, is trusting them, being loyal to them, not being lonely and depending on them; but the black sample does not emphasize these consequences nearly as much.

87

Theoretical Interpretation

It seems probable that differences in subjective culture emerge from differences in the availability of resources, in the presence of historical, economic and cultural factors suggested earlier. Clearly, whites have more resources than blacks, and the black hardcore have less resources than most blacks. The effect of extreme lack of resources, in addition to interpersonal competition, hostility and distrust, must be an attempt to make the few available resources stretch as much as possible. This can be done by finding novel ways to obtain gratification. This could result in a greater emphasis on immediate gratification. The lack of resources also means that the total level of reinforcements received might be considerably lower. This could have the effect of socializing children much less, thus increasing the probability of delinquency. Low levels of reinforcement will also have the effect of providing little cognitive connection between what one does and one's outcomes, leading to the expectation of external control of reinforcement, less imposition of social norms, thus leading to lower levels of normative clarity and less satisfaction with the total social situation, hence leading to anti-establishment attitudes. Finally, low levels of reinforcement may lead to a defensive self-esteem, which involves cognitive distortions which increase the virtues of the available resources and devalue the unavailable resources. In short, it is fair to say that when a society allows a large gap in levels of reinforcement, it is likely that there will emerge an unusual subjective culture, some features of which are likely to be undesirable.

I would like to emphasize here that I am not blaming the victims. As I see it, the historically established patterns of economic exploitation, reinforced by cultural mores, institutional racism and other features of the society have created a particular ecosystem for the hardcore unemployed, particularly if they are black. The subjective culture of this group is a natural outcome of this ecosystem. The ecosystem is not of their own creation. They are responding to it. Actually, our data suggest that they are responding adaptively. For example, they are more resigned to crime and other undesirable features of their environment than are people outside that environment, a reaction that is adaptive, in the sense that they find living in that environment more tolerable. This does not mean acceptable, only that it involves the realization that there is not much that they can do about it.

On the Consequences of Inequality

Inequality is not a new problem, nor is it a purely American dilemma. In the history of the world there have been many more examples of exploitation than examples of equality. The association of wage differentials with sex, age and ethnic groups has also had a long history. There are major problems of societal integration in India, in South America, in Africa. But what is novel in the United States is that we have the ideology and the resources to make progress toward the elimination of inequality.

Inequality leads to large differences in subjective culture (at least for some subgroups), which leads to undesirable behaviors by members of these subgroups, which leads to projection of these undesirable behaviors to all members of the minority group by majority members. Inequality increases the probability of crime by members of the subgroups which are most deprived; then the majority blames the whole minority group for the increased crime, not just those subgroups. Hence, the majority gives less status to the minority and justifies the inequality on the grounds of the lower morality of the minority group. Inequality thus creates a feedback which results in the reinforcement of inequality.

Integration as a Remedy

The major prevailing view is that integration is a remedy for this situation. When people use the word *integration* today, they mean merely putting people together, hoping that one group will become assimilated. Though I do not define integration this way, the popular press does, and it is important to distinguish the different meanings of the term. One over-optimistic view is that if we 'integrate' — i.e., put blacks and whites together in — our schools, industries and neighborhoods, we will have instant harmony. I used to agree with this view until I considered some other arguments; I now believe that we have not explored enough other alternatives. Let me first state why I feel that integration, in the form of putting people together, is not the remedy. As I see the evidence from integration studies, merely to put people together in a room, without creating conditions of interdependence, superordinate goals and superordinate normative regulators and associated sanctions for their implementation (Sherif, 1968) has little effect and can be counterproductive.

In a variety of situations around the world, mere contact has increased prejudice (Amir, 1976). This is perhaps too strong a statement, but it is consistent with the data when the status differences are large. Contact does generate prejudice, even among professionals who ought to know better. Consider, as an example, the stereotypes of professional personnel working for the Bureau of Indian Affairs (Hennigh, 1975). Teachers, nurses and physicians working in Alaska had much more negative stereotypes of Eskimos than those having little contact. Urban Indians who work among economically deprived rural samples often feel that the 'peasants are intolerably backward', while those with little contact have a positive though romantic view.

Amir's (1969, 1976) review of the contact literature showed contact to be beneficial only under particular specified conditions. Equal status contact is helpful; contact when holding superordinate goals, contact that receives institutional support, contact between cultural groups that are similar on dimensions other than status (such as on values), and contact under conditions of pleasurable stimulation (such as in camps, concerts or trips) can lead to improved attitudes. However, when such conditions do not hold, contact can lead to more prejudice. Unequal status contact, when mutually exclusive goals lead to zero-sum relationships, contact that is opposed by institutional norms, contact between groups that have very different subjective cultures, and contact under conditions of failure, anxiety or distress can all lead to increased prejudice.

When there is a difference between two groups, *A* and *B*, on an attribute that is related to status — for example, income, housing, education or anything else — contact is likely to make the difference more salient. Stereotypes develop when such differences are made salient (Campbell, 1967). Furthermore, in societies such as the US where there is an egalitarian ideology the status inequality becomes even more salient. People have to explain the inequality to themselves, so they generate cognitions that justify the inequality. For example, they may develop the stereotype *lazy* to explain observed differences in income.

In my studies of stereotypes of Greeks and Americans that were in contact with each other (Triandis and Vassiliou, 1967; Vassiliou *et al.*, 1972), the Americans devalued Greeks on dimensions of efficiency, skill and competence in getting things done, while the Greeks devalued Americans on dimensions of interpersonal warmth. In fact, both groups seemed to have an implicit personality theory in which work competence was negatively correlated with social competence, as measured by charm, warmth and friendliness. Thus each group appeared to observe the difference in the standard of living and translated it by means of their implicit theory — the Americans said that the Greeks are high in social competence and low in work competence; the Greeks said the same about themselves and saw the Americans as high in work competence, but low in social competence.

A similar situation is likely to prevail in black/white contact. Contact in situations of unequal status is likely to generate prejudice rather than reduce it, because some prejudice emerges as a justification of the status gap.

A Specific Proposal

Rather than integration, as it is conceived by the popular press, we need *additive multiculturalism*. I borrowed the idea, by analogy, from Lambert's (1973) discussion of additive and subtractive bilingualism. Lambert argues that when an English Canadian learns French he adds to his capacities; when a French Canadian learns English there is danger of assimilation into the vast North American culture and loss of the French identity. Whites who learn about black subjective culture and learn to appreciate the positive features of black culture become enriched. Asking blacks to become culturally white is subtractive multiculturalism. As Taylor (1974) wrote, perhaps too strongly, integration as advocated today is a white idea about how blacks would become psychologically white. That conception is subtractive multiculturalism. The way to reduce conflict is not for one side to lose what the other side gains, but for both sides to gain.

Some of the negative features of American society — including anxiety over achievement, which results in much 'Type A behavior' and a third of a million deaths from heart attacks each year — might be reduced if we adopt a more relaxed outlook, often found among blacks. (I am personally in need of reform, in this respect, as much as anyone else.) The pace is frantic. Too often we are in the situation of the passenger on an airplane who hears the pilot say, 'I have excellent news: our speed is breaking all records. Now for the bad news: we are lost.' Perhaps we should contemplate whether our crime, pollution, suicide and divorce rates are where they should be. In any case, we need to understand the feelings associated with each kind of multiculturalism. Desirable pluralism permits everyone to have additive multiculturalist experiences. Ideally, pluralism involves enjoyment of our ability to switch from one cultural system to another. There is a real sense of accomplishment associated with the skill to shift cultures. The balanced bilingual/bicultural person, or even more, the multicultural person, gets kicks out of life that are simply not available to the monolingual/monocultural person. There is a thrill associated with the competence to master different environments, to be successful in different settings. The person who delights in different social settings, different ideologies, different life-styles, simply gets more out of life. There are now effective ways to train people to appreciate other cultures (Brislin and Pedersen, 1976). We must use these procedures in our schools to broaden the perspective of most students.

At the simplest level, we find this broadening in the appreciation of different foods. Contrast the meat and potatoes diet of some people with the diet of those who have the means to explore the multinational cuisine of a large city. The ability to appreciate the full range of music produced in different parts of the world is another example. But, food and music appreciation are not as difficult to learn as the subtle ways of human interaction, and particularly intimacy. To be able to become intimate with many kinds of people who are very different is a great accomplishment. This should be the goal of a good education, and the essential step forward to a pluralist society.

A good education also means an education which is adjusted to the needs of the minority as well as the majority groups. Castañada *et al.*, (1974) outlined some of the ways in which schools must change to provide the best learning environments for Latin-background, black, and Native American children. Castañada, for instance, points out that frequently teachers punish behaviors that are learned in the child's home, thus making the school environment noxious. The Spanish-American emphasis on family, the personalization of interpersonal relations, the clear-cut sex-role differentiation and so on create a particular way of thinking, feeling and learning. A teacher who is not aware of these cultural influences can easily lose contact with a child. For example, teaching a Spanish-background child may be improved if the teacher sits close to the child, touches a lot, hugs, smiles, uses older children to teach younger children, involves the children in group activities, sends work to the child's home so the parents can get involved, arranges for Mexican foods to be cooked in class, teaches Spanish songs to all children and so on. Similarly, if monocultural American children understood why Native Americans have values stressing harmony with nature rather than its conquest, a present rather than a future time orientation, giving one's money away rather than saving it, respect for age rather than emphasis on youth, such children would broaden their perspective. The dominant American culture will profit from inclusion of such conceptions in its repertoire of values: harmony with nature is much more conducive to the respect that ecology imposes on technology in the post-industrial era, respect for old age may be much more functional in a nation where the majority is old as it will be soon, a present orientation may be more realistic in a society that can no longer afford to grow rapidly because of energy and resource limitations and so on. The majority culture can be enriched by considering the viewpoints of the several minority cultures that exist in America rather than trying to force these minorities to adopt a monocultural, impoverished, provincial viewpoint which may in the long run reduce creativity and the chances of effective adjustment in a fast-changing world.

Such goals are equally viable for minority and majority members provided we respect each other's cultural identity. We must not ask blacks to become culturally white. We must not ask them to lose their identity. Integration in the form of becoming like us implies by definition that their culture is inferior. Rather, what we want is to find more common superordinate goals and methods of interdependence that give self-respect to all. We need to be creative if we are to discover such methods.

Recent research by Johnson and Johnson (1983) has shown that cooperative schools, where children receive rewards for working together, teaching each other and helping each other, lead to improved intergroup relations, *as well as better learning*. The approach adopted by Aronson and his collaborators (Aronson *et al.*, 1978; Aronson and Osherow, 1980), called the jigsaw classroom, in which five or six students meet for about an hour several days a week to study one curriculum area, and engage in cooperative learning and peer teaching is another example. Such efforts have been successful in reducing intergroup tensions. But to achieve major tension reduction an even broader program is required — additive multi-culturalism.

To reach additive multiculturalism I see the need for a three-pronged strategy.
1   *Blacks and other minorities must seek power.* They need to develop a flexible, imaginative approach to acquiring it. To get power they need resources. They do have one important resource — a common fate. If they manage to communicate within each community the importance of concerted action for improving their position in American society, they will be able to engage in balance-of-power politics and thus acquire more resources than they now have.
2   *To learn about another culture one must be secure in one's own identity. The essence of additive multiculturalism is that those who have a firm identity — the well-established mainstream of America — must do the learning.* And they should learn not only about blacks, but also about Spanish-speakers, Native Americans and other ethnic minorities that exist in significant numbers in the US. To be educated in this country should mean that one is able to have good, effective and intimate relationships with the ten or more important cultural groups that exist here. Specifically, whites must learn to interact effectively with blacks. Right now, given the status of blacks and whites in this country, whites have no good reasons to learn how to get along with blacks. Unlike the American who, if he is to visit Paris should learn a bit of French, since otherwise he may not get much champagne or perfume, whites have little motivation to get along with blacks.

Note that I am emphasizing that learning to get along means learning new interaction skills. But this is exactly what additive pluralism is all about. It is being able to get along not only with one's own group but also with other groups. New techniques for culture learning (Brislin and Pedersen, 1976; Landis *et al.*, 1976;

Seelye, 1975; Triandis, 1975, 1976) are becoming available. These techniques can train people to engage in interactions where the rewards exceed the cost for both persons, with a large variety of ethnic groups. By extension some of these techniques can be used to improve relationships between men and women, old and young and so on. In short, whenever the life experiences of a group are sufficiently different from the experiences of another group, the gap in subjective cultures requires an effort to reduce misunderstandings. Each group must learn more about the perspective of the other groups than happens now.

3 *There is an urgent need for programs that guarantee jobs to every American who is capable of working.* Our data show the largest gap in subjective culture not between blacks and whites but between unemployed blacks and employed blacks. Current estimates of unemployment rates among young black males exceed 50 per cent. This is a totally unacceptable rate. A program of guaranteed jobs for those who can work, negative income tax for those who earn too little, job supportive services (such as public nurseries) and welfare payments for the old and disabled may eventually cost less than the 200 billion spent on various forms of welfare ('Progress against poverty,' 1976). Such a program can benefit both whites and blacks (though blacks will be helped proportionately more), the costs can be diffused through the income tax structure and it is consistent with the dominant values of this society — it puts people to work (Rothbart, 1976). I would add one more most important benefit: it creates the preconditions for successful contact. Given the importance of having a job within the American status system, the elimination of the unequal rates of unemployment via elimination of most unemployment would immediately reduce one of the important dissimilarities that make successful interracial contact difficult. I must emphasize that our evidence (Triandis, 1976), as well as that of Feldman (1974), suggests that working-class blacks are very similar in their subjective cultures to working-class whites; the discrepancies in subjective culture occur among the unemployed. Thus, by eliminating this category we would move toward another precondition of successful contact. Finally, by integrating the unemployed into the economy, we would create some commitment to the successful operation of the whole economic system, and a variety of superordinate goals.

For the guaranteed jobs plan to have the desired effects, however, these jobs must be identified not as government-jobs-specially-made-to-take-care-of-the-unemployment-problem but as legitimate jobs. This means that a variety of avenues toward full employment must be created simultaneously — stimulation of the private sector, identification of activities that have national priority (such as conservation projects), job training and other programs.

We Need More Research

Consider a theoretical model that describes black/white contact. There might be n dimensions on which two groups might be different. In the case of assimilated blacks, n tends to be close to zero; they differ little from whites. In the case of blacks with ecosystem distrust, it may be a very large number. Now consider m dimensions specifying the conditions under which contact is likely to lead to 'successful' interpersonal relationships, that is, relationships where the rewards exceed the costs for *both* blacks and whites. It is likely that in the case of work relationships (one of the *m* dimensions) this would be the case, while in the case of other relationships it may not be the case.

One of the research projects urgently needed is one that specifies how the *n* dimensions of difference are related to the *m* dimensions of successful contact. For example, a difference in trust in the American system of government might have strong implications for cooperation between a white and a black person in a business venture, while it may have little relevance for an intimate relationship; conversely, a difference in trust in the reliability of friends may have little significance in a relationship which is specified by a written contract but very large significance for an intimate relationship. We need to develop much greater understanding of how differences in subjective culture between blacks and whites have implications for some interpersonal relationships but not for others.

There is already enough research to indicate that acceptance in formal settings is more likely than acceptance in informal settings (Goldstein and Davis, 1973; Pettigrew, 1969; Triandis and Davis, 1965). We also know that when superordinate goals can be made salient, when contact receives institutional support and when contact is associated with pleasurable events, it is more likely to lead to successful interpersonal relationships. In short, we already know some of the *m* dimensions. But there might be others that we still need to discover.

On the antecedent side of the coin we know that certain characteristics of the groups in contact help to predispose successful interpersonal relationships. When two groups have similar status and know each other's subjective cultures, there is a high probability of successful interpersonal relationships in those social situations which induce cooperation. This is not so when people are of different status or do not know each other's subjective culture.

It follows from this discussion that contact without the preconditions of similarity in status, knowledge of the other group's subjective culture and similarity of goals may have undesirable consequences. Yet much of the current thinking on integration proposes exactly that kind of contact.

In addition we must learn a great deal more than we know now about successful intergroup contact. The aim should be to create in the shortest time the largest number of what we defined above as 'successful interpersonal relationships'. We must become an experimenting society (Campbell, 1969). As research on this topic gives usable answers, we might be able to create a new group of professionals — applied social psychologists — whose job it would be to counsel people on how to achieve successful interpersonal relationships in the shortest time. Such people might be called Human Relations Catalysts. In situations where people with different subjective cultures must interact they would act as consultants to provide the kind of training and perspective needed to establish a successful interpersonal relationship. The Human Relations Catalysts would know what skills, knowledge and attitudes are needed to be successful in particular job settings, in schools or in community activities. We already know much about this kind of problem (Brislin and Pedersen, 1976; Landis and Brislin, 1983), but we still have too many research gaps to be able to train such professionals well today. However, after only a few years of successful research I am confident we could do a very good job.

A Vision of the Future

What kind of society would emerge from such activities? As I see it, it would be one in which people would have more choices and their choices would be more acceptable to others. I see few situations that are more confining than unemployment. The unemployed person is forced to seek other avenues to gain status or income — crime is a common one. Yet that is often imposed by outside circumstances rather than a matter of free choice. Furthermore, a person with a steady job can seek better housing and better schools. This does not mean, in my view, that all blacks will want to live in white neighborhoods. Nor does it mean that all will want to send their children to integrated schools. But note the large difference between having to be segregated and deciding to be segregated. What I am advocating is increasing the number of times when people decide to adopt a particular life-style rather than have the life-style imposed on them via ideology, legal action or economic pressure.

The situation I visualize is that some blacks will go to all-black schools, some will work in all-black companies and some will live in all-black neighborhoods, but they will do so as a matter of free choice. The catalysts, who will often be black, after careful examination of each case might conclude that integration of a particular individual is premature or unlikely to lead to successful interpersonal relationships. They would so advise a client, giving reasons for that advice. Then the client might voluntarily choose to go to an all-black school, or what not. Hopefully, over time, fewer and fewer persons would receive such advice. My emphasis is on dealing with individuals and recognizing that there are individual differences. I can see the law as giving everyone the right to integrate, but it may not be to everybody's advantage to exercise this right immediately. A child with low self-esteem who is placed in a school where failure is guaranteed is not served well.

One of the ways in which the catalysts might operate would be the analysis of the subjective culture of various groups of clients in relation to the known subjective cultures of various mainstream groups. Then, by identifying the smallest existing gaps in subjective culture they would advise their clients about the right move, and would train them to be successful in the new social setting in which they will have to work, live or learn. Broadening the client's perspective concerning various subjective cultures seems to be an effective way to train for intercultural behavior (Triandis, 1976). It does increase cognitive complexity and makes a person more flexible in different kinds of social environments (Triandis, 1975). Thus, as I see it, the catalysts would keep constantly abreast of changes in the subjective culture, job requirements, specially needed skills and so on of different job settings and would advise their clients to move into those situations in which their clients would be likely to be most successful.

All of this discussion, however, does have a very strong overtone which I wish to dispel. All along I have been talking about contact across small gaps and what will happen over time. There are a few dimensions on which homogeneity is desirable. Total status is one of them. But in general I think homogeneity is undesirable. We need to learn to value different life-styles and assign equal status to them, in spite of the fact that they are different. Just as a Nobel-prizewinner in physics is different from a Nobel-prizewinner in literature yet one is not different in status from the other, so we must learn that different life-styles are perfectly viable. I suspect that we need cultural heterogeneity in order to have an interesting life, but also in order to invent the new life-styles needed in a fast-changing culture. What we do not need is the 'different is inferior' viewpoints that so frequently have characterized humankind's interpersonal relations.

Conclusion

Pluralism, then, is the development of interdependence, appreciation and the skills to interact intimately with persons from other cultures. It involves learning to enter social relationships where the rewards exceed the costs for both sides of the relationship, To achieve this state we need more understanding of social psychological principles and experimentation with new forms of social institutions, such as the catalysts.

My argument has been that our current attempts at integration, based on a legal framework, disregard individual differences and are attempts to eliminate cultural differences. I am advocating a shift from that perspective to one that provides for a marriage of the legal framework with our understanding of social psychological principles. Rather than integration, as conceived today, or assimilation, which involves the elimination of cultural differences, I am advocating *additive multicultural-ism* where people learn to be effective and to appreciate others who are different in culture. Additive multiculturalism is by its very nature something that needs to be developed in the majority rather than the minority of the population. As more members of the minority learn to integrate in jobs and are given a chance to do so, the majority must learn to relate to the minorities with a perspective of additive multiculturalism. Within that framework and over a period of many years, we should develop a pluralism that gives self-respect to all, appreciation of cultural differences and social skills leading to interpersonal relationships with more rewards than costs.

Our world is shrinking and is becoming more interdependent. For example, in 1964 it is estimated that 25 per cent of US products competed in the world market, and thus most US products were sold in the domestic market at prices that could ignore economic activities outside the US. In 1984 70 per cent of US products competed in the world market (*Washington Post*, national weekly edition of 7 May 1984, p. 17). Such rapid trends are continuing. Ignorance of multiculturalism is as much a deficiency of educational systems today as ignorance of history or geography. It is time for the educational systems to respond appropriately.

References

ABELSON, R.P. (1959) 'Modes of resolution of belief dilemmas', *Journal of Conflict Resolution*, 3, pp. 343–52.

ABELSON, R.P., ARONSON, E., McGUIRE, W.J., NEWCOMB, T.M., ROSENBERG, M.J. and TANNENBAUM, P.H. (1968) *Theories of Cognitive Consistency: A Sourcebook*, Chicago, Ill., Rand McNally.

AMIR, Y. (1969) 'Contact hypothesis in intergroup relations', *Psychological Bulletin*, 71, pp. 319–42.

AMIR, Y. (1976) 'The role of intergroup contact in change of prejudice and ethnic relations', in KATZ, P.A. (Ed.), *Toward the Elimination of Racism*, New York, Pergamon Press.

ARONSON, E., BLANEY, N., STEPHAN, C., SIKES, J. and SNAPP, M. (1978). *The Jigsaw Classroom*, Beverly Hills, Calif., Sage Publications.

ARONSON, E. and OSHEROW, N. (1980) 'Cooperation, prosocial behavior, and academic performance: Experiments in desegregated classroom', in BICKMAN, L. (Ed.), *Applied Social Psychology Annual 1*, Beverly Hills, Calif., Sage Publications.

BERKOWITZ, L. and WALSTER, E. (1976) 'Equity theory: Toward a general theory of social interaction', in *Advances in Experimental Social Psychology*, Vol. 9, New York, Academic Press.

BRISLIN, R.W. and PEDERSEN, P. (1976) *Cross-Cultural Orientation Programs*, New York, Gardner Press.

CAMPBELL, D.T. (1967) 'Stereotypes and perception of group differences', *American Psychologist*, 22 pp. 812–29.

CAMPBELL, D.T. (1969) 'Reforms as experiments', *American Psychologist*, 24, pp. 409–29.

CASTAÑADA, A., JAMES, R.L. and ROBBINS, W. (1974) *The Educational Needs of Minority Groups*, Lincoln, Nebr., Professional Educators Publishers.

DOWDALL, G.W. (1974) 'White gains from black subordination in 1960 and 1970', *Social Problems*, 22, pp. 162–83.

FELDMAN, J. (1974) 'Race, economic class and the intention to work: Some normative and attitudinal correlates', *Journal of Applied Psychology*, 59, pp. 179–86.

FOA, U.G. and DONNENWERTH, G.W. (1971) 'Love poverty in modern culture and sensitivity training', *Sociological Inquiry*, 41, pp. 149–59.

FOA, U.G. and FOA, E.B. (1974) *Societal Structures of the Mind*, Springfield, Ill., Thomas.

GOLDSTEIN, M. and DAVIS, E.E. (1973) 'Race and belief: A further analysis of the social determinants of behavioral intentions', *Journal of Personality and Social Psychology*, 26, pp. 16–22.

HENNIGH, L. (1975) 'Negative stereotyping: Structural contributions in a Bureau of Indian Affairs community', *Human Organization*, 34, pp. 263–8.

HOMANS, G.C. (1974) *Social Behavior: Its Elementary Forms*, New York, Harcourt Brace.

JANIS, I.L. (1972) *Victims of Groupthink*, Boston, Mass., Houghton Mifflin.

JOHNSON, D.W. and JOHNSON, R.T. (1983) 'The socialization and achievement crises: Are cooperative learning experiences the solution?' in BICKMAN, L. (Ed.) *Applied Social Psychology Annual 4*, Beverly Hills, Calif., Sage Publications.

JONES, E.E., KANOUSE, D.E., KELLEY, H.H., NISBETT, R.E., VALINS, S. and WEINER, B. (1972) *Attribution: Perceiving the Causes of Behavior*, Morristown, N.J., General Learning Press.

LAMBERT, W.E. (1973) *Culture and Language as Factors in Learning and Education*, Paper presented at the Symposium on Cultural Factors in Learning, Bellingham, Washington.

LANDIS, D. and BRISLIN, R.W. (1983) *Handbook of Intercultural Training*, New York, Pergamon Press.

LANDIS, D., DAY, H.R., McGREW, P.L., THOMAS, J.A. and MILLER, A.B. (1976) 'Can a black "culture assimilator" increase racial understanding?' *Journal of Social Issues*, 32, 2, pp. 169–83.

LEWIS, O. (1966) 'The culture of poverty', *Scientific American*, 215, pp. 19–25.

LEY, D. (1974) *The Black Inner City as Frontier Outpost*, Washington, D.C., Association of American Geographers.

MARX, G.T. (1967) *Protest and Prejudice*, New York, Harper and Row.

MOSTELLER, F. and MOYNIHAN, D.P. (1972) *On Equality of Educational Opportunity*, New York, Random House.

MURPHY, H.B.M. (1961) 'Social change and mental health', *Milbank Memorial Fund Quarterly*, 39, pp. 385–445.

MURPHY, H.B.M. (1965) 'Migration and the major mental disorders: A reappraisal', in KANTOR, M.B. (Ed.), *Mobility and Mental Health*, Springfield, Ill., Thomas.

MYRDAL, G. (1944) *An American Dilemma*, New York, Harper.

NAROLL, R., BENJAMIN, E.C., FOHL, F.K., FRIED, M.J., HILDRETH, R.E. and SCHAEFER, J.M. (1971) 'Creativity: A cross-historical pilot survey', *Journal of Cross-Cultural Psychology*, 2, pp. 191–8.

NISBETT, R.E., CAPUTO, C., LEGANT, P. and MARECEK, J. (1973) 'Behavior as seen by the actor and as seen by the observer', *Journal of Personality and Social Psychology*, 27, pp. 154–64.

NOVAK, M. (1972) *The Rise of Unmeltable Ethnics*, New York, Macmillan.

PETTIGREW, T.F. (1969) 'Racially separate or together?' *Journal of Social Issues*, 25, 1, pp. 43–69.

'PROGRESS AGAINST POVERTY: 1964–74,' (1976), *Focus on Poverty Research*, 1, pp. 8–12.

ROTHBART, M. (1976) 'Achieving racial equality: An analysis of resistance to social reform', in KATZ, P.A. (Ed.), *Toward the Elimination of Racism*, New York, Pergamon Press.

SCHUMAN, H. and HATCHETT, S. (1974) *Black Racial Attitudes: Trends and Complexities*, Ann Arbor, Mich., Institute of Social Research.

SEELYE, H. N. (1975) *Teaching Culture*, Skokie, Ill., National Textbook Co.

SELIGMAN, M.E.P. (1975) *Helplessness: On Depression, Development and Death*, San Francisco, Calif., Freeman.

SHERIF, M. (1968) 'If the social scientist is to be more than a mere technician . . .', *Journal of Social Issues*, 24, 1, pp. 41–61.

SIMONTON, D.K. (1975) 'Sociocultural context of individual creativity: A transhistorical time-series analysis', *Journal of Personality and Social Psychology*, 32, pp. 1119–33.

TAYLOR, D.A. (1974) 'Should we integrate organizations?' in FROMKIN, H. and SHERWOOD, J. (Eds). *Integrating the Organization*, New York, Free Press.

TAYLOR, D.M. and JAGGI, V. (1974) 'Ethnocentrism and causal attribution in a south Indian context', *Journal of Cross-Cultural Psychology*, 5, pp. 162–71.

THIBAUT, J. and KELLEY, H.H. (1959) *The Social Psychology of Groups*, New York, Wiley.

THUROW, L.C. (1969) *Poverty and Discrimination*, Washington, D.C. The Brookings Institution.

TRIANDIS, H.C. (1975) 'Culture training, cognitive complexity and interpersonal attitudes', in BRISLIN, R., BOCHNER, S. and LONNER, W. (Eds), *Cross-Cultural Perspectives on Learning*, New York, Halsted/Wiley.

TRIANDIS, H.C. (1976) (Ed.) *Variations in Black and White Perceptions of the Social Environment*, Urbana, Ill., University of Illinois Press.

TRIANDIS, H.C. and DAVIS, E.E. (1965) 'Race and belief as determinants of behavioral intentions', *Journal of Personality and Social Psychology*, 2, pp. 715–25.

TRIANDIS, H.C. and VASSILIOU, V. (1967) 'Frequency of contact and stereotyping', *Journal of Personality and Social Psychology*, 7, pp. 316–28.

TUCKER, L. (1966) 'Some mathematical notes on three-mode factor analysis', *Psychometrika*, 31, pp. 279–311.

TURNER, C.B. and WILSON, W.J. (1976) 'Dimensions of racial ideology: A study of urban black attitudes', *Journal of Social Issues*, 32, 2, pp. 139–52.

VASSILIOU, V.V., TRIANDIS, H.C., VASSILIOU, G. and McGUIRE, H. (1972) 'Interpersonal contact and stereotyping', in TRIANDIS, H.C. (Ed.), *The Analysis of Subjective Culture*, New York, Wiley.

WELDON, D.E., CARLSTON, D.E., RISSMAN, A.K., SLOBODIN, L. and TRIANDIS, H.C. (1975) 'A laboratory test of effects of culture assimilator training', *Journal of Personality and Social Psychology*, 32, pp. 300–10.

X (CLARK), C. (Ed.) (1973) 'The white researcher in black society', *Journal of Social Issues*, 29, 1.

7   The Canadian Brand of Multiculturalism: Social and Educational Implications

Ronald Samuda

Multiculturalism, as a demographic phenomenon, has existed since the beginning of written history. People of different races, languages, customs, ethnicity and culture have co-existed within the ancient empires of Persia, India, China, Rome, Greece and Turkey. Alexander the Great was one of the first to recognize the importance of respect for the dignity and preservation of the life-styles, language and customs of the people he conquered. Napoleon's initial successes were based on his recognition of the ethnic and linguistic differences of the alien nationals he coopted as fellow soldiers. In more recent times, despite English nationalism, the colonial administrators of the British empire succeeded largely because they accepted the differences of their colonial subjects and sought to find a compromise for governing within the peculiarities of the particular local ethos.

What is it, then, that is so new about multiculturalism of the present day? What, indeed, is the definition of multiculturalism? What are the events leading to the acceptance of multiculturalism as an ideal and as a policy in several countries of the world? And, more particularly, how does the Canadian brand of multiculturalism compare with that of other countries with a similarly culturally diverse society? Those are the questions which I shall seek to answer in this paper. As well, I shall provide an evaluative summary of the social and educational implications of Canadian multiculturalism based upon the results of research conducted in Canadian schools.

Some Comparative Immigration Trends

Perhaps the most potent factor in the emergence of multiculturalism lies in the sudden upsurge of migration after the Second World War. The devastation of war created an unprecedented demand for workers to man the factories of the developed countries. Soon after the war's end many European countries began competing for workers to augment industrial expansion. International competition for immigrant workers intensified in the 'fat' years of the late fifties and early sixties. The economic recovery of western Europe coincided with the drive of Canada and Australia to enhance their own economic and industrial development through planned and expanded immigration policies.

Workers from ex-colonial territories were asked to fill the gaps left by white workers after the Second World War. The major model developed in western Europe was the 'guest worker' program best exemplified in West Germany, in which there were nearly five million immigrant aliens representing 7.6 per cent of the population in 1983. In contrast, the United States, Canada and the United Kingdom have so changed their immigration laws that the preferential restrictions on the entry of people of non-European origin have become increasingly possible. Especially since 1965 in Australia and Canada immigration policies have been altered radically; the populations of both countries have increased dramatically in numbers and in diversity. Because of remarkable similarities between the two Commonwealth countries, I propose to draw certain parallels and to underscore the differences unique to the social and political realities of the Canadian brand of multiculturalism.

Changing Immigration Patterns

US immigration history has traditionally been based on preferential policies for western European settlers, supported by spurious theories of psychological assessment and eugenics advanced by such men as Carl Brigham, Henry Goddard and Robert Yerkes. It was the genetic interpretations of the results of the Army Alpha and Army Beta tests, administered to two million soldiers during the First World War, that provided the US government with 'scientific' arguments to systematically exclude those persons who differed markedly from the north-western European 'type' (Kamin, 1976). Even as late as 1952 the preferential quota concept was reaffirmed by the McCarran-Walter Act to justify the retention of quotas on the basis of assimilability and special treatment for immigrants from countries with historical and cultural ties with the United States (Keeley and Elwell, 1981).

Like the United States, both Canada and Australia depended on immigration for their economic prosperity and industrial development. Beginning in 1965 US policies moved progressively towards a more generous and regulated approach. In 1969, for example, 383,000 persons entered the United States; that figure increased year by year until in 1978 the total reached 600,000, including refugees from Cuba, Haiti, Indo-China and the Soviet Union (Kritz, 1981). Thus, there has been a sharp increase in the entry of people from such places as Asia, Latin America and the Caribbean. It may be that such a massive surge of radically different immigrants has forced American leaders to rethink their policy of the 'melting pot' and to begin making moves to a philosophy of multiculturalism.

Recent changes in the history of immigration in Canada and Australia have been even more dramatic. Despite some very obvious differences in the development of the two Commonwealth countries, there are nevertheless some remarkable similarities. Both have traditionally given preferential treatment to immigrants from the British Isles; in both there have existed restrictive policies which in effect barred the entry of non-Europeans. The result of such policies was that to the end of the Second World War there existed a preponderance of people of Anglo-Celtic origin and those of north-western European origin tended to meld into the society and to become so assimilated that the only remaining distinguishing feature was the name. In Canada the latter are called Euro-Canadians; they tend to be anglophone and monolingual.

In a general sense both Canada and Australia have initiated changes in their immigration laws which, beginning in the sixties, led to massive increases in population. What is of particular interest is the resultant change in the ethnic origin of the population. In contrast to its British-first policy, Australia permitted the entry of two million 'migrants' after the war of whom 60 per cent were non-British. By 1966 there was a considerable influx of people of Italian, Greek and other southern European origin. The white Australian policy was abandoned and by 1970 assisted passages were extended to Turks, Arabs and others from the Middle East (Fabinyi, 1971). Thus, by 1971 the combined proportion of foreign-born and native-born population of foreign parentage was about 40 per cent, exceeding the comparable Canadian figure of 33 per cent (Zubrzycki, 1981).

Australia has done a creditable job in coping with the immigrant population of non-British origin. Taft has documented the many programs and policies designed to help in the socialization of 'migrants' in Australia (Taft and Cahill, 1981). Integrative services for the entering migrant have been progressively extended to include special teacher-training programs, special classes for 'migrant' students in both elementary and secondary schools (Bhatnagar and Hamalian, 1984). Australian society has been enriched by the presence of different ethnic groups and although there still remain the vestiges of British cleavage among members of Australian society, attitudes towards migrants have become more tolerant and accepting (Taft, 1977). There exists an official and articulated policy based on the findings and recommendations of the Galbally Report on Post-Arrival Programs and Services to Migrants (Bhatnagar and Hamalian, 1984).

The Canadian Brand of Multiculturalism

Many Canadians would like to believe that there exists little or no 'racial problem' in the society. The national self-image tends to be that of a tolerant, law-abiding nation dedicated in practice and in ideology to democracy and peace (Hughes and Kallen, 1974). There are those of us who look with horror and disgust at the black-white confrontations of the sixties and who might even tend to feel smug in the belief that such events could not occur in Canada. Alas, such beliefs are not completely founded on reality. Until the sixties there still existed blatant and outright discrimination against the entry of black school children into certain schools. Racist ideologies helped shape pre-war Canadian immigration policies. In promulgating a 'progressive' early twentieth-century policy for immigration, Clifford Sifton referred to biological qualities as the criteria for and against the entry of ethnic groups. On such a basis the government ascribed to peoples of the southern climates, especially blacks, the labels of 'climatic unsuitability' for the harsh Canadian winters (Hughes and Kallen, 1974). Similarly, the vast prairie provinces were seen as very geographically appropriate for the introduction of people from the Ukraine. Between 1897 and 1914, 200,000 Ukrainians were settled in the prairie provinces of Manitoba, Saskatchewan and Alberta. By 1914 Manitoba contained 43 per cent of the Ukrainian population in Canada, who at that time were labelled Galicians, Bukovinians and Ruthenians. In the words of the government minister, Sifton, these immigrants were seen as 'the stalwart peasant, born on the soil, whose forefathers have been farmers for ten generations, with a stout wife and half a dozen children, is a very desirable settler' (Lysenko, 1947). Ukrainian settlement also occurred between 1924 and 1934 when over 70,000 immigrants arrived from the western Ukraine, and later, in 1947–55, 300,000 Ukrainian refugees were absorbed mainly into the farming, mining and industrial centres of the prairies. The result has been that the population of the prairie provinces, especially Manitoba, comprises a powerful and vocal group of Ukrainian ethnicity who have demanded economic and political parity as well as the right to have their children taught in bilingual programs emphasizing the retention of their Ukrainian heritage and fluency in Ukrainian language as well as English.

The Factor of Quebecois Nationalism

Multiculturalism in Canada is unique because of the peculiar nature of Canadian history. Unlike Australia and the United States, Canada has traditionally had two different charter groups each with its own language and culture, with distinct religious, ethnic and cultural differences which still exist.

In fact, it has been claimed that the Canadian aboriginal population has always been ethnically and linguistically heterogeneous (Berry *et al.*, 1977). When the French arrived in Canada in the sixteenth and seventeenth centuries, they found the 300,000 native Canadians comprising more than fifty societies with at least a dozen different linguistic groups. Even amongst the French differentiation occurred between the Acadians, who occupied the Atlantic region, and the Quebecois, each having their own distinct dialect and customs. In the intervening years the Metis emerged from French-Indian interbreeding. Soon after the British conquest came the influx of English, Irish, Scottish and Welsh, to be followed soon after by immigrants from north-western Europe like the Germans and the Dutch. Thus, in contrast to Australia, Canada's post-war population was de facto a multicultural society, although the prevailing trend was towards the assimilation of the non-French immigrants.

The movement towards official recognition of multiculturalism as government policy sprang from two major factors. One was the change in immigration policies in the early sixties. This was of paramount importance since it resulted in massive waves of immigrants from the countries of southern Europe, the Middle East, Asia and the Caribbean. But it was mainly the French-English conflict which spurred the change. As Burnet stated, 'the germs of nationalism had been incubating in Quebec for a long time' (Burnet, 1984). Added to the injustice and discrimination that the people of Quebec perceived, there was the fact of Anglo dominance and the feeling that they were being treated like the 'niggers' of Canada. It is probably no accident that the French-Canadian separatist movement coincided with the civil rights movement of Afro-Americans in the United States and with the call of Prime Minister Deifenbaker for a Canadian Bill of Rights.

Prime Minister Lester Pearson's response to the threat of the dismemberment of Quebec was to establish a Royal Commission on Bilingualism and Biculturalism in 1963. The issue of language was of particular importance to the emergence of multiculturalism. The deliberations of the commission and especially the concepts of bilingualism and biculturalism prompted the more powerful ethnic minorities — the Ukrainians in particular — to demand that their language and their culture should be recognized in what had in fact become a multiethnic and culturally pluralistic society.

The Official Languages Act of 1969 made French one of the two official languages of Canada and extended to Francophones outside of Quebec special language rights. But the special treatment of the French-Canadians ignited the 'other ethnic groups' who demanded that they too should be seen as part of the cultural mosaic (Jackson, 1977). It was mainly the Ukrainians, with the help of other powerful vocal ethnic groups, who were instrumental in changing the policy from biculturalism to 'multiculturalism' (Bociurkiw, 1978). Consequently, when Prime Minister Trudeau announced the federal policy in October 1971, it was entitled 'Multiculturalism within a Bilingual Framework'. In 1972 the liberal government appointed a Minister of State for Multiculturalism responsible for administering the new policies.

Beginning in 1962 all racial and ethnic criteria were abandoned in favour of an ethnic-blind point system based on education and training, personal qualities, occupational demand, skills, age and arranged employment, knowledge of English and French, presence of relatives and area of destination. The point system led to the highest annual immigration of the post-war period. No longer was Canada's policy restricted to Europeans (Kalbach, 1979). The doors were open to people from Asia and the Caribbean. From a mere handful of South Asians and West Indians residing in Canada in the two post-war decades, the numbers rose dramatically so that by 1977 nearly 300,000 immigrants arrived from India and Pakistan; more than 100,000 arrived from Jamaica and Trinidad; more than 50,000 came from Africa; Hong Kong and the Philippines became major suppliers of workers; and immigrants from southern Europe (Portuguese, Italians, Greeks, Yugoslavs) poured into Canada in unprecedented numbers.

Burnet's analysis of Canadian multiculturalism seems to place the issues in proper perspective (Burnet, 1984). She points to four myths which many Canadians would like to believe as fact. (1) She disputes the notion that many cultures can be maintained in Canada; except for the Hutterites, no ethnic group brings a total culture to Canada; it is ethnic identity (not culture) that can and does persist. (2) The multiculturalism policy pays insufficient attention to the special problems and interests of new arrivals — the immigrants; in this regard, Australia appears to have made significant innovations. (3) The policy aims at equality, but some groups are still economically and socially underprivileged. (4) The myth of early arrival is included in claims by Chinese, Ukrainian, Scandinavian, Polish, and French immigrants, and some British and Euro-Canadians claim to be the true Canadians.

The fact is that metropolitan Toronto has received close to 60 per cent of all immigrant students. The proportion of foreign-born students in that city rose from 31 per cent in 1951 to 42 per cent in 1971. The Director of Education, Duncan Green, estimated in 1977 that there were seventy ethnic groups or sub-groups with as many different languages and 400 ethnic organizations in Toronto alone. Thirty per cent of the students were foreign-born and 46 per cent had a first language other than English (Samuda and Crawford, 1980). Those figures are representative of one major city but similar conditions exist in such urban centres as Vancouver, Edmonton, Winnipeg, Ottawa and Montreal. Yet the potential for political clout can be perceived from the fact that the Canadian population still comprises a predominant proportion of people originating from the British Isles (45 per cent); those of French origin comprise 29 per cent; other ethnic groups make up about 26 per cent and the native Canadian population represents less than 2 per cent (Burnet, 1984).

What Does Canadian Multiculturalism Really Mean?

Quite apart from the rhetoric and the sentiments, multiculturalism in Canada represents a radical shift on the part of the federal government and the policy has been accepted by four of the ten provinces — Ontario, Manitoba, Saskatchewan and Alberta. It represents a recognition of the cultural diversity of Canadian society and equality of status for the various ethnocultural groups. Canadian multicultural policy recognizes the existence of two official languages but no official culture. In other words, cultural pluralism is the very essence of Canadian identity, based on the notion that every ethnic group has the right to preserve and develop its own culture and values within the Canadian context. It represents a sharing of culture — an extension of participation and control of social, political and economic institutions. It represents a greater choice of life-styles and of cultural traits, and a concern for and protection of the civil and human rights of people of different racial, ethnic and cultural origins. It connotes freedom of choice in matters of religion and equal access to social institutions. But, more importantly, multiculturalism in Canada means the acceptance of cultural diversity and the abandonment (at least in official statute and parlance) of the Anglo-conformity, bigotry, racism and ethnocentrism that formed the basis of government practice and intercultural relations until three decades ago.

Does Canadian Multiculturalism Work?

The multicultural policy was designed to serve the needs of established European ethnic minority groups (Samuda *et al.*, 1984). It represented a radical change in attitudes towards people of non-European ethnicity. The result has been that from the early sixties the schools of industrial urban centres have had an increasingly diverse school population. But the change came without preparation of teachers, administrators or counsellors. There was no planned in-service program; no integration of services by any federal department. Changes occurred on an ad hoc basis.

Breton *et al.* (1980) claim that the dominant groups tend to treat the issue as merely symbolic, that the recognition of minority cultures is granted as a token of cultural tolerance. The Anglophone majority of British and north-western European settlers have become assimilated into the Euro-Canadian majority. Relatively few immigrant settlers have become linguistically or culturally integrated into French Canada. Thus, the pattern of Euro-Canadian dominance has been retained. The French perceive the movement as denying them their special status. In Quebec the existence of small ethnic groups is seen as aggravating the demographic balance.

Kalbach's analysis of the occupational categories of immigrants reveals certain consistent patterns: US settlers are disproportionately represented in the managerial and professional categories; the Portuguese are concentrated in farming, construction, fishing, forestry and mining; South Asians tend to go into the sciences, engineering and mathematics; those from Hong Kong move into clerical and service occupations; and the Lebanese into fabricating, assembly and repair trades (Kalbach, 1979).

Occupationally selective immigration tends to concentrate immigrants from certain source countries in occupational groups of varying prestige and economic potential. The key to socio-economic status and mobility in the society is education. Without equality of opportunity for immigrants, the 'Vertical Mosaic' will persist. The most serious problems exist in the assessment, testing, placement and counselling of ethnic minorities. The concepts of multiculturalism are not yet integrated into the faculties of education, and many practising teachers still view education from the archaic assimilationist perspective.

As the results of our research in Ontario schools have shown, the use of IQ tests has been abandoned in some school boards. However, the teacher remains the arbiter in placement decisions (Samuda and Crawford, 1980). Classroom teachers and counsellors need training in dealing with the new Canadian. In summary, ethnocentric teacher training and insufficient emphasis on appropriate curriculum and counselling methods represent the failure of the educational system to adapt to the new Canadian school population. The fact of education as a provincial prerogative makes the all-Canada multicultural policy exceedingly difficult to implement. As well, the federal structure places multiculturalism in one ministry and immigration in another.

The 'visible minorities' have recently petitioned the government for a just share in the economic and political goods of Canadian society. A parliamentary committee has mandated research and structural changes to open up new opportunities. Porter's 'Vertical Mosaic' would appear to be persisting in the structure of Canadian society. Porter claims that Anglo- and Euro-Canadians still hold political and economic power. The Ukrainians, Italians and other European minorities occupy a middle stratum, with the French somewhere in between, and the visible minorities of Canadian blacks and native peoples remain at the bottom of the social totempole. Yet multiculturalism in Canada represents far more than mere government expediency to offset the French-Canadian threat of separation and to soothe other aggravated ethnic minorities.

Canada is still far from being an egalitarian mosaic. The school shares complicity in the process of social and economic structuring in terms of class and ethnic origin since children are still being measured and placed within what appears to be a democratic system. But the school is still a middle-class institution, manned by WASP middle-class teachers who uphold a mainly anglocentric curriculum which is often alien to the cultural and linguistic background of the students they teach. The just society remains a Canadian dream; but despite its untidy and uneven state of existence, Canadian multiculturalism is the kind of model which promises to correct the anomalies in our society.

Canadian multiculturalism represents the hope that, sooner or later, we shall evolve a social and political system where structural, institutional and personal racism will be replaced by the kind of ideal which prizes unity in diversity and where differences in ethnicity, language and culture will be viewed as differences rather than deviance. It is towards such an ideal that the Multiculturalism Directorate, the program officers and the consultative committees throughout the provincial system of government are aspiring. There is much to be done but multiculturalism is an idea whose time has come.

References

BERRY, J., KALIN, R. and RAYLOR, D. (1977) *Multiculturalism and Ethnic Attitudes in Canada*, Ottawa, Minster of State for Multiculturalism.

BHATNAGAR, J. and HAMALIAN, A. (1984) 'Comparative studies of immigrant adaptation', in SAMUDA, R. *et al.* (Eds), *Multiculturalism in Canada: Social and Educational Implications*, Boston, Mass., Allyn and Bacon.

BOCUIRKIW, B. (1978) 'The Federal policy of multiculturalism and the Ukrainian-Canadian community', in LUPUL, M. (Ed.), *Ukrainians, Canadians, Multiculturalism, and Separation: An Assessment*, Edmonton, Alta., The University of Alberta Press for the Canadian Institute of Ukrainian Studies, pp. 98–128.

BRETON, R., REITZ, J. and VALENTINE, V. (1980) *Cultural Boundaries and the Cohesion of Canada*, Montreal, Institute for Research of Public Policy.

BURNET, J. (1984) 'Myths and multiculturalism', in SAMUDA, R. *et al.* (Eds), *Multiculturalism in Canada: Social and Educational Implications*, Boston, Mass., Allyn and Bacon.

CLAYDON, L. (1980) *Refugee Letters: Some Aspects of Australia's Changed Institutional Response*, Victoria, La Trobe University.

FABINYI, A. (1971) 'More promising more dangerous', in TURNBULL, C. (Ed.), *Hammond Innes Introduces Australia*, London, Andre Deutsch.

GILCHRIST, J. and MURRAY, W. (Eds) (1968) *Eyewitness: Selected Documents from Australia's Past*, Adelaide, Rigby.

HUGHES, D. and KALLEN, E. (1974) *The Anatomy of Racism: Canadian Dimensions*, Montreal, Harvest House.

JACKSON, J. (1977) 'The functions of language in Canada: On the political economy of language', in Coombs, W. *et al.* (Eds), *The Individual Language and Society in Canada*, Ottawa, Canada Council, pp. 61–76.

Kalbach, W. (1979) 'Immigration and population change', *TESL Talk: Immigration and Multiculturalism: A Decade to Review*, 10, pp. 16–31.

Kamin, L. (1976) 'Heredity, intelligence, politics and psychology: II', in Block, N. and Dworkin, G. (Eds), *The IQ Controversy*, New York, Random House, pp. 374–82.

Keely, C. and Elwell, P. (1981) 'International migration: Canada and the United States', in Kritz, M. *et al.* (Eds), *Global Trends in Migration: Theory and Research on International Population Movements*, New York, Centre for Migration Studies, pp. 181–207.

Kritz, M. (1981) 'International migration patterns in the Caribbean: An overview', in Krist, M. *et al.* (Eds), *Global Trends in Migration: Theory and Research on International Population Movements*, New York, Centre for Migration Studies, pp. 208–33.

Lysenko, V. (1947) *Men in Sheepskin Coats: A Study of Ukrainian Assimilation*, Toronto, Ryerson.

Minsel, W. and Herff, W. (1985) 'Intercultural counselling: West German perspectives', in Samuda, R. and Wolfgang, A. (Eds) *Intercultural Counselling: Global Perspectives*, Toronto, Hogrefe.

Morrish, I. (1971) *The Background of Immigrant Children*, London, Allen and Unwin.

Nicholls, A. (1971) 'Newcomers', in Turnbull, E. (Ed.), *Hammond Innes Introduces Australia*, London, Andre Deutsch.

Petras, E. (1981) 'The global labour market in the modern world economy', in Kritz, M. *et al.* (Eds), *Global Trends in Immigration: Theory and Research on International Population Movements*, New York, Centre for Migration Studies, pp. 44–63.

Porter, J. (1965) *The Vertical Mosaic: An Analysis of Social Class and Power in Canada*, Toronto, University of Toronto Press.

Richmond, A. (1981) 'Immigration and pluralism in Canada', *International Migration Review*, 4, pp. 5–24.

Salt, J. (1981) 'International labour migration in Western Europe: A geographical review', in Kritz, M. *et al.* (Eds), *Global Trends in Migration: Theory and Research on International Population Movements*, New York: Centre for Migration Studies.

Samuda, R. (1975) *The Psychological Testing of American Minorities*, New York, Harper and Row.

Samuda, R. and Crawford, D. (1980) *Testing, Assessment, Counselling and Placements of Ethnic Minority Students: Current Methods in Ontario*, Toronto, Ministry of Education.

Samuda, R. and Woods, S. (1983) *Perspectives in Immigrant and Minority Education*, Washington, University Press of America.

Samuda, R., Berry, J. and Laferriere, M. (Eds) (1984) *Multiculturalism in Canada: Social and Educational Implications*, Boston, Mass., Allyn and Bacon.

Taft, R. (1977) 'Coping with unfamiliar cultures', in Warren, N. (Ed.), *Studies in Cross-Cultural Psychology*, London, Academic Press.

Taft, R. (1982) 'The social and ideological context of multicultural education in immigrant countries', Paper read at a Symposium organized by Wenner-Gren Foundation, Stockholm.

Taft, R. and Cahill, D. (1981) 'Education of immigrants in Australia', in Bhatnaga, J. (Ed.), *Educating Immigrants*, London, Croom Helm.

Zubrzycki, J. (1977) 'Australia as a multicultural society', *Proceedings of the Australian Ethnic Affairs Council*, Canberra, Australian Government Publishing Service.

Zubrzycki, J. (1981) 'International migration in Australia and the South Pacific', in Kritz, M. *et al.* (Eds) *Global Trends in Migration: Theory and Research on International Population Movements*, New York, Centre for Migration Studies, pp. 158–80.

8 Remodelling Australian Society and Culture: A Study in Education for a Pluralistic Society

David Dufty

In 1988 most Australians will be involved in some way in 'The Bicentenary' which, according to official publications of the Bicentennial Authority, 'celebrates not only 200 years of European history but the entire span of human life in Australia from the mysteries of Aboriginal antiquity to the possibilities of the future.' It should be different from the United States Bicentenary which was a less than satisfactory celebration since it was planned in an era when multiculturalism as a policy was still only emerging and when indigenous people were not fully aware of their rights and powers. The American Indians played a very limited role in the US celebrations; they were also conspicuously absent from the Opening Ceremony of the Los Angeles Games. Australians ought to be more sensitive to such matters. Multiculturalism has been an official policy of federal and state governments for a decade and Aboriginal people are highly conscious of their rights and powers.

The immediate challenge of the Bicentenary and longer-range issues of life in this pluralistic society raise questions with implications for the world-wide debate on multiculturalism. What sort of society has evolved in Australia? Is the society which has developed one which all Australians will want to celebrate? How could the society be improved? What role can education play in helping people understand what their society is like and in influencing its future development?

Pluralism as Ideal and Reality

Whatever else it may be, Australian society has always been diverse in nature. The original inhabitants of Australia were far from homogeneous. There were some physical differences, and considerable linguistic and cultural differences between coastal, desert, tropical and cool temperate Aboriginal tribes.[1]

The British invaders destroyed many of the indigenous societies and cultures and established outposts of British society. The newcomers were far from homo-geneous, however, since there were distinctions between convicts and free settlers, officers and men, rich and poor, establishment and rebels, including political dissidents from Ireland. The Protestant-Catholic division continued in its new setting and the immigrants brought with them their ethnic differences, including Irish, Scottish, Cornish and Welsh. The Welsh even preserved their language for a generation or two. Chinese came in large numbers during the gold rushes. Italians, Greeks and Germans were amongst early immigrants. However, the mythologies and the dominant ideologies and institutions were of British origin, modified by the attempt in the 1890s to create an aggressive Australian nationalism with the help of the *Bulletin* magazine. The 1890s were also a period of droughts, strikes and class conflict between labour and management. Upper and lower houses of parliament perpetuated class-based institutions. Women began their struggle for the vote but socially remained in the home.

Despite some further migration from southern Europe and Lebanon, Australia was institutionally, and in the eyes of its dominant majority, an Anglo-Saxon, or perhaps an Anglo-Celtic country, until the close of the Second World War. During the war, however, there had been a turning towards the USA in strategic and economic matters. After the war some four million migrants arrived from more than 100 countries. For the period 1947–78, 45 per cent were British, while 55 per cent were from non-English-speaking countries. By mid-1978 some 30 per cent of the total population comprised post-war immigrants and their children.

The arrival of large numbers of non-British migrants speaking languages other than English forced Australians to rethink their social and cultural policies. Major attention was paid to the settlement problems of these migrants, to their learning of English and to the adaption of their children to Australian schools. After attempting policies of 'assimilation' and 'integration', the Australian government, influenced by vocal migrant leaders, by progressive politicians and academics, and by trends in other countries, decided on a policy of 'multiculturalism'; Australia was designated 'a multicultural society'. But is this a descriptive term indicating what Australia is like, or is it a prescriptive term telling us what Australia ought to be like? Some reports recognized this ambiguity and noted both meanings of the term,[2] others were idealistic and optimistic and offered definitions such as the following: 'The term multiculturalism is used to describe an ideal society where groups would co-exist harmoniously, free to maintain many of their distinctive religious, linguistic or social customs, equal in their access to resources and services, civil rights and political power and sharing with the rest of society particular concerns, which have national significance. There would be diversity, equality and interaction through sharing.'[3]

During the 1980s migrants have continued to flow in from varying countries but a new 'non-discriminatory' policy has restricted migrants to people with needed skills, to those with close family in Australia, and to refugees. Since most of these refugees have come from Asia a major debate has developed (discussed below) which relates to aspects of this definition, including the degree of difference possible and the amount of sharing needed for harmonious co-existence.

Multiculturalism, Polyethnicity or Pluralism?

The debate on what to call Australian society continues, although some are weary of it. Bullivant believes the term 'multicultural society' has so many shortcomings that it should be abandoned.[4] He prefers the term 'polyethnic' which emphasizes the central role of the ethnic group in the current debate. 'Multiculturalism' as a socio-cultural theory, he argues, fails to take into account the effect of socio-economic classes. His ideal society might be described as 'integrated polyethnic', after Tumin and Higham, and is 'pluralist at the family, local and private levels of ethnic group life — the essence of polyethnicity — but, of necessity, integrated at the other common levels of government, the law, the economy and so on'. Education for pluralism 'must include consideration of the dynamics of economic and political power — how and why minority groups, whether they be of ethnic, social class, or cultural origins, are disadvantaged in relation to dominant groups in society.'[5]

Bullivant is critical of another Australian theorist of multiculturalism, George Smolicz. He describes him as being concerned with 'multicultural butterfly collecting' due to his efforts to describe various types of multiculturalism.[6] Smolicz however is well aware of the cultural domination of the Anglo-Celtic group and is very much concerned to promote the growth of ethnic cultures, including their linguistic, religious and familial cores. These ethnic cultures are 'developed in balance with the shared values, for the benefit of all Australians, who are in this way brought closer to cultures from many lands.'[7] Bullivant is more concerned with helping migrants to gain survival skills, including the use of the English language, in order to operate effectively in the dominant culture. Bullivant and Smolicz had an 'interesting dialogue' on the subject at a conference in 1982 which was summed up rather tersely by Barbara Falk: 'You could say Australia is a polyethnic state and it therefore ought to be a multicultural society. There is little point in further debating which is the correct formulation.'[9]

The position taken in this chapter is that there is considerable evidence that Australia is both polyethnic and highly diverse in many other ways, and it should now be possible to move into an era in which ethnic diversity is accepted as a major aspect of pluralism. In addition other aspects of pluralism are recognized and studied and Australians are educated for general social and cultural literacy and not only for awareness of ethnic diversity. The richness of life brought by migrant groups is acknowledged, including their languages, but the importance of migrant experience in Australia is also stressed and the contributions to the culture of other social groups, and of people dwelling in different regions of Australia, are also recognized.

Social and cultural literacy involves awareness of the existence of varied micro-cultures, as well as the emergent Australian macro-culture, and awareness of which groups are dominant and which individuals and groups are discriminated against. It involves knowledge of human rights, of law and of political skills needed to influence decision-making and reduce discrimination. It involves awareness of global issues and global interdependence and is not ethnocentric in its world view.

David Dufty

Towards a More Comprehensive View of a Pluralistic Society

Multicultural education has tended to concentrate on issues related to ethnicity. A broader concept of Australian society and social education is needed for people to become more fully aware of the many dimensions of their pluralistic society.

These dimensions include differences associated with:

- ethnicity and race, manifested in differences in language, mores and customs, and varying according to the degree of identification with the ethnic or racial group:
- income, type of employment or non-employment, level of education, type and place of residence, in other words, differences in socio-economic class as it is manifested in Australia;
- strong ideological convictions and membership of groups with very distinctive beliefs, values and behaviour patterns, including active political and religious groups;
- gender;
- age;
- health, disability and handicap;
- the region in which people live.

Each of the above dimensions has been the subject of unending debate and some illustrative comments follow.

(a) Ethnicity and race are confused and contentious matters in Australia. 'Ethnic' has been a term popularly applied to non-British migrants. In N.S.W. members of the Multicultural Education Centre of the N.S.W. Education Department have made efforts to explain to students in schools that a person has both a national identity and an ethnic identity, that these identities are complementary, and that ethnic identity can be a matter of choice and self-perception and varies in importance to different people.[8]

'Race' is a term which would seem applicable to Aboriginal people but the current concept of who is an Aborigine does not make reference to physical characteristics; it defines an Aborigine 'as a person of Aboriginal or Torres Strait Island descent, who identifies and is accepted as such by the community with which he or she is associated.'[9] Aboriginal people tend to reject being categorized with other ethnic groups, or as a third wave of migrants, as suggested in a recent postage stamp series. They are the original inhabitants of the country.

Being the original people gives Aborigines claims to the land which was taken from them without even the token treaties made with indigenous people in North America and New Zealand. At the time of writing debate has flared up again over rights by mining companies to prospect and mine on Aboriginal lands.[10] The Liberal Opposition has said it will repeal the Hawke Government's Land Rights Act if it gets into power, and the UN Working Group on Indigenous Populations is listening to submissions by government and Aboriginal representatives.[11]

Race is also a major public and political issue in regard to immigration policy. The current debate has been precipitated by increasing numbers of refugees from

Vietnam, Laos and Kampuchea entering Australia; by the activities of small but active racist groups; by racist reactions by conservative groups such as the Returned Soldiers League; by a provocative statement by leading historian Geoffrey Blainey; by the media playing up controversial issues; and by the Liberal Opposition using the issue as political capital. Blainey was reported as saying that the policies of the Hawke Government on immigration favoured Asians, were anti-British and were running ahead of public opinion. He denies being a racist, as do the politicians, and argues, presumably from a historical viewpoint, that a country cannot cope with too great a rate of change. He also points to the danger of too many Asian migrants at a time of high unemployment.[12]

Arguments also arise as to whether everyone should speak 'the Australian language'. Pluralists point out that rather than there being one Australian language there are many. Many different Aboriginal languages have been spoken in Australia for thousands of years, while in 1976, 12.3 per cent of the Australian population over the age of 5 reported using 'community languages' other than English.[13]

(b) Ethnic and racial differences are clearly important but so also are differences in income and socio-economic class. Studies of poverty have revealed that some two million of the fifteen million people in Australia are living below the austere poverty line developed by the Poverty Inquiry of 1975.[14] The culture of poverty involves buying only specials at supermarkets, buying second-hand clothes, relying on friends, relatives and charities for handouts, no security of employment or accommodation, lack of outings, high incidence of stress, child abuse, family breakdown and suicide.[15] Over 9 per cent of the workforce is unemployed at the time of writing and this is much higher in depressed areas. Young school leavers, women and some migrant groups also have high rates of unemployment. There is no simple 'ethclass' relationship but multiple factors are involved in studies of disadvantaged groups in Australian society.[16]

(c) The present Prime Minister, Bob Hawke, has had considerable success in bringing together private industry, the unions and the government and in establishing a wages and prices accord. Nonetheless, there are major ideological differences even within the Labor Party, with its varied factions ranging from Left, to Centre Left, to Centre Unity, to Right. There are also major ideological divisions within ethnic groups.[17]

Religion can no longer be regarded as providing a unifying ideology for Australian society. A recent report by the N.S.W. Anti-Discrimination Board[18] points out that more than 20 per cent of N.S.W. people do not claim to be Christians and that these include Muslims, Jews, Buddhists and a growing number with 'no religion'. There are those who argue that Australian Rules Football is the religion of many people in Melbourne. More seriously there are many for whom environmental and/or peace and anti-nuclear beliefs are central to their world-views. Nuclear issues can also cut right through political parties and church groups.

(d) Slightly more than half the people of Australia are women. Women now make up about one-third of Australia's paid work force; however, they are concentrated in traditional female occupations such as clerical, sales, keyboard operators, domestic service, process working, teaching and nursing.[19] The women's movement, non-sexist resource centres and special programs to widen the interests of girls[20] have contributed to a considerable change in the images held by both women and men of the role of women in Australian society. The present Sex Discrimination Act aims to assist people to understand the law and to make a positive contribution to the reduction of discrimination.[21]

Male and female homosexuals are now of considerable significance as distinctive cultural groups with their own values, customs and social networks. As yet, however, the Queensland education system does not recognize the existence of this phenomenon in social studies programs.

One further gender-related issue is that of single parents of both sexes, who with changes in divorce laws have increased in numbers and created interest groups to provide mutual support.

(e) The proportion of older people in Australia is swiftly growing. Life expectancy has increased and by 2000 it has been estimated that one in every ten Australians will be over 65. While far from being homogeneous these old people share many interests and values and are becoming a political and economic force in the society. Age and poverty when combined, sometimes with handicap, create major challenges for society and government.

(f) Improvements in medical science have contributed to the survival of many handicapped people, and the recent successes of Australians at the Handicapped Olympics have brought a small amount of attention. Greater public awareness is still needed, however, especially when handicapped people are confused with sick people.

(g) There are significant differences between regional sub-cultures in Australia, and this has been true from Aboriginal times. The differences not only have substance in varied climatic experience, group activities and affiliations, values and customs and political viewpoints but are also perceived differences. Some Queenslanders and Western Australians have contemplated secession. Tasmanians are acutely conscious of being left off maps of Australia and states rights became a major issue when the Federal Government used its powers to stop the flooding of the Franklin River by the Tasmanian Government.

The above factors operate in varied combinations to produce distinctive social groups such as an Aboriginal community in an inner-city setting, which is very different from an isolated 'homeland' group in Arnhem Land, or an upper-middle-class Anglican retirement community at a seaside resort, or a Sikh community involved in banana production on the north coast of N.S.W., all of which are set within the wider Australian society and culture. Members of such groups may experience disadvantage, discrimination or lack of perceived political power. In an ideal pluralistic society there should be awareness of disadvantage and means to reduce such disadvantage.

Can We Change the Stereotypes?

In 1977 I questioned students in a number of senior high schools in Japan regarding their images of Australia. The pictures in their minds were fairly predictable. They wrote about kangaroos, koalas, sheep, cattle, wide open spaces and significantly 'the White Australia Policy'. I have asked groups of Australian students the same questions and found that they too have rather stereotyped images of Australia and Australians with meat pies, beer, Vegemite and the wide brown land prominent, rather than more multicultural or less materialistic symbols. The myths of the Lucky Country and Australia as a middle–class society where everyone can have 'a house of our own' still prevail, despite the poverty noted above and the problems frequently mentioned in the press of people losing their jobs and subsequently their homes.[22]

Is it desirable and possible, as the Bicentenary approaches, to do something further about remodelling the images which have been passed down as authentically and typically Australian due to the hegemony of the dominant social groups: to reconceptualize Australian society and culture in the minds of political leaders, academics, educators and members of the general public? There is space only for the following brief responses.

Rewriting Australian History

Of basic importance is the rewriting of Australian history books, including all school textbooks.[23] For example, the concept of the 'discovery' and 'first settlement' of Australia (meaning by Europeans) needs to be replaced by 'the invasion of Australia', since Australia was fully settled by tribal groups in 1788. Major attention needs to be paid to 40,000 years of Aboriginal prehistory as well as to the rapid and tragic destruction of Aboriginal tribes by the white settlers. The roles played by women in Australian history need to be emphasized.[24] Alternative paradigms of Australian history, for example, those by radical social historians such as Humphrey McQueen,[25] need to be compared with traditional viewpoints, which centre on political leaders and prominent events.

Changing the Maps and Spatial Perceptions

Australians need to be familiar with maps showing how Aboriginal tribal areas extended across the continent in 1788. Even earlier maps are needed to help reconstruct human, animal and plant life before and after the last ice age which was part of the lived experience of the ancestors of some present-day Australian people.[26] Bicentennial atlases and geography textbooks will need to help Australians in one region to gain a greater understanding of life in other regions. For example, people in the north-west of Western Australia experience a different climate, have a different perspective on the rest of the continent, and are struggling to express through the media, writing and the arts something of their distinctive life situations. World maps are needed which show the areas from which Australian ethnic groups trace their origins and which show the many interconnections between Australia and its Asian and world neighbours. Historical maps and timelines are needed to show the plurality of world civilizations, all of which are part of Australia's many rich heritages.

Strengthening and Multiplying Identities

A new interest in family history is growing in Australia and in other countries as people strengthen their family identity. Convict origins which were once anathema are now prized. Ethnic identity based not only on overseas experience but also on social life of the ethnic group in Australia is being strengthened by the publication of literature written by ethnic group members. There are many ways of experiencing and defining reality and in the past the dominant group has monopolized access to knowledge, its construction and its distribution as public knowledge.[27] The Bicentenary can make a major contribution by assisting in making minority group and regional literature publicly accessible.

Developing an Australian identity relates partly to identification with the land of Australia, and painters like Russell Drysdale, poets like Judith Wright and novelists like Patrick White have assisted this process. Some Aboriginal artists, writers and dancers have also shared their sense of identity with the land with other Australians. Smolicz would argue that we also need to share certain values with all Australians, including our parliamentary system, our belief in the rights of the individual, our belief in multiculturalism and our acceptance of the unity of the Australian state.[28]

In a rapidly changing society multiple identities assume major significance. For example, at a time when work is vulnerable to sudden changes it is important for many people not to think of themselves in terms of one lifetime vocation but as capable of changing that work identity if necessity demands. As already pointed out, ethnic identity in a pluralistic society is partly a matter of choice. One can choose to be more or less Greek. In a school a Greek boy managed to join the dominant football group, which was mainly Anglo-Celtic in origin. He was accepted as a 'football wog' and so had an additional identity added to his set of identities.[29]

New Symbols and Analogues

Controversy rages as to whether Australia should have a new flag by the Bicentennial Year. In Queensland the government insists that 'God Save the Queen' be played, despite the Federal Government's decision that 'Advance Australia Fair' is the national song, now that the sexist 'Australia's Sons' has been changed to 'Australians All'. The symbolic significance of Anzac Day may well fade as the veterans die off and the peace movement gains in strength.

In a more ideal pluralistic society, new analogues, new terms for explaining what the society is like are necessary. Some people have tried to replace the 'melting pot' analogue with the 'mosaic' but this is a very static concept.[30] Al Grassby provided the phrase, the 'Family of the Nation', but it did not catch on. The Bicentennial theme is 'Living Together'. It may be somewhat complex, but an interactive social ecology model of society would be more appropriate to show the dynamic nature of the society and its setting in both the continent of Australia and regional and global settings.[31] Unless the Bicentenary is developed very clearly in a world context it could well become an exercise in jingoism.

Remodelling the Schools

In all states there have been major developments in education for the polyethnic society, including Language Centres for new migrants, English as a Second Language programs in schools, teaching of 'Community Languages' (a preferred term to migrant languages) both within the school day and at Saturday schools, use of ethnic aides, multilingual teaching materials, plus ongoing experiments and debate on bilingualism.[32] More recent policy statements, such as those produced in N.S.W. in 1983, [33] stress the role of parent and community participation in the task of multicultural education, and emphasize whole school policy aimed at educating all children for the multicultural society, not just assimilating migrant children.

However, one must look not only to multicultural programs but also to programs like the Australian Schools Commission's 'Participation and Equity Program' which is concerned with the pluralistic task of 'making changes to secondary schools organisation to accommodate more adequately the social, economic and cultural diversity of students.'[34] Other comparable programs have been The School to Work Transition Program and the Disadvantaged Schools Program. All clearly reflect the economic bases of pluralism in addition to its ethnic aspects. The Curriculum Development Council in Canberra will be involved in a major enquiry into Australian Studies both as it is taught in schools and as to how it ought to be taught in the future.

Restructuring Society

A more radical viewpoint on pluralism would be that it is not sufficient to change the images through education, even if that is possible; one must change the structures of society as well. Some progress has been made in regard to the reduction of prejudice by means of anti-discrimination laws, and by institutions such as the Human Rights Commission and the Office of the Commissioner for Human Relations.[35] However, the deepest divisions and injustices in the future may well depend on our answer to the question: 'how can knowledge, employment and income be equitably shared so that there is not one privileged, technocratic class of haves and one class of have-nots, without knowledge, power or adequate material benefits?'

Conclusion

The rhetoric about, and governmental support for, multiculturalism have served a major purpose in the 1970s and early 1980s but there is a need to rethink the basis of pluralism in Australian society in the light of changes in immigration, in social institutions and values, and in technology. The Bicentennial Year presents an unusual opportunity for a rethink of educational and social policy, since it is concerned not only with Australia's past but also with Australia's future. Other countries may find some value in monitoring this opportunity to remodel Australian society and culture.[36]

Notes

1 Blake, B.J. (1981) *Australian Aboriginal Languages*, Sydney, Angus and Robertson.
2 *Participation* (1978) Sydney, Ethnic Affairs Commission.
3 *Education in a Multicultural Society*, Federal Education Portfolio Discussion Paper, Canberra, Department of Education, 1979, p. 18.
4 'Politics of multiculturalism versus multicultural butterfly collecting in Australian education', in Falk, B. and Harris, J. (Eds) (1983) *Unity in Diversity: Multicultural Education in Australia*, Carlton, Victoria, Australian College of Education, p. 169.
5 *Race, Ethnicity and Curriculum* (1981) Melbourne, Macmillan Company of Australia, p. 15.
6 Falk and Harris, *op.cit.*, p. 166.
7 'Principles of Australian pluralism', in Falk and Harris *op. cit.*, p. 32.
8 See Mathews, P.W. *et al.* (n.d.) *Ethnic Studies: A Base Paper*, Sydney, N.S.W. Department of Education, and (n.d.) *Our Multicultural Society*, Sydney, N.S.W. Department of Education.
9 Quoted in *Aboriginal Education Policy* (1982) Sydney, N.S.W., Department of Education.
10 *Sydney Morning Herald*, 3 May 1984.
11 *Sydney Morning Herald*, 1 August 1984.
12 *Sydney Morning Herald*, 1 May 1984.
13 Clyne, M.G. (1982) *Multilingual Australia*, Melbourne, River Seine Publications.
14 *Poverty in Australia* (1975) Commission of Inquiry into Poverty, Canberra, Australian Government Publishing Service.
15 Smith, P. (1982) *Living on the Edge*, Sydney, Australian Council of Social Service.
16 See, for example, *About Migrant Women* (1984) Canberra, Australian Government Publishing Service.
17 See Encel, S. (Ed.) (1981) *The Ethnic Dimension: Papers on Ethnicity and Pluralism by Jean Martin*, Sydney, Allen and Unwin, p. 49. See also Jupp, J. (1984) *Ethnic Politics in Australia*, Sydney, Allen and Unwin.
18 *Discrimination and Religious Conviction* (1984) Sydney, N.S.W., Discrimination Board.
19 *Women in Australia* (1979) Canberra, Australian Government Publishing Service.
20 Foster, V. (1984) *Changing Choices: Girls, School and Work*, Sydney, Hale and Iremonger.
21 *Putting the Sex Discrimination Act into Practice* (1984) Canberra, Human Rights Commission.
22 See Dwyer, P. (1977) *How Lucky Are We*, Carlton, Victoria, Pitman.
23 Note the work in progress on *Australians: An Historical Library*, a Bicentennial project using a 'slice of life' approach. Sections are 'Australians to 1988', 'Australians 1838', 'Australians 1888', 'Australians 1938', 'Australians 1939–1988' (publishers John Fairfax, David Syme and Kevin Weldon).
24 See, for example, Summers, A (1975) *Damned Whores and God's Police*, London, Allen Lane.
25 McQueen, H. (1978) *A New Britannia*, Harmondsworth, Penguin.
26 Geoffrey Blainey has written a very interesting account of early Aboriginal society in (1975) *The Triumph of the Nomads*, Melbourne, Macmillan.
27 See Martin, J. (1978) *The Migrant Presence*, Canberra, ANU Press, p. 23, and Houbein, L. (1978) *Ethnic Writers in English: A Bibliography*, Adelaide, ALS Working Papers.
28 *Culture and Education in a Plural Society* (1979) Canberra, Curriculum Development Centre.
29 Walker, J., 'Louts and legends: Male youth culture in an inner city school', unpublished

paper, Sydney University, Department of Education.

30 De Lacey, P.D. and Poole, M.E. (1979) *Mosaic or Melting Pot: Cultural Evolution in Australia*, New York, Harcourt Brace and Jovanovich.

31 The Society and Culture Syllabus of the N.S.W. Board of Senior School Studies is based on an integrative, dynamic model of Australian society in a global setting. For further details refer to D. Dufty, Department of Education, University of Sydney.

32 A useful summary of developments can be found in Wilkinson, P. (Ed.) (1981) *Education for a Multicultural Society: A Kit for Educators*, Richmond, Victoria, Clearing House on Migration Issues.

33 *Multicultural Education Policy Statement* (1983) Sydney, N.S.W, Department of Education.

34 *Participation and Equity in Australian Schools* (1983) Canberra, Commonwealth Schools Commission, p. 1.

35 See the Annual Reports of the Commission and the book, *Let's End the Slander: Combating Racial Prejudice in Teaching Materials*, (1979) Canberra, Office of the Commissioner for Community Relations.

36 For details of the Bicentenary contact The Australian Bicentenary Authority, GPO Box Aus 1988, Sydney, NSW., 2001, Australia.

9   Teaching and Learning about Racism: A Critique of Multicultural Education in Britain★

Mike Cole

Schools: We're all equal here.

Black students: We *KNOW* we are second-class citizens, in housing, employment and education.

Schools: Oh, dear. Negative self-image. We must order books with Blacks in them.

Black students: Can't we talk about the Immigration Laws or the national Front?

Schools: No, that's politics. We'll arrange some Asian and West Indian Cultural Evenings.

It is necessary to ask: who are the socially constituted speakers and initiators of the social practice of the discourse (of multiculturalism)? Clearly, they are not the ethnic minorities themselves but the representatives of dominant social forces to whom 'Blacks' are a problem. Concrete political and economic conditions and contradictions that face both black and white alike are not addressed but are contained within and deflected by the concept of multiculturalism.[1]

Introduction

Traditionally multicultural education has been seen (overwhelmingly) as 'teaching' children about other cultures, thereby instilling respect for such cultures by white

★ This chapter is dedicated to the young people in my class at Middle Row Primary School, Ladbroke Grove, London in 1975 who taught me a great deal about racism and the diverse ways in which it affects their lives.

indigenous children and improving the self-image of non-white immigrant and indigenous children, partly as a result of the positive images thus engendered. It was also expected to have had the spin-off of generating tolerance and understanding *between* minority groups.

That it has been felt possible for (white) teachers and, by implication, (white) teacher trainers to undertake such a gargantuan task as acquainting themselves with a number of cultures to such an extent that they can 'teach' those cultures even to *members* of such cultural groups is quite staggering. Learning about cultures in institutions as a mere part of a three- or four- or even one-year course leads at best to meaningless platitudes, at worst to racist stereotypes. Multicultural education, moreover, has assumed a 'homogeneous (British) national culture innocent of class or gender differences' into which other equally generalized Caribbean or Asian cultures can be integrated.[2] This approach excludes economic and political relations of domination and subordination. It also tends to lack a historical dimension and thereby ignores the dynamic nature of culture, of forms of resistance and struggles within cultures and between dominant and subordinate cultures. The school (and the classroom) is seen as a neutral arena and all that remains is for the teacher to provide the right materials,[3] to 'teach' a list of unchanging attributes. Curriculum materials tend to limit black culture, to reduce it to the artefacts produced with in a specified number of safe 'cultural' sites — the arts, religion, food.[4] Where teaching transcends these confines, pariticularly in the teacher-training context, to, for example, 'the family', this often leads to racist and sexist stereotypical constructs like the domineering West Indian woman and the passive Asian woman.

This approach aims not only to increase respect for minority cultures but also to 'improve self-concept' as a result of the content of the teaching. Self-concept is also to be enhanced by the general attitude of the teacher. That it has been believed that teachers are morally equipped to enhance black self-concept means that dangerous assumptions have been made about the capacity of white 'middle-class' teachers to 'do good' to young blacks. Such an approach is patronizing and allows the teacher to avoid examining her/his own racism and encourages an aura of cultural superiority. Moreover, Stone has questioned the whole notion that black children need their self-concepts raised.[5]

Although the approach favouring 'teaching about ways of life' and 'improving self-concept' has formed the dominant paradigm within multicultural education it would be foolish to dismiss everything enacted under the name of multicultural education. As Green argues, initially it was 'an educational philosophy espoused by progressive teachers who sought support of the struggles of black students and parents to oppose the racism in schools.' However it has also been 'the banner under which the state intervenes.'[6]

Multicultural education, as Green notes, contains a number of contradictions. It is our task to open up these contradictions, to show the inadequacies of the dominant interpretation of multicultural education and to attempt to develop a progressive theory and practice for both further and higher education and for schools. It should be clear why I say 'our' task. Implicit in the brief critique above is a general acceptance of a Marxist analysis of contemporary society.

I would like to make my position clear from the outset. The term 'Marxist' is greatly misunderstood, open to a wide range of interpretations and usually used by those in positions of power as a term of abuse. What I mean by a Marxist analysis is one which recognizes capitalism as a system of exploitation of one class by another. According to Marx, this exploitation is an objective fact (rather than a subjective opinion) since the dominant class (the capitalist class) does not pay the worker the full fruits of her/his labour but appropriates the surplus created in every act of productive labour. For example, a worker making, say, a table produces a value greater than the sum of the original materials; if the materials had a value of £50 and the table a value of £100, the worker is paid less than the £50 value she or he has created. The appropriated surplus is the source of capital accumulation, the driving force of capitalism. Marxism also sees the establishment of a democratic, socialist society as the only effective means to end the waste and misery which is a direct result of this capital accumulation. I do not consider the Soviet Union and other Eastern European countries as socialist in the sense Marx intended and am not competent to judge whether socialism even exists in a true form at the moment. I also do not believe that Marx had all the answers, nor that his work does not need developing. In particular I believe that in concentrating on social class, he seriously underestimated identities of gender and race.

I would argue that capitalism precludes equality of class and race and sex, and that therefore it is absolutely vital to develop a Marxist theory of racism which demonstrates the need for a socialist society in which black and white, female and male are genuinely free and equal.[7] Although in Marx's time there were black people living in Britain,[8] it was not until after the Second World War that black workers entered Britain in substantial numbers. Moreover, Marx noted that whereas the state went 'naked' in the colonies, at home it tended to assume 'respectable forms'.[9] For these reasons, it is understandable why racism directed at black people did not figure prominently in Marx's writings.[10]

Marx was also blind to gender. Although he showed awareness of the importance of the household to the continuance of capitalism, he seriously underestimated its centrality. I would agree with Seccombe that it should be regarded as a second site of the labour process where labour power consumed in production is restored, where domestic (unpaid) labour disappears (becomes insignificant, is not real work, is a 'labour of love') and where women in paid employment typically do a second day of labour.[11] Marx further lacked awareness of the way in which men attempt to wield power over women. While capitalist power over male workers is derived from the former's ownership of the means of production and (male) capitalist power over female workers is, in part, derived from such ownership, power has a further and separate dimension, the power of all men over women. As Dworkin explains, the power of men is a metaphysical assertion of self which exists a priori and is indifferent to denial or challenge, 'I want and I am entitled to have, therefore I am.' She goes on to identify further aspects of male power which although in part maintained by the distribution of wealth cannot be totally explained by a reduction to economic, namely physical strength, the capacity to terrorize, the power of naming, the power of sex (originating in the penis).[12] In Marx's time, women were faced with massive civil subordination and feminists concentrated on obtaining basic equality before the law. Marx can therefore be forgiven for not showing awareness that patriarchy as a system of oppression needs to be opposed as strongly as capitalism as a system of exploitation. Marxists writing today cannot.

How then might a Marxist theory of race which centralizes gender proceed?[13] I would like to begin by stressing that there can be no general or universal Marxist theory of race. As Lawner argues, Marxism is not about abstract dogma: 'The point of departure for a Marxist thinker is always culture as a whole and not, as many people argue abstractly, a presumed set of Marxist doctrines torn from their original context.'[14] By that she means that Marxists have to *start* at the cultural and therefore superstructural level;[15] that the starting point of their analysis has to be specific cultural formations or identities. By implication also, such cultural formations are necessarily firmly set in time and place. However, they are, of course, products of history and liable to continuous change and transformation.

Starting at 'the superstructural', however, does not mean one has to stay there. Nor, is it necessary to collapse the cultural into the economic. 'Staying there' tends to lead to idealism (political and educational forces alone can solve the problem); economism tends to lead to crude reductionism (for example, the notion that racism is *all* to do with the capitalist economy).

How, then, do we begin to understand racism in contemporary British society; how can we draw out the complex interplay between economic, political and educational forces which have shaped the position of young blacks today?

As we have argued elsewhere large numbers of young black people un-employed and on the streets can be explained by the need for Capital to restructure in post-imperial, post-boom economic situations.[16] However, the increasing conflict between young blacks and the police, for example, needs to be explained politically. In Britain the counter-hegemonic stance taken by increasing numbers of young blacks, though not posing any current real revolutionary threat, may be seen as a political response. (In Gramscian terms the resistance is conjunctural not organic.) As Sivanandan has said, 'As though to confirm the dialectics of History they, the British born, carry the politics of their slave ancestry.'[17] Hall *et al.* have reminded us they have two histories not one.[18] Although this response is related to young blacks' structural location in a more advanced mode of production (corporate capitalist Britain as opposed to, for example, earlier colonial Jamaica) its political manifest-ation would not be apparent if young blacks had been successfully hegemonized. In fact, harsh economic realities make control via hegemony increasingly difficult.

> English racism, both as a material structure and as an ideological presence, cannot be explained away to black youth as a temporary aberration. It is how the system works. In their experience English society *is* racist — it *works through race*. They did not — cannot — share the optimism of their parents that things will get better — in fact things have got worse — in terms of more restrictive immigration legislation (and increasingly, lack of employment opportunities), the political mobilisation of white hostility and above all police harassment on the streets. Nothing makes one aware

of living in a 'colony' so much as the permanent presence of an 'occupying force'.[19]

Black women, of course, are also oppressed by the forces of patriarchy which give street harassment a massive extra dimension.

Marxism encourages us to think dialectically and to see schools as sites of struggle. There are strong reasons for a renewed and major intervention informed by Marxism. In the 1960s, as now, government intent was to contain black resistance. However, whereas in the 1960s government rhetoric excluded anti-racism, the new offensive seems to include anti-racist education as part of the package. This contradicts state policy of subordinating all ethnic (and all non-bourgeois) cultures.[20] However, as Hatcher and Shallice argue, especially since the 1981 'riots' anti-racism has been forced upon at least one arm of the state, central government.

> The principal contradiction is between the role of racism in the Tories' overall political strategy, and their need to retain and reassert hegemony over the black population and restrain the more counter-productive manifestations of racism. One does not need to subscribe to a 'functionalist' view of racism to recognise the part that it plays in the Tories' attempts to manage the crisis.[21]

There are signs that the inclusion of anti-racism in multicultural education is more than mere rhetoric. Although, they argue, the black community has been particularly under attack in terms of unemployment, legislation (and policing) since 1979.

> playing the racist card unleashes several potentially dangerous dynamics. The first is the opposition of the black communities, in the form of unacceptable social conflict in the streets and also the loss of Tory seats in the cities. The second is that white racism may express itself in excessive and therefore counter-productive ways. The third is the undermining of the concept of equality of opportunity as a key ideological pillar of British society. To contain these three tendencies the state has combined repression with the elaboration of a range of integrationist measures: the Race Relations Act, the Community Relations Councils, and especially since the 'riots' a straightforward attempt to buy off black militancy by handing out money to black community organisations. This is the context in which the Tories are now taking on board a version of multicultural education (a version which includes anti-racism).[22]

This follows in the wake of the Scarman Report and the Rampton Report which both openly acknowledge the possibility of racism in British society.[23] Hatcher and Shallice continue:

> In opening up a new space for anti-racist activity in the schools (however) ... they run the risk of accelerating the politicisation of one area of schooling, just when they are anxious to *de*-politicise (in their terms) the curriculum (for example, the denunciation of peace studies as CND propaganda, and the exclusion of social issues from physics exams and YTS

programmes). The extent to which the Tories favour translating the rhetoric of anti-racist education into practice will depend upon the amount of pressure they feel themselves under from the black communities and their allies. They are caught in a contradiction of balancing the price of concessions in education and thereby risking an unwelcome politicisation of schooling, against the price of not giving ground and so risking a more militant response from the black communities.[24]

To this I would add that successful politicization in schools may increase the likelihood of a more militant response, but perhaps one which is itself more politicized.[25]

How might this politicization occur? How, in the light of the new offensive, are we to intervene to draw out the lessons from the struggles which were waged under the old banner? How are we to develop a theory and a practice of anti-racist education, a praxis which is also anti-sexist? We must stress anti-racism, to the exclusion of the *traditional* concept of multiculturalism. (If we do not do this, there is a very real danger that anti-racism will be just a part of the package, to be swamped by more traditional approaches.) Not only is there now space to argue for this; there is, *at the time of writing*, the actuality of practice, e.g., the anti-racist policies of the Inner London Education Authority (ILEA), since Ken Livingstone became leader of the Greater London Council (GLC).[26]

Racism: A White Not a Black Problem

To begin with, and this is my first main point, we must insist that racism is very much a white problem (just as sexism is a male problem). Although this is implied by Tory advocacy of anti-racism, the Tory philosophy overall which reflects popular racism, I would argue, still sees racism as a black problem, rather than as the *white* response to black people living here.

There is a prevalent common-sense view (the way I am using 'common-sense' is discussed shortly) which sees racism as a two-way problem, which states that blacks are/can be equally racist against whites as whites are/can be against blacks. I totally reject this view since racism (and sexism) implies power. It is white males who are in control of power and resources. We must present the argument that resistance is a rightful defensive (and aggressive) posture. Issues of separatism, be they based on race or gender (or both), are for relevant oppressed groups to make decisions on, NOT for white males.

It has been extensively argued that racism has changed.[27] During the days of the Empire a genetic inferiority model flourished whereby imperialism was ideologically justified by labels like 'coon' or 'native'. Now the official emphasis is on the alien character of the blacks, their different way of life, fears that they might 'swamp us'.[28] This is the essence of 'the new racism'. An excellent example of an academic treatise which sees blacks as a problem on account of their 'differentness', which epitomizes the stereotyped 'common-sense' view is the main chapter of Cashmore and Troyna's *Black Youth in Crisis*.[29]

I am using 'common-sense' in a very specific sense here, defined well by Errol Lawrence:

> By 'common-sense', we mean that body of knowledge about the world that has been forged in the practical experience of everyday life and which embodies, therefore, solutions to everyday problems as encountered by determinate groups of people throughout their history. That is to say that common-sense is more or less 'directly in touch with the practical struggle of everyday life' of those groups of people. However, a part of that practical struggle is the struggle 'in ideas' between those groups, situated in relations of dominance and subordination within a social formation. Since the ideas of the dominant groups are the 'ruling ideas' they will tend not only to form the parameters within which thought takes place but also to be embodied within the dominant institutional order and will, therefore, 'discipline' subordinate groups in *practice* as well as in 'mind'. Inevitably then, the ruling ideas will inform or shape common-sense and (what is more important) will actually become embedded within it, will in fact become a part of the common-sense of those subordinate groups . . . common-sense . . . is contradictory and fragmentary, it is also unsystematised, containing 'all those ideas which can be tagged onto existing knowledge without challenging it' in any direct way, indeed (as Stuart Hall *et al.* have pointed out in *Policing the Crisis*) it is inconsistent precisely *because* what is *common* about it is that 'it is not subject to the tests of internal coherence and logical consistency' — it is, in short, knowledge that is 'taken for granted'.

Lawrence also emphasizes that 'common-sense' contains elements of opposition to the status quo. However, as he goes on, referring to some earlier work of Cashmore and Troyna (and others), that sort of intellectual work, far from strengthening such opposition, tends to lend to the dominant interpretation (based on racism) a 'scientific' veneer of objectivity.[30] As far as the *Black Youth in Crisis* chapter is concerned, any such veneer can only be derived from Cashmore and Troyna's status as 'academics' since the chapter is virtually void of theory. Unlike some of the mainstream sociologists of race who oscillate between Marx, Weber and Durkheim,[31] Cashmore and Troyna present no macro-theory of society.[32] Nevertheless, they articulate a very dangerous form of thinking about black people and I would like to examine the chapter in detail. Moreover, its influence has extended beyond the normal academic community to the local press and to the police.[33] Cashmore and Troyna, in fact, offer a full-blown social pathology model of young blacks. One scarcely needs to go further than the title of the chapter (and the book they have edited) to guess what is coming. The title, *Black Youth in Crisis*, following the popular racist imagination, sees racism as a black problem. It is thus not the white patriarchal racist state which is in crisis but 'black youth'. I have less interest in the intentions or sincerity of the authors in writing this chapter than in the way in which I believe it contributes to racist theory and practice.

I Lost count of the number of times the problem was presented in terms of 'black youths' rather than white racism, so will quote only some typical instances. They are all based on the premise, stated in the introduction of the book, that Cashmore and Troyna 'believe that there are *problems* unique to young blacks and [their] work is about exposing these *problems*' (p. 14, my emphasis).

> From the ghettos, emerged a special group, a group which did not regard itself as having a *problem*, not one which could be resolved through conventional measures, anyway. (p. 15, my emphasis)
>
> Too long have sentimental journalists and liberal social investigators emphasised the black man [sic] as the receiver of pressures or the reactor to conditions. Well-meaning they may be, but we try not to let naiveté cloud our conception of the black youth. What we wish to do is stress the constructive element of these postures. Black youths were not simply jettisoned out of the mainstream of society and left to survive at the margins; they were not smashed around by the big bad bats of society like ping-pong balls. Generally, they developed and refined their own attitudes, orientations and postures in relation to the rest of society. In this sense, *they created their own 'problems'*. (p. 17, my emphasis)
>
> Collectively [black youths] promoted a *social problem* the likes of which had not been provided by any group in the history of migration to England. (p. 15)

In the Open Door Programme, *It ain't half racist Mum*,[34] Maggie Steed and Stuart Hall, on behalf of the Campaign against Racism in the Media (CARM), argue that misinformation, stereotyped images and the presentation of popular prejudice (even if subsequently corrected) can form an indelible imprint on one's consciousness. Hall *et al.* explain well the process by which the *description* of 'pathological symptoms' can serve to avoid calling into question the fundamental structural characteristics of society.[35] It is into this vacuum, they argue, that emerge the most powerful mechanisms for resolving the problems ideologically — *public images*. Since it is 'public images' more than anything else which saturate Cashmore and Troyna's chapter, it is worth quoting Hall *et al.* at length.

> A 'public image' is a cluster of impressions, themes and quasi-explanations, gathered or fused together. These are sometimes the outcome of the features process itself; where hard, difficult, social, cultural or economic analysis breaks down or is cut short, the resolution is achieved by orchestrating the whole feature so as to produce a kind of composite description-*cum*-explanation — in the form of a 'public image'. But the process is somewhat circular, for these 'public images' are frequently already in existence, derived from other features on other occasions dealing with other social problems. And in this case the presence of such 'public images' in public and journalistic discourse [and academic discourse] feeds into and informs the feature treatment of a particular story. Since such 'public images', at one and the same time, are graphically compelling, but also stop short of serious, searching analysis, they tend to appear *in place of analysis* — or analysis seems to collapse into the image. Thus at the point

where further analysis threatens to go beyond the boundaries of a dominant ideological field, the 'image' is evoked to foreclose the problem.[36]

What is the 'public image' of young blacks evoked by the chapter in question, a chapter in which the authors claim that they 'do not intend to caricature [black culture]' (p. 32)? It is an image of a group of people with 'bizarre needs' among whom 'street offence and theft convictions spiralled ominously' and 'feelings of disengagement intensified'.

> Black youth became objects of consternation, accounts of fecklessness, improvidence, violence, laziness and dishonesty were not uncommon and there were indications that West Indians did not bring up their children in a completely satisfactory manner with dire consequences for subsequent achievements at school. (p. 15)

Black (i.e., Afro-Caribbean) youths, moreover (unlike whites and Asians?), we are told, like forming gangs!

> Arrogant, rumbustious, contemptuous towards whites — these were some of the popular traits attributed to young blacks. They were not far off the mark. Young blacks retreated into their gangs where they cultivated postures *vis-à-vis* the rest of society and those postures could have been bespoken to engender these kind of negative responses. (p. 17)

Just in case we might overlook the racist nature of the society in which they live, we are reminded that young blacks 'faced the pressures, racialism was rife' (p. 17). But Cashmore and Troyna want 'balance'. By this they mean that we need to know that

> Young blacks actively and deliberately contributed to their own positions. They were a cultural phenomenon and cultures do not evolve spontaneously: they are worked at, constructed. Let us not fail to take into account the parts played by the blacks in provoking the outcast label slapped on them. They *were* arrogant, rumbustious and contemptuous. And perhaps with good reason. (pp. 17–18)

Shortly afterwards they issue a warning about the conclusion they are moving towards. It is going to concern a problem 'we all know [about]', 'the problem surrounding young blacks' (p. 18). This is a clear working example of Althusser's central thesis on ideology, the interpellation of subjects [37] whereby

> . . . we act and respond to ideology as if we were the originators of the ideas and values within it. In other words, when the *Sun* or *The Daily Mail* speaks of what 'the public' 'wants', 'needs', 'is fed up with', 'has had enough of' this strikes a chord with all the other organs of ruling-class ideology — the rest of the media, the various apparatuses of the state. Because we are largely trapped with one view of the world — capitalism/patriarchy/racism — it all 'makes sense' to us. This isn't logical — but as Stuart Hall once said — ideologies don't work by logic — they have logics of their own.[38]

Before Cashmore and Troyna reveal what the problem is, the problem 'we all know [about]', they ask whether the problem can be solved. By Black Studies perhaps? No, Black Studies they see as limited in that they divert blacks' attention to history rather than to the present. They also see such studies as dangerous 'because in creating a sense of identity and hence solidarity they can have a polarising effect' (p. 24). Is the problem 'because they are young' (p. 25)? No, they are young but they are also black.

> And it is this dimension which separates young blacks from their white counterparts. Youth has its own problems; being black its own problems; put them together and you have a whole new set of problems which tend to dispel the optimism of those who believe rather sanguinely that youthful exuberance will subside as maturity comes to the fore. We understand these problems to have a more solid potential. (p. 26)

The problem is that they are different. Although a great many blacks 'seemingly integrate into mainstream occupations, work towards qualifications, entertain harmonious relations with whites', beyond this . . . the crucial realisation of being *different*, being black remains' (pp. 27–8, my emphasis). 'The culture of disengagement' emerges from 'the link between blackness, differentness, and crucially disprivilege' (which, the preceding analysis would suggest, is partly of their own making).

Being different is not only in black youths' consciousness. It is one of Cashmore and Troyna's 'objective conditions' of black youth culture: 'Sharing the problems common to all black people in the UK. . . . means coming to terms with being black and being *different*' (p. 32, my emphasis). The new racism has arrived. What form does this 'difference' take? The problem 'we all know [about]' is now to be revealed. 'There is a penchant for violence within the West Indian culture' (p. 32). This 'possibly [stems] from the days of slavery.' But it does not really matter; 'whatever the sources of this violent proclivity, there can be no denying its existence: black youths do have a certain fascination for violence.' Ideological closure is apparent. 'What we all know [about]' has been 'proved'. 'The incredible enthusiasm' for Kung Fu and the martial arts exemplifies this![39]

To Cashmore and Troyna there is no stated solution except a vague notion of attitude change which is 'unlikely' anyway.

> The prospect is not pleasant, but it has to be faced; the situation is dire, but it has to be reckoned with. Measures we have at our disposal are cosmetic: they mask the real discontent beneath the surface. Nothing short of a wholesale transformation of attitudes, orientations and postures towards young blacks and, crucially, on the behalf of young blacks, will suffice in defusing a potentially explosive future. *People expect things of black youths and the latter expect things of others; both sets of expectations are usually fulfilled. These expectations are therefore unlikely to be changed and, without such changes, there can only be a further slide into the kind of ugly crisis of violence that we both find abhorrent, yet have unwillingly to concede is a menacing probability.'* (p. 34, my emphasis)

Quite obviously, Cashmore and Troyna are talking about black *males*. However, we are also warned that the 'girls (who) have organised themselves into gangs and have demonstrated a willingness to engage in such tactics' (p. 34). These sorts of conclusion are potentially very dangerous. Racists and even well-meaning liberals[40] could deduce that there is only one way to deal with 'the problem' which makes ' an ugly crisis of violence' 'a menacing probability'; send it away, get rid of it, repatriate it.

Whereas early functionalist sociology coincided with hopes of assimilation, and Weberian-dominated sociology helped the state 'manage the underclass', the current atheoretical approach (unless we see attitude orientation and posture transformation as a statement informed by theory) written after 'the riots' and exemplified by Cashmore and Troyna, the most dangerous to date, albeit unwittingly is exemplary of the new racism and prepares the ground for repatriation. (I am emphatically NOT suggesting that Cashmore and Troyna are racists or would in any way favour repatriation. I am arguing that to all but the committed or partly convinced anti-racist their writing could have this effect.) At the same time it totally mystifies and obscures the real problem — white racism, and the real solution — an anti-racist, anti-sexist socialist society.

Empire, Politics and Patriarchy: The Formation of a British Racism

My second major point about the teaching of anti-racism in teacher training establishments and subsequently in schools is that the specificity of a British racism of the 1980s cannot begin to be understood without a thorough examination of the requirements of developing capitalism, imperialism and patriarchy on the one hand, and political forces on the other. We need to explain that it is the former which created the supply of cheap labour in the first place. We need to put forward an alternative explanation of Empire to the one currently offered in schools. We need to stress that the Empire arose as the drive for capital accumulation took capital beyond national boundaries, rather than as a result of benign attempts to 'civilize' the third world. We need to stress that imperialism drained the third world of capital and rendered its inhabitants workless. (Since capital was brought back from the colonies to Britain, the movement of (colonial) labour power back to labour-hungry Britain too was a logical consequence.) Black people were, of course, actively recruited to Britain.

We also need to point out that this history cannot be understood without an analysis of the role of female labour power. Asian and Afro-Caribbean women have tended to do the lowest paid and most menial work. A recent report by the West Midland's County Council low-pay unit states that a fifty-hour week at £1 per hour is the norm, while wages of £25 for a forty-hour week, where the legal miminum is £47.60, are not uncommon. Ninety per cent of Britain's sportswear is made in the West Midlands, mainly by Asian women. Conditions are said to be appalling, with work taking place in derelict buildings with leaking roofs, and the women having to pay for their own heating (usually paraffin heaters). Many premises have inadequate fire exits, often blocked by stocks of cloth. Workers supply their own toilet paper, rarely have access to hot water and are without eating facilities. Shared toilets for men and women usually fail to flush, first-aid kits are rare and child labour is common. According to *The Observer*, which summarized the report, most of these 400+ small firms are Asian-owned.[41] While it is British racism which ultimately bears responsibility for this state of affairs, this minority of black businessmen cannot be exonerated from blame for colluding with the white dominated structures of exploitation and oppression.

Black women have also suffered as a result of racist immigration legislation. As Parmar points out, Asian women are exposed to British racism even before they arrive in Britain in the form of long and rigorous interviews in the embassies of the Indian sub-continent. Women are also asked very intimate questions about themselves in order to 'prove' marital status.[42] In the late 1970s sexual examinations were commonplace at London's Heathrow airport in order to determine virginity and to test for venereal disease. As Parmar points out, examinations to 'prove' whether a woman is a virgin can only be seen as acts of violence and intimidation against black women by the British state, since the 'testing' is based on the racist and sexist assumption that Asian women are always virgins before they get married. Moreover 'one cannot prove virginity by poking a finger up a vagina — not every woman has a hymen.[43] As far as venereal disease is concerned, a former General Secretary of the Joint Council for the Welfare of Immigrants stressed that 'it was a fairly frequent occurrence that ... young girls, straight from their grandmothers' houses, would be taken to Holloway prison, their pubic hair shaved off, and examined for VD.[44] Asian women are viewed at one and the same time as submissive, meek and tradition-bound (virgins before marriage) and promiscuous from an early age (potential carriers of VD).

Asian women have been active in struggling against oppression both in the sub-continent and in Britain. They led the strike at Grunwicks, at the Chix sweet factory at Slough and at Fritters in North London.

> Asian women have not only been active at their workplaces but have also been involved in struggles and campaigns against other forms of oppression and repression. Asian women's groups, with a strong and culturally specific form of feminism, have emerged and actively campaigned against virginity testing, the use of Depo-provera, immigration legislation, racist attacks in schools, for better housing, against the racist practices of DHSS and the NHS, and every other area of their lives.[45]

Moreover, as Sivanandan points out:

> In fighting for educational and social and welfare services for the whole community, Asian and Afro-Caribbean women pinpointed the parallel histories of a common racism. In health care, for example, black women fought against the neglect of 'black disease'. Simultaneous campaigns were mounted in Brent against sickle-cell anaemia (affecting West Indians) and

Vitamin D deficiencies causing rickets (affecting Asians). And issues such as forcible sterilisation, arising from the health services' obsession with black fertility, or the easy consignment of black women to mental hospitals, arising from its stereotyped understanding of 'black psyches in captivity', were fought by black women from both communities.[46]

At the time of writing, black women in support of the Afia Begum Campaign Against Deportations (ABCAD) are touring Europe campaigning against the racist and sexist nature of immigration and deportation legislation.

Racist Immigration Legislation

We need to explain that successive immigration legislation has changed the status of the black ex-colonial citizen from British subject to 'guest worker' (the European model). We further need to point out that this change of status has to be justified ideologically. Here are two examples:

> The imposition of mass immigration from backward alien cultures is just one symptom of this self-destructive urge reflected in the assault on patriotism, the family — both as a conjugal and economic unit — the Christian religion in public life and schools, traditional morality, in matters of sex, honesty, public display, and respect for the law — in short, all that is English and wholesome. (Alfred Sherman, Tory ideologue, 9 September 1979)[47]

> If we went on as we are, then by the end of the century, there would be 4 million people of the New Commonwealth or Pakistan here. Now, that is an awful lot and I think it means that people are really rather afraid that this country might be swamped by people with a different culture. And, you know, the British character has done so much for democracy, for law, and done so much throughout the world, that if there is a fear that it might be swamped, people are going to react and be rather hostile to those coming in. (Margaret Thatcher, recently elected Prime Minister, 12 October 1979)

— The distance between these two quotations is small, both in time and in depths of racism. Although the rhetoric of Thatcher is (necessarily) milder, its implications of 'hostile reactions' could be thought of as more dangerous.

The advent of Thatcherism, I would argue, represents a moment of profound triumph for the British (and international) ruling class. Since 1979 we have seen unprecedented offensives against the working class as a whole, against women as a whole, and particularly relevant to this book, against black women and men. The 1981 Nationality Act, which came into force in January 1983, completed the process of eroding the rights of black people. The *official* stated purpose of immigration restrictions is to control numbers. However, both the 1971 Immigration Act and the 1981 Nationality Act, while restricting black immigration, actually increased patrial (i.e., white) rights to come to Britain. It is significant that 'immigrant' has become synonymous with 'black'. White immigrants are not normally even described as such, whereas black *Britons* are often called 'immigrants'. As Macdonald explains, quoting a former Home Secretary, the former act gave this right to 'possibly millions of people, who never previously had the right [while the latter] consolidates this situation by extending the acquisition of British citizenship by descent to those whose mother or father was a CUKC (Citizen of the UK and Colonies). At a stroke countless numbers of citizens of Australia, New Zealand and Canada acquire dual nationality by obtaining the additional benefits of British citizenship.'[48] Moreover, as Macdonald argues, if numbers were the real problem, some attempt would have been made to control the immigration of Irish people who are exempt from contro.[49]

The Nationaity Act is also sexist.[50] For example, women are discriminated against in terms of rights to bring husbands and children here, loss of right to be here if they marry overseas students or if marriage to men here temporarily breaks up. Marriage to patrial men (men totally free from immigration control) after 1 January 1983 does not give patriality to women. There is, however, one step towards sex equality in the Act; children born abroad to British mothers are able to inherit their mother's nationality. However, children born here after 1 January 1983 are British only if either of their parents is allowed to stay here permanently. This means that, for the first time, *stateless* children can be born in Britain to non–British women who are unable to transmit their own citizenship to such children. Lastly, if a man is deported, his wife can be deported with him. If a woman is deported, her husband cannot. The rules are very strict but can be broken. This gives the Home Office worrying authority, but also opens space for campaigns against aspects of the Act.

Unless these facts are brought into the open and discussed in classrooms, we have no hope of counteracting racism. A Marxist analysis of racism, informed by feminism, allows us to locate race to time and place and to realize the economic and political forces underlying it.

Experience

My third point is to do with experiential aspects of race and their relationship to gender and class. While no white person knows what it is like to be black, and no male knows what it is like to be female, most of our pupils (and some of our student teachers) know what it is like to be working–class. It needs to be stressed that we live not only in a society which is racist but also in one which is patriarchal and capitalist. It must be demonstrated that history is a history of class struggle *and* struggle between the sexes as well as racial conflict, that in a very real sense if we are to fulfil human potential all oppressed peoples have a vested interest in opposing all forms of exploitation and oppression.

These forms of exploitation and oppression are, where relevant, experienced simultaneously. Hatcher and Shallice quote the work of Catterall which serves as an excellent practical example of the experiential approach. Regretfully, in what they quote, the dimension of sexism is missing, so I will include its *possibilities* (in square brackets) in summarizing his otherwise admirable suggestions. We could, he suggests, focus on the effects of monetarism on East London — the decline of dockland, the rise of racism [the worsening of the position of women as workers, part-time and full time, trapped in the home, as mothers]. Urban studies or environmental studies, he concludes, must explore the possible connections between the forms and intensity of racism [and sexism] and, for example, social decline occurring largely as a direct result of monetarist policy.[51]

Through such methods we are able to show the material as well as the ideological dimensions of exploitation, the way in which inequality is *constructed* (something rendered impossible by the traditional multicultural approach), how all oppressed groups are made less equal and how

> Increasingly rigid immigration laws designed to limit black entry into Britian, police harassment and inequalities in housing and employment are not just detrimental to the interests of the black community, but they actually construct certain racial groups as 'less equal' than others.[52]

In these material conditions it is hardly surprising that black students *know* they are second-class citizens — in school as much as anywhere else.[53] Indeed, it can be argued that this knowledge is one of the major reasons for low achievement in schoos,[54] rather than liberal arguments about low self-image.

By exploring these complex relationships in schools radical teachers are able to start from experience but then to transcend it. Too often teachers fail to provide the 'intellectual baggage', and classroom discussion tends to degenerate to the 'airing of prejudice'. All students must be encouraged to state their feelings but unfortunately 'uninformed "discussion" is valued more highly than the careful, structured development of theoretical skills combined with the acquisition of necessary empirical data.'[55]

Language

Implicit in such development is a facility for language. My final point is to do with the language of liberal discourse[56] and how it might be transformed. Language, I would argue, is both a medium of communication and the embodiment of ideas. I will deal with the latter first. The ideas which language embodies are bourgeois, patriarchal and racist. However, as Dodgson and Stewart argue, describing Carby's discussion of the work of Bruce Boone, there comes a time when the language of the dominant group becomes unheard and we only recognize those voices which deviate from the norm.[57] Our counter-hegemonic role associalists must be to multiply and celebrate these deviant voices, to develop a discourse which is Marxist/feminist/anti-racist.[58]

Significant strides, have already been taken. Many nineteenth-century bourgeois conceptions have already been successfully challenged, and have taken on socialist connotations, for example:

liberty	–	liberation
democracy	–	democratic socialism

137

upper class   —   ruling class
lower class   —   working class

Similarly, man-made language is constantly being demystified, revealing some of the mechanisms whereby the male supremacist society is maintained through language,[59] for example:

man   —   people
he/him/his   —   s/he her/him her/his
chairman   —   chair
Mr, Mrs, Miss   —   Ms, Mr

The development of an anti-racist discourse is also crucial. This discourse must replace the voice of multiculturalism which is the voice 'of the dominant group, the white middle class, which positions the blacks and working class as subjects of the discourse; multi-culturalism excludes the language and alternate set of meanings of subordinated groups.'[60] Nevertheless, as we know, blacks have resisted.

> Young people of African and Asian descent refer to themselves (proudly) as they are ('black' as opposed to 'white'), rather than using the cautiously ambiguous term, the derogatory term, 'coloureds' so long prominent in liberal discourse. The Rastafarian movement is of considerable importance. As Gilroy has argued

> > *It is often forgotten that blacks arrived here bearing traditions of anti-colonial struggle wherever they set out from. Older West Indians have encountered the discourse of Rasta before, and though sometimes critical of it, many ... were happy to recount tales of their contact with the Garveyites 'at home' ... the solidarity [the movement] provides the whole community appears to offer a refuge from the new pressures of popular racism.*

> Rasta discourse, he argues, is communalist and able to convey commitment in a selective or intermittent manner. It invites speakers, furthermore, to appropriate the ideas which appeal to them without being pigeonholed by the oppressor. The operation of a shared language 'far more than the colours and vestimentary codes of dread style, marks the frontiers of a discursive community in which deep disagreement is possible without condemnation or schism.'[61]

All forms of ethnic minority language must be equally valid, whether a 'form' of English like Rasta discourse or a completely different language. This is emphatically *not* to suggest denying a facility for Standard English to black students. (A recent study in two infant schools showed that mother-tongue teaching can increase proficiency in Standard English.[62]) On the contrary, in order for black (and white) students to overcome their oppression, in order for the preceding strategies to work, excellence in Standard English is of paramount priority.

Students must at the same time know how Standard English is used and how it can be transformed. They must understand the dominant language in order to undermine it. This has been movingly put by Chris Searle.

In opposition to the code of imperialism and death — that language of Thatcher, Saatchi and Saatchi, of Rupert Murdoch and the *Sun* — as teachers we must bring into our words and into our classrooms a new language of life, to re-invent a language of meaning and hope, a language that means unity and struggle for our students and ourselves that will begin to sustain us and fight with us in the next crucial years against the advance of all that is backward and threatens to disintegrate us. In doing so, together we shall transform our language as we transform our world, and truly make our common words the messages of a new creation.[63]

Secondly, I would like to look at language as a *medium* of communication, how *the way we use language* as opposed to its content can crucially alter its ideological impact. Barker and Beezer's excellent critique of the Scarman Report on the Brixton riots shows how descriptions of rationality were continuously used to describe the actions of the police as compared to descriptions of emotionality commonly used to describe young blacks. It is our duty as teachers, I would suggest, to encourage our students to look at both official and unofficial texts in similar critical manner. In the Scarman Report (and Barker and Beezer provide a number of examples):

The police are described as concerned, seeing dangers, being informed, exercising judgement, taking decisions and accepting responsibilities; as having good intentions and making imaginative decisions; and even where there was failure, they were able to salvage retrievals.[64]

On the other hand, the people of Brixton, described by Scarman as 'a people of the street'(!),

do not take decisions, but are the subject of rumours by which they are swayed. They do not act, but are driven into action by feelings; they feel insecure in all manner of ways; they believe and feel rather than know and act, and their activities, because so prone to rumour, are likely to end in a limbo of half remembered and half distorted attitudes. At the stroke of the magician's pen, they disappear, not into a cloud of smoke, but into a cloud of emotions, atmosphere and feelings.[65]

As Barker and Beezer argue, whereas the former is the language of rationality and reason, the latter 'is subtly oppressive; it denies the possibility of taking stock of situations and moving from information and knowledge to positive action, purposive action. This is the language of emotion, disconnected from reasoning.'[66] To reinforce their point, they go on to reverse the language of some typical paragraphs. To do justice to the point they are making, I will need to quote them at length.*

Consider the police-eye view of the 'sad, little incident' (Para. 3.24) said to have sparked off the first day's clashes:

---

* Reproduced by the kind permission of the Editor, *International Socialism Journal*, 34 PO Box 82, London E2.

> At about 6.10 pm on the warm evening of Friday 10 April 1981, Police
> Constable Stephen Margiotta (PC 643L) was on duty in uniform in
> Atlantic Road, when he noticed that the traffic had come to a standstill.
> Crossing the road and walking toward the junction of Atlantic Road and
> Coldharbour Lane he saw a black youth in the road running towards him.
> The youth appeared to be very distressed and was apparently being
> pursued by two or three other black youths. PC Margiotta thought that
> this youth might have committed some offence and decided to try and stop
> him. After an initial unsuccessful attempt the youth tripped and fell and
> PC Margiotta fell over him. (Para 3.4)
>
> When PC Margiotta and the youth stood up, the officer noticed that
> his own arm and shirt and the back of the youth's shirt were covered in
> blood. The youth broke away, but stopped on the north east corner of the
> junction of Atlantic Road and Coldharbour Lane where PC Margiotta,
> who had been joined by another officer, PC 523L Sanders asked the
> youth what was the matter and the youth replied by taking off his shirt to
> reveal a wound some three or four inches long just below the centre of his
> back in between the shoulder blades. The wound was bleeding profusely.
> The youth was clearly distressed. He was also struggling to get away.
> (Para 3.5)

So the narrative begins. All our presumptions are mobilised by its
seeming reasonableness. PC Margiotta, going about his normal work,
'noticed' something. A black youth — a 'person of the streets' — was
running towards him, away from three others 'chasing' him. Naturally, PC
Margiotta assumed that a black youth in a distressed state might well have
committed some offence. What other motive could there be for such
behaviour? Despite his distress which, it was now evident, had a physical
cause (the stab wound) the youth still tried to get away despite the police's
'evident' desire to help him (even if they had to fall over him and then
corner him in order to convince him of this). A wise judgement by the
police is in the offing.

This is all so obvious and self evident, and the way the story is told
helps to make it so. We have been well prepared to read it this way, since
the whole of the preceding section of the Report has informed us of the
problems of Brixton, the difficulties of adjustment West Indians face in
coming here, and how they are a people fond of hanging around the streets
and liable to become involved at any time in criminal activites. PC
Margiotta is the epitome of level-headedness and clear, incisive thinking in
the midst of emotions and myth-living.

It is difficult to escape this understanding of the disorders, but not
impossible. It could have been different, so let us make it so. Let us put the
police at the centre of the narrative, but in a different way, as the *problem* in
Part II. In this section of background information, imagine that we were

informed of long standing arguments over the need for controls over the Metropolitan Police, of the difficulties of recruiting which had led over the years to the present poor quality of the recruits (requiring only four O-levels). Most of these came from educationally disadvantaged areas. The class division between these recruits and those above Inspectorate level, who came from solidly upper middle class backgrounds, was the cause of resentment and a general atmosphere of tension and hostility. (This might even be compounded by their tendency to hang around the canteen, when off duty, endlessly swapping grievances.) And so on. Let us imagine finally that the Lambeth Working Party report had been mentioned here, with its summary of prejudiced behaviour by many police against local black people. This behaviour had particularly been displayed by the white youth of the force. How might that story have looked then?

It is hard to conceive it being told any longer over the shoulder of PC Margiotta. Conceive it instead like this:

> *At about 6.10 pm on the warm evening of Friday 10 April 1981, Dave Shepherd, a young black resident of Brixton had been forced into a fight, in the course of which he sustained a knife wound. Managing to escape from his aggressors, he was making his way quickly for help when he came across three of his friends. They warned him that there were police youths about, spoiling for trouble. Ignoring their warnings, he continued down the road quickly. Mr Shepherd was in considerable pain. When he came to the road junction, he saw one of the police youths, who began running towards him. Reasoning that the youth might be about to harass him, he attempted to leave, but was grabbed and forced to the floor, with the police youth on top of him. This caused considerable further pain, and increased the flow of blood from the wound. Fearing that the police might arrest him and so delay his finding medical assistance, Mr Shepherd once again attempted to leave; but the degree of pain he was suffering forced him to pause on the north east corner of the junction of Atlantic Road and Coldharbour Lane. Meanwhile the first police youth had been joined by another, and together they cornered Mr Shepherd. In an effort to persuade them not to delay him, he showed them the wound in his back. Once again he attempted to leave, in order to seek the medical help he knew he urgently needed, but once again they prevented him.*

The feel is different, isn't it? Now the calm rationality of the police is not so self evident, especially as this narrative has been preceded by the section dealing with the tensions within the police, the difficulties young officers have in adjusting, and their disadvantaged background. The obvious follow-up to this would be to explore the nature of myths and stereotypes held by the police, which could lead to such unreasonable attitudes towards a person such as Dave Shepherd.'[67]

Mike Cole

Conclusion

I would like to conclude by insisting that we as teachers need to *learn* as much as to teach. We have to listen to the demands and wishes of members of the black community. It is up to *that* community to prioritize current needs. There will be occasions when learning about aspects of black culture will be appropriate, but this must come from within that culture outwards to us. (White) teachers must also be in dialogue with the labour movement, with the trade union movement, with the women's movement (where appropriate). For education to become truly liberating, it must push against the forces of oppression, be they centred on class, race, gender or all three. Race, like gender, must not be marginalized as it so often is by the conventional left. The current miners' strike (May 1984) is, of course, crucial. But so is Greenham Common and so is black resistance in the community, in the inner city. The time is past to see production as the only site of struggle. One of the advantages of teaching and learning about the *reality of* race is not only what it tells us about race but also what it tells us about the whole nature of the society in which we live.

In my experience of teaching young black people in inner-London about ten years ago and being taught by them was that what concerned them most was racist abuse and attacks, conflicts with the police, bad housing, employment prospects. Now unemployment is even more central than it was then. We cannot and must not rely on multiculturalists to protect and further the interests of young blacks. Unless we, as teachers, confront these real issues, unless we address a culture which is relevant and pressing, we have no hope of making meaningful contact with our students. Multiculturalists avoid political issues, seeing the role of institutions like the Home Office, the police or the immigration authorities as 'outside' education. But these state institutions are racist and bring black people directly into conflict with the state. Multiculturalists rely on the police to protect blacks under attack. Anti-racists are not so naive, and recognize the need for black communities to mobilize and defend themselves.[68]

I hope that what I have outlined in this chapter demonstrates the wider implications inherent in teaching and learning about racism. It represents much more than 'suggestions to undermine racism'. If we come to terms with what lies behind some of these ideas, we are talking about a major transformation which goes beyond the boundaries of race, and, of course, about a new conception of teaching and learning (which will be much contested by the ruling forces). I will leave the last word to Stuart Hall.

> There are no guarantees against the growth of a popular racism, but there is always, in the factual everyday struggles of those who resist racism, the possibility of an anti-racist politics and pedagogy.
> Somehow we have to tread that difficult line whilst not selling short the complexity of the issues with which we are dealing. Instead of thinking that confronting the questions of race is some sort of moral intellectual academic duty which white people with good feelings do for blacks, one has to remember that the issue of race provides one of the most important

ways of understanding how this society actually works and how it has arrived where it is. It is one of the most important keys, not into the margins of the society, but to its dynamic centre. It is a very good way of getting hold of the political and social issues of contemporary Britain because it touches and connects with so many facets.[69]

Acknowledgements

Once again I am indebted to Audrey Page for her work in getting this chapter word processed so efficiently. Madan Sarup kindly offered some suggestions on an early draft.

Notes

1 Carby, H.V. (1979) *Multicultural Fictions*, Centre for Contemporary Cultural Studies, Stencilled Occasional Paper SP No. 58, available from The University of Birmingham, PO Box 363, Birmingham B15 2TT. The dissemination of 'information' about ethnic minorities' 'culture' and 'ways of life' has not only taken place at 'Cultural Evenings'. It has been passed on extensively by white teachers and white teacher-trainers as part of their mainstream teaching.

2 Carby H. (1980) 'Multi-culture', *Screen Education*, 34, Spring, p. 64.

3 *Ibid.*, p. 65. The multicultural approach also ignores different forms of racism (rooted in a different colonialism) and consequent different forms of resistance. This point was exemplified in a recent talk by Avtar Brah and Rosemary Deem.

4 *Ibid.*, p. 67.

5 Stone, M. (1981) *The Education of the Black Child in Britain: The Myth of Multi-racial Education*, Glasgow, Fontana. Stone argues that there is no basis in fact for the belief that black children have poor self-esteem or negative self-concept. And, as Andy Green has suggested, 'high self-esteem may well co-exist with low morale and pessimism in the black child; a feeling that however good I am, racism will keep me down'. Green, a. (1982) 'In defence of anti-racist teaching; A reply to recent critiques of multi-cultural education', *Multi-Racial Education*, 10, 2, p. 28.

6 Green, *ibid.*, p. 20. In Marxist analysis (discussed shortly), the state is more than merely central and local government, and encompasses also hierarchies in the civil service, the judiciary, the police, the military, as well as owners and controllers of the media. For an examination of contrasting Marxist theories of the state see Cole, M. and Skelton, B. (1980) 'Capital, the state and youth', in Cole, M. and Skelton, B. (Eds), *Blind Alley Youth in a Crisis of Capital*, Ormskirk, Hesketch.

7 Capitalism, racism and sexism are intimately connected in modern capitalist societies, and for this reason functionalist and Weberian accounts (referred to below) are inadequate as 'solutions' to the exploitation of black women and men and white women. For an examination of some of the connections see, for example, Cole, M. (1984a) 'The American connection: Race, gender and capital accumulation today'.

8 For a history of black migration to Britain, see, for example, Walvin, J. (1973) *Black and White* London, Heinemann. For a briefer version see Kum Kum Bhavnani's three articles in *Spare Rib*, February, March and April 1982.

9 Marx, K. (1853) 'The future results of British rule in India', *The New York Daily Tribune*, 8 August, quoted in Stone, J. (Ed.) (1977) *Race, Ethnicity and Social Change*, London, Wadsworth, pp. 5–9.

10 Marx does write, however, of racism directed at the Irish:

> In all *the big industrial centres in England* there is profound antagonism between the Irish proletariat and the English proletariat. The average English worker hates the Irish worker as a competitor who lowers wages and the *standard of life*. He feels national and religious antipathies for him. He regards him somewhat like the *poor whites* of the Southern States regard their black slaves. This antagonism among the proletarians of England is artificially nourished and supported by the bourgeousie. It knows that this scission is the true secret of maintaining its power.

Karl Marx, confidential communication, quoted in Anderson, C.H. (1974) *The Political Economy of Social Class*, London, Prentice Hall, p. 65.

11 For a discussion of 'the double day of Labour' and the notion of the household as a second site of the labour process, see Seccombe, W. (1980) 'Domestic labour and the working class household', in Fox, B. (Ed.) *Hidden in the Household*, The Women's Press. See also Cole, M. (1984a) *op. cit.* For some suggestions about the implications of the effect of the current needs of capitalism and Thatcherism on the double day of labour, see Cole, M. (1984b) *Recession and Education: The Thatcher Offensive*, in preparation.

12 Dworkin, A. (1981) *Pornography: Men Possessing Women*, The Women's Press, Ch. 1.

13 It is crucial that gender be central to the analysis, not only because authentic socialism means equality for *all* workers, black and white, male and female, but also because at least half of the black population of the world are women.

14 Lawner, L. (1979) in the introduction to *Antonio Gramsci: Letters from Prison*, Quartet Books, p. 45.

15 The superstructure refers to levels of society such as the political, the ideological, the educational, the cultural, as distinct from the economic base of society where workers are exploited by capitalists in production.

16 Cole and Skelton (1980) *op. cit.*, p. 17.

17 Sivanandan, A. (1976) *Race Class and the State: The Black Experience in Britain*, London, Institute of Race Relations, p. 365.

18 Hall, S. *et al.* (1978) *Policing the Crisis*, London, Macmillan.

19 *Ibid.*, p. 354.

20 Hatcher, R. with Shallice, J. (1983) 'The politics of anti-racist education', *Multi-racial Education*, 12, 1, pp. 5–6.

21 *Ibid.*, p. 5.

22 *Ibid.*

23 Cmnd 8427, *The Brixton Disorders 10-12 April 1981: A Report of an Enquiry by the Rt. Hon. Lord Scarman*, London, 1981; Cmnd 8273, *West Indian Children in Our Schools. Interim Report of the Committee of Inquiry into the Education of Children from Ethnic Minority Groups*, Chairman [sic] Anthony Rampton OBE. The Scarman Report is discussed below.

24 Hatcher with Shallice (1983) *op. cit.*, p. 6.

25 I realize that this statement might suggest a patronizing attitude, that I might face the accusation of arrogance. However, as I hope will become clear in this chapter (and indeed as its title suggests), in fighting racism, teachers must be equally prepared to learn as to teach, that the teaching/learning situation is a two-way process.

26 However, as Hatcher and Shallice point out, although ILEA's policy documents represent 'the most advanced attempt by any Local Authority to promote racial equality in schools,' even they are weakened by their divorce from class realities. They assume that there is no fundamental conflict of class interest in education (that their proposals can serve the best interests equally of the employers, the individual and the nation), that the British people have a long history of resistance to injustice (which they don't) and that schooling can be considered as an entity separate from capitalist society (which it can't) (Hatcher with Shallice, *op. cit.*, pp. 11–12).

27 See, for example, Barker, M. (1981) *The New Racism*, London, Junction Books.

28 This, however, does not preclude a return to 'official' labels of inferiority in times of crisis. Take the case of the (neo-colonial) Falklands War where 'our lads' fought 'the Argies' — often depicted in grotesque caricatures in the popular press. What is crucial is that both forms of racism, the old and the new, are *white* problems but are presented 'universally' as problems inherent in those on the receiving end of the labels.

29 Cashmore, E. and Troyna, B. (1982) 'Black youth in crisis', in Cashmore, E. and Troyna, B. (Eds), *Black Youth in Crisis*, London, George Allen and Unwin.

30 Lawrence, E. (1981) 'White sociology, Black struggle', *Multiracial Education*, 9, 3, pp. 4–5, 7. Ernest Cashmore and Barry Troyna have, in fact, replied to this critique. See (1981) 'Just for white boys? Elitism, racism and research', in *Multiracial Education*, 10, 1.

31 See, for example, the works of John Rex who has moved from functionaism plus a bit of Weber (*Race, Community and conflict*, 1967) to Webcrianism plus a bit of Marx (*Colonial Immigrants in a British City*, 1979) to functionalism plus a bit of Marx (class analysis/imperialism) ('West Indian and Asian youth', in Cashmore and Troyna, *op. cit.*). Notwithstanding this eclecticism, Rex (following Weber) believes ultimately in the possibility of an ethical capitalist society (see his chapter in UNESCO (1980) *Sociological Theories: Race and Colonialism*).

32 In fact, they do not even demonstrate a working awareness of Marxism. 'Hostility to whites' by black political organizations is to them 'dependent on the amount of marxist input to the ideology' (p. 29). Why Marxism should or can make blacks hostile to whites they fail to explain.

33 Both the *Birmingham Evening Mail* and the *Wolverhampton Express and Star* emphasized the arguments that there is a 'penchant for violence' in black culture and the active contribution that young blacks have made to their own problems. Both saw the book as a warning that 'more violence is on the way'. (See John Solomos's review of the book in *The Sociological Review*, August 1983, p. 566.) Meanwhile a new review in *Police* noted that the analysis forms the basis for the argument that 'young blacks are not only active participants in the process of race-relations, their participation may often be far from helpful'. (See Errol G. Lawrence's review of the book in *Race and Class*, 25, 2, pp. 96–7.) Troyna has subsequently expressed regret at some of the arguments of that chapter (see his letter to *New Society*, 2 December 1982). I realize that the chapter forms part of a larger book; however, I make no apologies for concentrating exclusively on that chapter, nor for not referring to Troyna and Cashmore's other works. My intention is not a critical review of the book nor of the works of Troyna and Cashmore; rather I am citing this chapter as exemplifying the stereotyped common-sense images of young blacks.

34 This went out on BBC2 on 4 March 1979. A film or video of the programme can be obtained from The Other Cinema, 12/13 Little Newport Street, London WC2H 7JJ (tel. 01 734 8508/9).

35 Hall *et al.* (1978) *op. cit.*

36 *Ibid.*, p. 118.

37 See Althusser, L. (1971) *Lenin and Philosophy and Other Essays*, London, New Left Books, pp. 171–83.

38 Cole (1984b) *op. cit.*, p. 23, footnote 14. The thesis of the interpellation of subjects is a useful and underworked means of understanding ideology in a very practical sense. In this paper I apply the thesis of the interpellation of subjects to the rhetoric of Thatcherism. The reference to Stuart Hall is Hall, S. (1978) 'Racism and reaction', in BBC/CRE, *Five Views of Multi-Racial Britian*.

39 Cashmore and Troyna's 'analysis' could also be used on the Greenham Common Women. It would probably be called something like 'Peace Women in Crisis' and would go something like this: The Greenham Common Women present *problems* and these problems cannot be solved by conventional measures. Moreover, they have contributed to these problems themselves. After all, no one forced them to abandon their families and go to Greenham Common. The women are seen as dirty, irresponsible and a general nuisance. 'Arrogant, rumbustuous, contemptuous' towards cruise missiles, they therefore

retreat into gangs to engender negative responses towards the bomb. We might then have a quick reference to the dangers of nuclear warfare: 'Of course, the possible destruction of the world does pressurize these women.' But a balanced account must look at the way they have provoked the labels attached to them. They would then probably issue a warning that they are going to mention the unmentionable, 'what we all know'. But before they do, can the problem be solved? By CND studies perhaps? No, that would polarize women too much. No, the problem is . . . they're different — what form does this difference take? They're women, they're non-violent.

40 I recently read the first draft of this paper as far as Cashmore and Troyna's concluding paragrah, i.e., before discussing its implications, to a group of first year students. The first question I was asked by a concerned student was, 'Have there ever been any studies on whether black people *want* to be repatriated?'

41 *The Observer*, 13 May 1984.

42 Parmar, P. (1982) 'Gender, class and race: Asian women in resistence' in CCCS *The Empire Strikes Back*, London, Hutchinson, p. 245.

43 *Ibid.*

44 Wilson, A. (1978) *Finding a Voice: Asian Women in Britain*, Virago, pp. 74–5.

45 Parmar (1982) *op. cit.*, p. 269.

46 Sivanandan (1982) 'From resistance to rebellion: Asian and Afro-Caribbean struggles in Britain', *Race and Class*, 33, 2/3, pp. 147–8.

47 Sherman, a. (1979) 'Britain's urge to self-destruction', *The Daily Telegraph*, 9 September, quoted in CCCS (1982), *The Empire Strikes Back*, London, Hutchinson, p. 27.

48 McDonald, I.A. (1983) *Immigration Law and Practice in the United Kingdom*, London, Butterworth, p. 15.

49 *Ibid.*, p. 16.

50 The following information is a summary of some of the points made in an article by Sue Shatter (1983) and the Spare Rib collective which appeared in *Spare Rib*, April, pp. 32–3.

51 Hatcher and Shallice (1983)

52 *Ibid.*, p. 10.

53 Carby, H. (1980) 'Multi-culture', *Screen Education*, 34, Spring, p. 64.

54 Green (1982) *op. cit.*, p. 33.

55 Ferguson, B. (1981) 'Race and the media; Some problems in teaching', *Multi-racial Education*, 9, 2, quoted in Hatcher with Shallice (1983) *op. cit.*, p. 10.

56 In less liberal countries more Orwellian language tends to be required. In South Africa, for example, the term 'apartheid' has long been out of favour in official circles, the latest vogue phrase being 'group determination'. The Minister of Native Affairs became the Minister for Bantu Administration and then the Minister for Plural Relations and now is the Minister for Cooperation and Development, to fit in with the idea of 'group determination'. 'South African . . . Ministers . . . are often heard talking warmly of South Africa as a "multi-racial" society. They mean only that it is a country in which different races live — side by side but not, so far as is possible, together.' Finally, south Africa is apparently described by the government as a 'consensus (rather than majoritarian) democracy' which describes a process of bargaining between different racial groups! (*The Times*, 11 April 1984).

57 Dodgson, P. and Stewart, D. (1981) 'Multi culturalism or anti-racist teaching: A question of alternatives', *Multi-racial Education*, 9, 3, p. 48. as Hazel Carby has argued, the very concept of multiculturalism mobilizes a 'race relations' discourse (Carby (1980) *op. cit.*, p. 65).

58 These arguments are developed in Cole (1983) *op. cit.*, pp. 479–85.

59 See Spender, D. (1980) *Man Made Language*, London, Routledge and Kegan Paul.

60 Dodgson and Stewart (1981) *op. cit.*, p. 48. They are discussing Carby's use of the work of Bruce Boone (Carby (1979) *op. cit.*).

61 Cole (1983) *op. cit.*, p. 483. The reference to Paul Gilroy is 'Steppin' out of Babylon — race, class and autonomy', in CCCS (1982) *op. cit.*, pp. 292–3.

62 For details, see Twitchin, J. and Demuth, C. (1981) *Multi-Cultural Education Views from the Classroom*, London, BBC pp. 135–6.

63 Searle, C. (1983) 'A common language', *Race and Class*, 25, 2, p. 74.

64 Barker, M. and Beezer, A. (1983) 'The language of racism: an examination of Lord Scarman's Report on the Brixton riots', *International Socialism*, 18, Winter, p. 113 (available from International Socialism, PO Box 82 London E2).

65 *Ibid.*, pp. 113–14.

66 *Ibid.*

67 *Ibid.*, pp. 121–3.

68 Hatcher and Shallice (1983) *op. cit.*, p. 19.

69 Hall, S. (1980) 'Teaching race', in James, A. and Jeffcoate, R. (Eds) *The School in the Multicultural Society*, London, Harper and Row.

10 An Initial Typology of Perspectives on Staff Development for Multicultural Teacher Education

James Lynch

In the very title of this book may be assumed to reside an element of impatience with the still embryonic state of multicultural teacher education in the United Kingdom. Indeed, there can be little doubt that British teacher education has not distinguished itself in either the alacrity or quality of its response to the newer and changing perceptions of British society as being multiracial and multicultural, which have arisen in the last two decades. The catalogue of the tardy and grudgingly minimal reactions of teacher education to the earnest admonitions and explicit exhortations of successive reports and official documents to take greater account of this newer 'fact' of British society in its programmes has been protrayed with depressing accuracy elsewhere, based both on descriptive surveys and other documentary and evaluative evidence,[1] and it would serve no useful purpose to repeat them here.

The reasons for this relative failure may reside in the epistemological continuity of British teacher education since Robbins, so graphically illustrated and persuasively argued and portrayed by Alexander.[2] They may be located in the preemptive and traumatic fixation furnished by successive systemic and institutional convulsions since that time. They may perhaps be unkindly attributed to the increasing obsolescence of the bulk of teacher educators' experience, embalmed in sepia intellectual snapshots of schools of yesteryear. Some may seek to find the reasons in the very potent subjugation of institutions of teacher education to other culturally conservative and elitist organizations, institutions and disciplines, themselves expressive of even more monist predispositions and values. Others may advance alternative rationales to explain the cultural stagnation of teacher education which, it is increasingly argued, must be subject to urgent and radical change if the goal of a more equal and harmonious multicultural society is to be effectively pursued. All of this would be speculation, for we simply do not know the cultural rationale for a professional situation seen as distressing and unsatisfactory by many individuals and groups both within and without teacher education.[3]

What is known is that by 1984 few institutions of teacher education had undertaken a systematic reappraisal and revision of their epistemological and organizational *Aufbau*, to make them more congruent with the norms and values deriving from an ethic appropriate to a multicultural and multiracial society, let alone altered the 'economic' and power-political make-up to wider policies expressive of those values. The dominant epistemological and organizational structures remained inured. There were, for instance, no Professors of Education from any ethnic minority community in any university or polytechnic in that year. Few members from such communities were permanent members of staff and, where they were, they tended to be in junior and less influential roles. Few members of ethnic minority communities sat as equals on School and Faculty Boards; none on the Councils of such professional bodies as the Polytechnics' Council for the Education of Teachers; and few, if any, on the Boards of Governors and analogue committees in institutions offering teacher education. None was invited in mid-1984 to be a member of the new, national Council for the Accreditation of Teacher Education in England and Wales.

What little action had been taken in teacher education by that time was at first additive, often folkloric, and optional to the mainstream epistemology of the curriculum. More recently the commitment to multicultural teacher education was dissipated, sometimes to the point of invisibility, by means of a so-called 'permeation' curricular approach. A small minority of institutions had offered special access courses in an effort to increase the flow of numbers of ethnic minority teachers,[4] and a handful had begun to formulate an overall policy, including staff recruitment and development, research and the appointment, in one institution, of an external consultant on anti-racist teaching.[5] There was one brief case study of a School of Education totally 'rejigging' its structure and curriculum to focus it closely on the requirements of a multicultural society.[6] However, even where any concerted action had been taken, the overall impression was ad hoc and piecemeal approaches, inchoate from each other and *vis-à-vis* the system as a whole, such that existing hierarchies could remain undisturbed. Teacher education could not escape a strong impression of tissue-rejection, and evasion strategies of innovation in response to the need and demands for fundamental change,[7] and this impression was reinforced by the announcement in late 1984 of the membership of the new Council for the Accreditation of Teacher Education without a single member from a visible ethnic minority community, and the entering of a note of reservation by the United Kingdom to a Council of Europe recommendation on the introduction of intercultural teacher education which was signed by twenty-three European countries.

Looked at in the context of the above dreary catalogue, two other events in 1984 may come to be seen as forming something of a watershed for teacher education. In March of that year the second version of a significant discussion document in the field of multicultural teacher education was produced by a working group of the national public sector higher education validating body, the Council for National Academic Awards. It sought to 'suggest principles in respect of multicultural and anti-racist education', together with a checklist of items for possible inclusion in courses of teacher education.[8] The writ of this document did not, of course, run to the university sector of teacher education', where evidence of such agenda was more elusive, nor even to a large part of the public sector of teacher education at that time validated by universities. Nonetheless, in spite of its 'minority' audience, it is worthwhile summarizing its orientation and its aspiration.

The document espoused more expansive and, by then, largely acceptable commitments to the appreciation and the utilization of the richness of cultural variety in Britain, let alone the world, in educational curricula at all levels; the development of cultural sensitivity towards the cultural identity and practices of various groups; and the development of a clear understanding of the importance of achieving equality of opportunity in social and economic life. In addition, the document set out what were seen as five necessary areas of professional education, including equipping teachers: to prepare all young people for life in a multicultural and racially harmonious society; to have awareness and understanding of racism; to have an awareness of intercultural relations; to be able to teach, recognizing any particular needs of ethnic minority pupils and students; and to interact effectively with colleagues in relation to these issues.

The overall orientation of the paper was to curriculum rather than institutional or systemic considerations, although there was brief reference to some minimal but necessary institutional initiatives. There was no reference to assessment and its role in knowledge control (there was one reference to examinations in the context of minority languages). Neither prejudice acquisition nor pedagogical strategies for prejudice reduction with regard to students on teacher education courses nor the children they teach were referred to. There can be no doubt that the document (and the follow-up checklist of items meriting consideration in the development and validation of teacher education courses, derived from the discussion document),[9] in its explicit acceptance of anti-racist education, is an advance on previous attempts in Britain to map the practical implications of implementing multicultural teacher education, and yet the implications in terms of staff development of the lecturing staff who are to be entrusted with its implementation remain unexplored.

Two months later the pressure group NAME, the National Association for Multiracial Education, published an important and far-reaching statement on teacher education.[10] The statement aimed: to achieve an urgent demonstration of NAME's view of the need for essential change in teacher education to eliminate racism and promote the development of a just and pluralist society; to emphasize the need for a reflection in education of the perspectives of all local communities including a black perspective; and to offer a range of practical recommendations for consideration and action. More exclusively focused on anti-racism than the CNAA document, the document calls for interventionist education to counter racism and achieve social justice. More broadly than the CNAA document referred to above, it calls for explicit policies addressing institutional management, staffing, recruitment and the assessment of students, provision of courses and staff development opportunities, course content, evaluation and resources.

The document calls for the conferment of qualified teacher status to be dependent on the demonstration of 'skills, knowledge and personal qualities appropriate to teaching in a multiracial society' and 'the adoption by students of an anti-racist approach in classroom practice'. All courses are to be scrutinized to ensure that due emphasis is given throughout to 'antiracist perspectives', and courses are to include the development of strategies for anti-racist teaching. The statement concludes by urging all bodies involved in teacher education to recognize the urgent need for essential change in teacher education. The document is neither concrete nor specific with regard to what knowledge, skills, competences and approaches advocated might be necessary nor how they may be translated into behavioural consequences, not least for the teacher educators themselves.

Whether these two statements will have any more effect on a recalcitrant teacher education than two decades of previous exhortation remains to be seen. What both documents do, however, is to change the terms of reference for future discourse for, with all their limitations, they are landmark documents in the long journey towards a more just and humane pluralist society from which racism and other forms of prejudice have been banished. They force teacher education, system, institutions and individuals, to express through their actions — or inactions — where they stand *vis-à-vis* that goal.

A number of organizations and individuals, in the United Kingdom and abroad, have set down in some detail what multicultural teacher education may mean in terms of new course patterns. An early document, published jointly by the former Community Relations Commission and the former Association of Teachers in Colleges and Departments of Education, saw three broad dimensions diffused throughout the whole training of student teachers: informational, technical and affective.[11] It also set down the need for experiential (e.g., contacts with minority groups) and philosophical (e.g., the generation of an appropriate ethos) dimensions, and pointed to the need for the involvement of all staff.

Notwithstanding earlier developments in teacher education in the late 1940s as part of the Intergroup Education Movement, it was not until 1976 in the United States that multicultural standards were set down for the accreditation of teacher education programmes.[12] Two years later the eminent American teacher educator and expert in multiethnic education, James Banks, in an address to a conference sponsored by the American Association of Colleges for Teacher Education, expressed the view that a 'philosophy of ethnic pluralism must permeate teacher education institutions before ethnic studies curricula and materials can be effectively integrated into the teacher education curriculum.'[13] In addition to this basic requirement, he envisaged the implications of a multiethnic ideology for teacher education to lie in the development of cross-cultural competency, greater self-understanding, and the establishment of personal contact situations and dialogue. In these proposals we can see once again the identification of the need for a philosophical/moral baseline or ethos and experiential as well as other means of learning envisaged by the CRC Report, together with a commitment to the discourse of a democratic pluralism.

In 1980 the Commission on Multicultural Education of the American Association of Colleges for Teacher Education published a series of documents examining strategies for implementing multicultural teacher education, including conceptual and speculative writing, a collection of thirteen case studies, an annotated bibliography and guidelines for the implementation of such a strategy.[14] A survey of strategies for the implementation of multicultural teacher education in Australia has been conducted,[15] and as reported earlier there are isolated case studies of multicultural teacher education outside the United States.[16]

In a more recent paper addressing the issue of what precisely multicultural teacher education means, Gay points to the fact that most Americans (and Britons?) are ethnically illiterate, living in ethnic enclosures, isolated from all but superficial and transitory interactions with ethnic others.[17] She proceeds to identify some essential baselines for what pre-service courses for teachers should comprehend, including:

> basic information about ethnic and cultural pluralism;
> knowledge acquisition and values clarification about ethnic groups and their cultures;
> how to combat racism;
> linguistic knowledge of black students in its historical, economic, cultural and political contextuality;
> competences for perceiving, believing, evaluating and behaving in different cultural contexts;
> skill development in translating 'multicultural' knowledge into programmes, practices, habits and behaviours of classroom instruction;
> competences in making educational objectives, curriculum content and learning activities meaningful to the experiential backgrounds and frames of reference of all students (their values, perceptions, cognitive processes and language);
> skill in achieving teaching and learning style congruency;
> psychology and sociology of ethnicity, including issues of human behaviour and learning.

She concludes by stating that many of the above areas represent lacunae in current American (and British?) teacher education, and she draws attention to the great benefit of perspective which multicultural education can bring to conventional teacher education.

But it is also clear that what Gay is suggesting is not merely the provision of baseline substantive and didactic knowledge, but the translation of that knowledge into individual and group methodologies of interaction in the classroom, involving inevitably all levels of Bloom's taxonomy up to the highest levels of mental functioning and skills to interpret that functioning into responsive behaviour in the instructional process.

For that level of cognitive, moral and professional sophistication, it is clear that students and staff need to be involved not solely in informational and awareness-raising activities. As with the pupils, whom they must teach to celebrate diversity and reduce and occlude prejudice, students need to be involved in enquiring, experiencing, creating, skill training, modelling, interrelating and social actioning activities, addressing the development of dispositions and values, competences, skills and abilities, learning and thinking techniques, interpersonal relations and practical competences, articulated to the prismatic cultural reality of the ethnic pluralism of society and its currently effective prejudices.[18]

Let us assume for the moment that teacher education takes on board the broad implications of the documents and proposals quoted above. Then the question arises of how those implications can be translated from the easy lucidity of rhetoric and recommendations into the difficult and mostly uncharted realm of effective action and how, in time, the effectiveness of the action is to be monitored and appraised, by teacher education staff who may be highly inexperienced and untrained in this area of work: perhaps even as yet unconvinced of the priority to be afforded to this particular new dimension of their work.

Most staff and students in teacher education derive their cultural biography from an Anglo-centric socialization of many years' duration and manifest efficiency, so that the question inevitably arises of where the expertise is to come from to implement such revolutionary and innovatory programmes, even given the dubious hypothesis that the consensual will exists.

In a paper on the effects of teacher prejudice on student growth and development, bearing on a large body of research and writing (and years of conventional wisdom in teacher education), Gay describes teacher prejudice as valuative screens through which pupil motivation, interpersonal relations, the processes of instruction and curriculum content are 'filtered, interpreted and assigned meaning relative to the perceived characteristics and capabilities of students.'[19] As most teacher educators are 'one-time' teachers, it seems logical to assume that they may be subject to similar restricted cultural perceptions, distorting in turn the cultural perceptions and professional behaviour of their students, at best, as Gay suggests, condescendingly aiming to save ethnic minority students from themselves, at worst ignoring their alternative cultural realities altogether. Given that the expectations of teacher educators influence students in performing in prescribed ways, it may be said that the 'cultural predispositions' of teacher educators achieve their 'classroom' instructional effect through the proxy of their students' behaviour: a recipe for a cyclical process of restrictive, monist continuity in teacher education, unless drastic measures are addressed to the teacher educators themselves, not solely their programmes, institutions and students.

Thus, what is required is nothing less than the moral, intellectual, social, cultural and professional 'rejigging' of a whole generation of teacher educators, within a context where large elements of teacher education courses are, in any case, taught in many institutions by staff who are not and do not consider themselves to be teacher-educators! The scope and comprehensiveness of such an exercise is daunting but not impossible, if the goals are especially espoused, clearly articulated and their implementation appropriately resourced and monitored at both institutional and systemic levels. This is a far cry from the assumptions underlying any folkloric tinkering with the curriculum of teacher education, resting on the dubious assumption that staff have the cultural and intellectual, social and moral prerequisites already and that structures, procedures and governance are not on the agenda.

One pathfinding initiative to this goal, and possibly the only such national initiative, is the *Training the Trainers* programme, established in late 1982 and directed by Professor Maurice Craft of Nottingham University. Originally implemented by six teacher education institutions (three Polytechnics, three Universities) in the major conurbations, within two years the programme had involved sixteen such centres, both urban and rural, in the provision of focused short courses for lecturers, advisers and senior teachers working in initial and in-service teacher education. Funded through DES regional in-service channels (and also by Shell UK and Boots Charitable Trust), the impact of the programme upon participants' institutions/Authorities is being evaluated on a DES grant.

Certain prerequisites would appear to be essential to the introduction of genuine programmes of multicultural teacher education, committed to democratic dialogue and involving discourse and appeal to the judgment of participants rather than indoctrination, if the absence of overarching paradigms, lack of definition, specificity and coherence, etc., currently affecting the development of all curricular designs in the field, are to be resolved. A number of helpful guidelines, for example, may be derived from contemporary literature in the field of multicultural teacher education. *Culturally*, for instance, the socialization framework for such programmes would appear to require a priori a heterogeneous student and staff body; *morally*, the credibility of such programmes necessitates, for the generation of an appropriate ethos, beyond a philosophical commitment, an active engagement for policy goals deriving from the basic ethics of multicultural education, such as prejudice reduction and erasure; *pedagogically*, such programmes require intercultural teaching strategies, geared to facilitating personal value clarification, to evoking insights, mediating competences, etc; and *experientially*, teacher educators need to be afforded opportunities for personal and professional contact situations, including work in a variety of multiracial settings, schools and communities which will provide them with the necessary first-hand professional socialization.[21]

In an earlier paper, which reviews some of the conceptualizations of multicultural teacher education and appraises the potential relationship between competency-based teacher education, social studies and multicultural education, Gay seeks to offer a paradigm to achieve greater specificity, coherence, organization and sequential development in designing multicultural programmes.[22] This paradigm may provide one way of mapping out, by extrapolation, what new demands for staff development teacher education faces in responding to documents such as those produced by NAME, CNAA and other bodies, which require or advocate the introduction of 'anti-racist' teacher education. Drawing on the traditions of competency-based teacher education, she specifies five areas of competence:

1 knowledge: addressing cognitive understanding;
2 performance: specifying teaching and instructional behaviour and attitudes;
3 consequence: identifying student behaviour resulting from teacher (i.e., for our purposes, lecturer) behaviours;
4 affective: indicating attitudes to be demonstrated by lecturers;
5 exploratory or expressive: detailing experience to be undertaken by lecturers.

If these five dimensions are coalesced with the four outlined above, cultural, moral, pedagogical and experiential, and overlap eradicated, a coherent outline sketch emerges of the staff development required, specific to individuals, institutions and systems, if multicultural teacher education is to be introduced. Whilst each individual teacher educator may not have to assume sole responsibility for all these dimensions in his/her own professional biography, there are certain essential and indispensible elements for all and the demands of the system and institutions are tantamount to a global commitment as outlined in Figure 1.

The commitments involved in the staff development dimension of introducing multicultural teacher education as shown and *categorized* in Figure 1 may be clarified as follows:

1   If we take the contextual dimension first, it is clear that in spite of the valiant efforts of those institutions involved in the initial schemes of access courses, much still needs to be done to make both staff and student bodies 'multicultural'. Direct and potent representation is needed from immediately circumambient ethnic minority communities and their organizations, from organizations such as the CRCs and CRE at system and institutional levels, as, for example, the CNAA, the new Council for the Accreditation of Teacher Education, the new Local Committees on teacher education, Senates, Boards of Governors, Faculty and School Boards, Course Teams, etc; equal representation and financial support is needed for all denominations in chaplaincy and other pastoral schemes; 'new blood' appointments of staff from ethnic minorities are required and the appointment of manifestly well qualified staff from ethnic minority communities at senior levels.

2   In terms of the moral and affective dimensions some few institutions are beginning to formulate 'norm-encouraging' policy statements and a number of validating bodies are seeking to do likewise. But there is still no systemic policy statement and issues of multiculturalism are rarely discussed by Academic and other Boards in a way which would generate, through interaction with ethnic minorities, intercultural competences and consensual norms of custom and morality as a base for action. Programmes, activities and experiences to help staff to analyze, clarify and, as appropriate, change their racial, sex and class values, attitudes and behaviour within a liberal democratic tradition are rare indeed, and those aimed at assisting staff to help students to do this are almost non-existent. Sometimes the whole hope for 'affective' progress seems to lie with one 'co-ordinator' or consultant rather than with attitude-generating corporate and collegial discourse or, on the other hand, with the introduction of compulsory workshops such as those recently criticized by Jeffcoate as tending to indoctrination and totalitarianism.[23] Yet, if their students are to be aware of the way in which British education may perpetuate discrimination and prejudice and ready to affirm cultural, racial, sex and other individual differences in their professional interactions with children in schools and with their parents and the broader community, so also teacher educators will require affective dispositions of that kind as part of the normative culture within which their interactions with their students take place and have effect. In very many cases this involves a reorientation of existing norms and values, both

Figure 1. An Initial Typology of Staff Development Needs for Teacher Education

DIMENSION	1 CULTURAL/ CONTEXTUAL	2 MORAL/ AFFECTIVE	3 COGNITIVE	4 PEDAGOGICAL PERFORMANCE	5 CONSEQUENTIAL	6 EXPERIENTIAL
General Example	e.g. Heterogeneous staff and student body:	e.g. Philosophical/ policy commitment to ethics of multicultural education:	e.g. Knowledge of bases of prejudice acquisition and reduction:	e.g. Specific teaching and instructional behaviour and professional attitudes:	e.g. Behaviour in students resulting from lectures' competences in 3 and 4:	e.g. Working in multiracial and supplementary schools and other 'new' intercultural experiences:
Level						
Individual	Vicarious through interethnic contacts, friendship and professional association in research, teaching, writing, etc.	Essential at level of knowledge and active commitment	Essential as a personal and professional baseline but differentially according to role and responsibility	Essential but differentially according to role of individual in teacher education	Collegial and community task rather than individual one, but communities are made up of individuals	Essential dependent on role of individual
Institutional	Essential at all levels of hierarchy and in controlling bodies such as Faculty Boards and Boards of Governors	Essential in forms of policy statement and implementation appraisal individual and 'departmental'	Essential — perhaps 'pooled' on an inter-institutional basis	Essential, e.g., through inter-cultural teaching strategies	Indispensible part of institutional evaluation strategies	Indispensible part of institutional staff development for some substantial proportion of staff
Systemic	Essential in form of political involvement of all ethnic groups, monitoring, etc.	Desirable if other two levels are to be effective	Essential for detailed planning, overview and monitoring	Essential, e.g., through research and development work, coordination, etc.	Necessary for potency of other two levels	Necessary moral, resource and coordinating role

personal and institutional, deriving from collegial and wider community discourse and leading to planned and systematic change of the existing normative culture. Unless provision is made for the cultural re-education through democratic discourse of those who are to implement such planned and systematic change, it is highly unlikely that anything other than chimera commitment and ineffective lip-service will emerge, even in response to more 'rational' or 'power-coercive' measures such as legislation, regulation, mandatory standards or advisory guidelines.

3   With regard to the cognitive dimension, similar to what Gay calls knowledge competences, slightly more progress has been made in clarifying and defining content for teacher education, through which we can perceive the implications for teacher educators: a knowledge of the microcultures of society,[24] of ethnic minorities and their cultures, alertness to bias, ethno-centrism, stereotyping, prejudice and racism and their educational, social and economic impact; an understanding of race relations and the impact of nationality legislation; a knowledge of the pedagogical implications of work on prejudice acquisition and reduction, cognitive styles and research on field dependence and independence, vocational guidance, etc; an awareness of the issues associated with testing, assessment and examinations in a multicultural society, of educability and achievement as social constructs deriving from specific cultural assumptions; the implications of cultural diversity for the curriculum and teaching methods of schools; the availability of materials to support the multicultural curriculum and of criteria to evaluate them for their fidelity to that concept. Some of this material is well documented and readily available.[25] Some already resides in the curriculum of teacher education and merely needs to be 'converted' and adapted by means of appropriate conceptual coalitions with existing disciplines, areas and modules.

Gay's work, for instance, is helpful in identifying, summarizing and systematizing, but also in indicating some of the *conceptual coalitions* which may be necessary if the existing curriculum is not to reject the newer cognitive areas. Although she is writing with regard to teacher education programmes, it will be apparent that, once again, by extrapolation, what she proposes can be scrutinized for its direct implications for staff development such as the ability:

- to identify Bloom's taxonomy in questioning strategies:
- to describe the major steps in the inquiry mode of teaching;
- to understand the taxonomy of affective objectives in the context of specific subject or discipline teaching;
- to distinguish between inductive and deductive reasoning and among different modes of scientific inquiry;
- to characterize the different stages of moral reasoning;
- to define a fact, concept, generalization and theory.[26]

It is clear that what Gay is proposing is a commitment to higher-level mental functioning across areas which should already be a part of teacher education curricula, and therefore already residing within the expertise of at least some teacher educators. Through a process of interlearning with their colleagues and of conceptual alliance with existing areas of the curriculum, it may be no great task to achieve the necessary cognitive reorientation of staff.

4/5 Adopting a similar approach to what she calls performance and consequence competences (before proceeding to identify in detail critical content for all three areas of competence: cognitive, performance and sequential), Gay draws our attention[27] to the need for the cognitive, affective and contextual gains to lead to behavioural change in professional action as well; improved intercommunicative and broader intercultural competence; pedagogical modes that positively and manifestly value diversity and democratic discourse; eschewing of racism, sexism and cultural prejudice in their presentations; scrutiny of recommended texts and materials for their fidelity to the ethic of multiculturalism; selection of a variety of cultural exemplars as illustrative material; inclusion of different cognitive modes in discussions of educability; avoidance of stereotyping; acceptance of the necessary inclusion of other cultural contributions in their teaching; expansion of the cultural criteria for assessment and broader evaluation; ability to study their own practice, evaluate it against multicultural criteria, and culturally expand and amend their criteria for professional judgment, etc. These are some of the consequential pedagogical competences which are appropriate to a teacher education committed to democratic cultural pluralism in its very ways of working. In the United Kingdom, however, there has so far been no baseline identification of the pedagogical staff development competences which will need to be addressed if teacher educators are to adopt multiculturally congruent pedagogical styles and to seek to evoke such behaviours in their students. Empirically, there is nothing about the knock-on effects of specific multicultural teaching strategies by lecturers onto student values, attitudes and behaviour, let alone the analogue of those dimensions amongst pupils in classrooms. Yet one of the major aims of the complex recipe for teacher education staff development, proposed above, must remain to change what happens in the classroom and through that how pupils relate to each other in our culturally pluralist society.

6 Concerning the experiential dimension of the typology suggested above, recent changes in the pooling regulations[28] make it possible for teacher education staff to be released to 'review' their school teaching experience and for the institution to claim the costs involved from the central Advanced Further Education Pool. It will be necessary for a substantial number of staff undertaking such experience to do so in multiracial schools and for some to have experience by arrangement and where possible in supplementary schools and community organizations,[29] if personal contact situations such as those envisaged by Banks are to be achieved and intercultural competence developed, if the cultural lag of teacher education is to be made good, and the whole initiative to introduce multiculturalism

into the deep structure of teacher education is not to be frustrated. Some of this work could be undertaken initially on a 'seed' lecturer basis until the multicultural capital of teacher education has been built up.[30] Accounts exist of rationales for the incorporation of cross-cultural experiential learning into teacher education programmes and to their potential contribution to classroom affectiveness and personal growth, which may provide extrapolated models for teacher educators.[31]

In the context of an increasing clamour for anti-racist teaching from a number of different directions, it may be useful to refer briefly to an early paper by Carl Grant on how multicultural in-service teacher education may be best achieved. Using the well-known conceptualization of planned organizational change strategies: empirical-rational; power-coercive; and normative-reeducative, he emphasizes the limited effect of the first two and the importance of the third if the normative culture which guides people in their actions, personal attitudes and cognitive modes is to be changed.[32] Slightly reformulating Grant's work, several principles for 'multicultural' change emerge from his insightful writing as follows:

1 For normative-reeducative change to be effective a framework of empirical-rational and power-coercive measures is necessary but not sufficient (e.g., research, legislation, etc.);

2 While strategies for information provision and correction of misinformation are necessary, it must be recognized that the 'problems' may lie in the attitudes, values, norms and external and internal relationships of clients;

3 The effective use of new knowledge, therefore, requires the elimination, or at the very least attenuation, of negative attitudes and pathological norms from the teacher's repertoire of beliefs and values;

4 Only normative-reeducative change can achieve fundamental value, habit and meaning reorientation;

5 Democratic discourse is an indispensible part of such a change strategy, involving what Stenhouse called appeal to the judgment of participants, involvement of the 'clients' in working out the change programme themselves and in its implementation and evaluation;

6 Planned change relating to cultural pluralism demands mutual and collaborative effort and dialogue to define openly and resolve problems and to bring into consciousness non-conscious elements; this involves support and involvement by other dimensions of the pluralistic culture;

7 The resources, concepts and methods of a variety of behavioural sciences, used selectively, relevantly and appropriately, will be a necessary alliance for the implementation of programmes of change;

8 Clients involved in such a planned and systematic normative-reeducative programme of change may travel through three major and overlapping phases: awareness and recognition; acceptance and appreciation; and affirmation and full commitment. Baker, in a similar model for the training of teachers, proposes a sequence ranging from the acquisition of knowledge, through the development of an appropriate philosophy to the implementa-

tion of multicultural education, and this might be seen as the parallel cognitive and pedagogical dimension to Grant's mainly affective ill-ustration.[33] Not all will reach their goal;

9   For the above, a 'whole-institution' approach is required.[34]

Adopting Banks' preliminary typology of the emerging stages of ethnicity,[35] and applying it in an institutional manner to institutions of teacher education, one may expect teacher education to move through a number of stages from its present predominantly ethnocentric emphasis to a future state where institutionally and systematically, philosophically and practically, it would manifest an explicit and active commitment to multicultural education as one of its central core of values. These stages are illustrated in Figure 2 and the dimensions of staff development as illustrated in Figure 1 would need to address such a progression.

It is now becoming urgent for British teacher educators to reverse the long history of inertia in responding to the democratic cultural pluralism of British society. But inherent within the very concept of democratic cultural pluralism is a commitment to professional dialogue and discourse, which rules out the illusory solution of authoritarian or totalitarian strategies, and which endorses — not undermines — the basic ethic of multicultural education: respect for persons, their cultures and their human rights.

Writing over a decade ago, James Banks made this comment on the situation at that time in the United States: '*Our society is becoming increasingly polarized and dehumanized, largely because of institutional racism and ethnic hostility.*'[36] Such a commentary may well be thought to apply also to British society of the 1980s. Schools are not omnipotent but neither are they totally impotent in avoiding such polarization and dehumanization. It they are to make their contribution to a more humane and just, pluralist society, however, teachers can legitimately expect professional training appropriate to that goal as part of their initial and in-service education. For that an appropriate teacher education is indispensible which in its very values, structures, epistemologies and procedures endorses the goals of democratic cultural pluralism.

This brief chapter has been able to do no more than offer a brief, incomplete and no doubt inadequate outline commentary and conceptualization, derived from contemporary writings about multicultural teacher education, of the staff develop-ment prerequisites necessary for teacher education to be effective and to have at its core an active engagement with issues of cultural pluralism in a democratic society and education for prejudice reduction.

If the present lamentable situation of teacher preparation for multicultural education is to be changed, the initiative will rest centrally, in the first instance, with a group which currently comprises predominantly white, middle-class teacher educators. They will not be able to achieve the necessary normative-reeducative change, however, without potent and creative discourse with representatives of other dimensions of our cultural pluralism and without recognition of the 'plight' of teacher educators as a central resource priority for in-service education. In that sense the 'interminable debate' of the title of this book cannot but continue, for

Figure 2.   Stages in the Development of Multicultural Teacher Education: A Preliminary Typology

Stage VII	Systemic Multiculturalism	Norms and values of system and all components attuned to core ethic of multicultural education, e.g., active commitment to prejudice reduction in system and society.
Stage VI	Total Institutional Multiculturalism	All variables and factors in total environment permeated by multicultural ethic.
Stage V	Institutional Multiculturalism	For example, multiethnic staff and student bodies; involvement of ethnic minorities in government, etc.
Stage IV	Holistic Policy Multiculturalism	For example, policy formulations at institutional and systemic levels.
Stage III	Curricular Multiculturalism	For example, new programmes for students.
Stage II	Ad Hoc Multiculturalism	For example, isolated initiatives (mainly addressing cognitive gains).
Stage I	Ethnocentric Captivity	For example, predominantly monist culture, epistemology, structure including staff and student bodies, evaluation and assessment strategies and few, and if any, only formalistic non-potent links with ethnic minorities.

democratic cultural pluralism requires 'interminable' discourse as the sustenance for its continued existence.[37] The problem in teacher education is that the debate has begun so late and progressed so little.

Notes

1 Craft, M. (1981) *Teaching in a Multicultural Society: The Task for Teacher Education*, Lewes, Falmer Press.
2 Alexander, R. (1984) 'Change and continuity in teacher education curricula', in Alexander, R. *et al.* (Eds), *Change in Teacher Education: Context and Provison since Robbins*, Eastbourne, Holt Saunders, pp. 103–60.
3 There is no shortage of advocates of multicultural teacher education, only of detailed analyses of what the implementation of such a policy implies for the staff development of teacher educators. See, for example, Hobbs, M. (1982) 'Teacher education for a pluralist society: The British case', *European Journal of Teacher Education*, 5, 1–2, pp. 29–44, and Hannan, A.W. (1983) 'Multicultural education and teacher education: The British case with some American comparisons', *European Journal of Teacher Education*, 6, 1, pp. 79–86.
4 A report of these Access Courses was produced in late 1982 as part of a DES project, 'Evaluation of special pilot courses for entry to higher education'. See Millins, P.K.C. (1982) 'Progress and performance of students on special preparatory courses 1981–2', Ealing College of Higher Education, October.
5 Although the example is now somewhat dated, relating to the period 1976–79, it still remains one of the very few descriptive accounts of its kind. See Lynch, J. (1981) 'Multicultural education and the training of teachers: A case study', *The South Pacific Journal of Teacher Education*, 9, 1, pp. 43–54.
6 Sunderland Polytechnic, Faculty of Education appointed an eminent black headteacher as consultant on anti-racist teaching to the Faculty with effect from September 1983.
7 See Millins, K. (1981) 'Rampton's basic lesson', *The Times Educational Supplement*, 3392, 4, 26 June.
8 Council for National Academic Awards, Committee for Education, Multicultural Working Group, (1984) 'Multicultural education: Discussion paper', London, CNAA, April, cyclo.
9 Council for National Academic Awards, Committee for Education, Working Group on Multicultural Education, (1984) 'Notes on multicultural education paper', London, CNAA, October, cyclo. The Committee for Education had decided in the agreement of the original document (CNAA, April 1984) that 'the substantive issues should not now be reopened for discussion', *ibid.*, frontispiece.
10 National Association for Multiracial Education (1984) 'Statement on teacher education', May.
11 Community Relations Council and Association of Teachers in Colleges and Departments of Education (1974) *Teacher Education for a Multicultural Society*, London, CRC/ATCDE, reprinted and republished by the Commission for Racial Equality, 1978, especially Chs. 2, 3 and 4.
12 National Council for the Accreditation of Teacher Education (1977) *Standards for the Accreditation of Teacher Education*, Washington, D.C., NCATE, p. 4.
13 Banks, J.A. (1979) *Multi-ethnic/Multicultural Teacher Education: Conceptual, Historical and Ideological Issues*, Rosslyn, Va., National Clearinghouse for Bilingual Education, p. 18.
14 American Association of Colleges for Teacher Education, (1980) *Multicultural Teacher Education* (Volume I: Preparing Educators to Provide Educational Equity; Volume II: Case Studies of Thirteen Programmes; Volume III: An Annotated Bibliography of Selected Resources; Volume IV: Guidelines for Implementation), Washington, D.C., AACTE.
15 Lynch, J. (1980) 'Multicultural teacher education in Australia: The state of the art', Report prepared for the Education Research and Development Committee, Canberra, ERDC, cyclo.
16 For example, Lynch (1981), *op. cit.*
17 Gay, G. (1983) 'Why multicultural education in teacher preparation programs',

Contemporary Education, 54, Winter, pp. 79–85, *loc. cit.*

18 I have developed these considerations further in a recent article. See Lynch, J. (1985) 'Human rights, racism and the multicultural curriculum', *Educational Review*, forthcoming.

19 Gay, G. (1979) 'Teacher prejudice as a mediating factor in student growth and development', *Viewpoints in Teaching and Learning*, 55, 2, pp. 94–106, *loc. cit.*, p. 100.

20 See Press Release, Craft, M. (1983) 'Teacher education in a multicultural society: Training the Trainers', June. The six institutions initially involved were: Birmingham Polytechnic, Liverpool University, London University, Manchester Polytechnic, Nottingham University and Sunderland Polytechnic. These were later joined by Bedford College of Higher Education, Bristol Polytechnic, Moray House College of Education, St Martin's College, Lancaster, Southampton University and University College, Cardiff, with Avery Hill College, Bradford University and Middlesex Polytechnic also planning to participate and several further centres also considering participation. By late 1984 this project had attracted £30, 000 of external funding and, in an otherwise gloomy scene, gave cause for some optimism that the tide had begun to turn.

21 Some of these prerequisites are based on Justiz, M.J. and Darling, D.W. (1980) 'A multicultural perspective in teacher education', *Educational Horizons*, 58, 4, pp. 203–5.

22 Gay, G. (1978) 'Interfacing CBTE and multicultural education in social studies teacher preparation', in Felder, D. (Ed.), *Competency Based Teacher Education Professionalizing Social Studies Teaching*, Washington, D.C., National Council for the Social Studies, 6, pp. 85–101.

23 Jeffcoate is particularly critical of the Brent LEA's approach to Racism Awareness Courses. See Jeffcoate, R. (1984) *Ethnic Minorities and Education*, London, Harper, p. 150.

24 Gollnick, D.M. and Chinn, P.C. (1983) *Multicultural Education in a Pluralistic Society*, St Louis, Mo., C.V. Mosby.

25 For example, Banks J.A. *et al.* (1976) *Curriculum Guidelines for Multiethnic Education*, Arlington, Va, National Council for the Social Studies, has specific suggestions for teacher education programmes involving cognitive, affective and pedagogical dimensions.

26 Adapted from Gay (1978), *op cit.*, p. 87. She also provides a useful summary of conceptualization generated by others as a basis for the design of multicultural curricula in teacher education.

27 Gay, G. (1981) 'Multiculturalizing teacher education', *Urban Education*, 5, 2, Winter, pp. 12–20, identifies goals for the instructional application dimension, including the analysis and study of their own attitudes and professional actions.

28 Department of Education and Science (1984) 'Guidance on pooling', April.

29 An interesting account of a diploma course for teachers, which requires teachers to work closely with a local community organization, is given in Jones, C. and Street-Porter, R. (1983) 'Anti-racist teaching and teacher education', *Multicultural Teaching*, 1, 3, pp. 9–12. Such a pattern could be adopted for teacher education staff.

30 An interesting example of a 'seed' teacher approach to developing teacher competence in this field in the south-eastern counties of Texas is to be found in Yao, E.L., (1983) 'A training program in Asian-American culture for elementary school teachers', *Contemporary Education*, 54, 2, pp. 86–93.

31 Wilson, A.H. (1982) 'Cross-cultural experiential learning for teachers', *Theory into Practice*, 21, 3, pp. 184–92.

32 Grant, C.A. and Melnick, S.L. (1976) 'Developing and implementing multicultural in-service teacher education', Paper presented at the national Council of states on In-Service Education, New Orleans, 17–19 November.

33 Baker, G.C. (1983) *Planning and Organising for Multicultural Instruction*, Reading, Mass, Addison Wesley, pp. 51–60.

34 Banks emphasizes that the total school environment must be involved if an effective multiethnic educational environment is to be created and sustained. The same seems to me to apply to teacher education institutions and particularly where professional socialization

is such a large part of the institution's task. See Banks, J.A. (1981) *Multiethnic Education: Theory and Practice*, Boston, Mass., Allyn and Bacon, diagram p. 31 *et passim*.

35 The typology is used in a number of his writings. See, for example, Banks, J.A. (1984) *Teaching Strategies for Ethnic Studies*, 3rd ed., Boston, Mass., Allyn and Bacon, p. 58.

36 Banks, J.A. (1972) 'Imperatives in ethnic minority education', *Phi Delta Kappan*, January, pp. 266–9.

37 This argument is the central feature of a more recent publication by the author. See Lynch, J. (1986) *Multiculture Education: Principles and Practice*, London, Routledge and Kegan Paul.

11 The All Black School: Development and Implications

Roger Homan

Introduction

The basis of this contribution is empirical. It was researched by structured interview, unstructured observation and in some places participant observation in a total of fifteen educational agencies in Bedford, Birmingham, Bradford, Coventry, Hackney, Haringey and Manchester. The only common feature of those fifteen organizations was sponsorship within the ethnic minority communities. Most but not all were called schools, either by their sponsors or by their observers. My initial comment must be one of appreciation to all those who allowed me to observe and interview them, among whom I am especially grateful to Mr Orville Woolford, headmaster of the John Loughborough middle and secondary school in Tottenham, and Mr Mohammed Afzal, warden of the Sparkbrook Islamic Centre in Birmingham.

The purposes of this chapter are to survey the genesis and rationale of the 'supplementary school' and its related forms and to explore the implications of these for state education. These will be approached by means of the study of three cases which reflect the range of organizational types.

Theory and Practice

Every curriculum has its omissions. In some education systems such as those of eastern Europe these are institutionalized: school occupies only the morning of the day and creative and sporting activities are left over for the afternoon when the children visit the youth house under the auspices of the *komsomol* or Young Pioneers.[1] Arguably there has existed such a complementarity between schools in the British system and uniformed youth organizations such as the Scouts, Guides and Boys' Brigade. And religious education, while being charged to the school by the 1944 Education Act, has been conducted on the assumption that parents who desired strong doses for their children would take them to appropriate places on a Saturday or Sunday — and, more recently, on a Friday. It is the Sunday School tradition of Robert Raikes, borrowed and adapted in the nineteenth century for the purpose of socialist education, that provides the model of the supplementary school which comes into being at two levels. First, the supplementary school is sponsored by a community as a consequence of the failure of local provisions to meet the needs of its children: state schools are variously perceived as having low expectations of minority group children, as sustaining a moral climate not considered desirable by parents, and as providing conditions in organization and content in teaching inappropriate or inadequate for children of a particular religio-cultural background. Second, the supplementary school is a response to individual aspirations that exceed those achievable within the school day: of such an order are the 'crammers' which children attend early in the morning in Japan and the German Federal Republic, and such institutions have their counterparts in the West Indies.

While often co-existing, these separately identifiable tensions in the demand for supplementary schooling are important to distinguish. The first mode is often characterized by a strong sectarian element of world rejectionism. The moral order of the state system is denounced for its permissiveness, greed, indulgence and attitudes to sex and chastity. In both West Indian and Islamic organizations there prevails a marked puritanism which is found by its apologists to be increasingly out of step with trends in secular Western thought. The second mode accounts for the formal pedagogy and traditional agenda of contents that prevail in many supplementary schools. The academic levels in these schools are by design especially demanding and the pupils are said to respond favourably.

The rationale of the supplementary schools derives from the influential work of Bernard Coard who highlighted the effect upon educational achievement of depressed expectations[2] and elaborated a strategy of self-help:

> We need to open Black nursery schools and supplementary schools throughout the areas we live in, in Britain. Our nursery schools should have Black dolls and books and pictures, and story-books about great Black men and women, and their achievements and inventions. Our children need to have a sense of identity, pride and belonging, as well as mental stimulation, so that they do not end up hating themselves and their race, and being dumped in ESN schools. Pride and self-confidence are the best armour against the prejudice and humiliating experiences which they will certainly face in school and in the society.
>
> We should start up supplementary schools in whatever part of London or Britain we live, in order to give our children additional help in the subjects they need. These classes can be held on evenings and Saturday mornings. We should recruit all our Black students and teachers for the task of instructing our Black children. Through these schools we hope to make up for the inadequacies of the British school system, and for its refusal to teach our children our history and culture. We must never sit idly by while they make ignoramuses of our children, but must see to it that by

hook or crook our children get the best education they are capable of! Some supplementary schools have already been started in parts of London. Don't be the last to get your child in one![3]

Mosque, synagogue and church have always offered provision for their young at evenings or weekends. The systematic development of a general curriculum corresponding in some measure to that of the state school and pursued under the direction of institutions of the minority groups is, however, a phenomenon of the last seven or eight years. And there has been an historic provision of denominational day schools by Christians and Jews; only in the last few years, however, and even now only on a scale dictated by financial resources, have there appeared schools sponsored by the minority communities.

There are broadly four organizational types of which three are explored by case study below. These are:

1 The Sunday School, which has a strong confessional basis and offers doctrinal and moral education based on biblical teaching. Unlike the Sunday schools of the traditional English churches, those of the West Indian churches are often attended by adults as well as children.
2 The Evening School, some forms of which meet also or instead at weekends. This is attached to a religious centre and offers teaching in the sacred or community language and culture transmission.
3 The Day Schools, which are as yet few in number. These are recognized as full-time schools and are reckoned to provide a moral, intellectual and spiritual climate appropriate though not necessarily exclusive to the children of the communities they serve.
4 The Supplementary School, which does not have a religious base but which, like the Day School, operates in a full range of curriculum subjects. Schools of this kind are again few in number at the present time. There is a notable example in the London borough of Redbridge which has been established by the Black People's Progressive Association. The practice of the Supplementary School is explored by Maureen Stone who describes a school that operates five evenings a week from 4.00 to 9.30 p.m. 'on the basis that children learned nothing in school so it was their duty to provide some kind of education.'[4] The timetable here included English, art, sociology, human biology, creative writing, maths, French, German and dance/drama.

In communities in which commitment is maintained by competence in the mother-tongue as well as by religious allegiance, language classes are widely offered under the auspices of the religious organization as an adjunct though not as a dimension of its manifest function. So it is with Polish, Italian, Greek, Urdu and many other languages. Chinese classes, however, are organized by the Chinese community without the advantage of a religious foundation and a suitable network of accommodation. A recent survey of these by the Commission for Racial Equality estimated that there were some sixty Chinese language classes in existence with enrolments ranging from 20 to 900.[5]

Case 1: The Sunday School

The Sunday school characterized in this paper is that of the black pentecostal churches, the principal of which to be found in Great Britain are the New Testament Church of God and the Church of God of Prophecy. Modern pentecostalism started at the beginning of this century among American blacks. It was imported to Europe within three or four years and there survive here the Elim Pentecostal Church, Assemblies of God, the Apostolic Church and other smaller fellowships. The black pentecostal churches are distinguished by their music, fervour, the power of ecstatic utterance and the stamina of the faithful, whose sessions of worship are seldom shorter than two hours. Accordingly, black and white pentecostals have tended to keep their organizations apart.

Where accommodation allows the black pentecostal Sunday school is a large and complex organization. That which I attended in Lozells, Birmingham, had an attendance of about 300 and classes were segregated by age and gender. This is afforded in the many cases in which the church has taken over the premises of a nonconformist church such as the Methodists or Congregationalists whose buildings, now so often surplus to needs, were invariably designed as complexes of schoolrooms, lecture rooms, catering facilities, vestries, galleries and so on. The Sunday school convenes at 10.00 a.m. for an hour and a half or so (advertized times are not closely observed!) and then is rounded up for morning worship.

The norm of pedagogy is catechism. There are recognized answers to questions and the purpose of the class is to learn these set responses. The relationships between pupil, teacher and supervisor are also formal. One stands up to answer a question and the teacher likewise defers to the school supervisor who pays a visit to the class and checks control and learning:

Q. What must you do to get the new birth?
A. You must be born again.
Q. I would ask the pupils to stand to give their responses.
    It shows a little bit of — well, I can't find the word.
A. (Standing) You must be born again.
    Thank you, sir.

And:

Well, that is good, but I am not altogether satisfied. A source is something which has within it something, am I not right Brother Lewis?

Detailed Bible study forms the basis of the morning's lesson. In the adult classes allegiance to the church is general and strong while the pupils of the younger classes are sent by parents who believe in the value of religious instruction for their children even if not for themselves.[6] The didactic function of the black pentecostal Sunday school is assigned to it by the nature of corporate worship which is expressive rather than instrumental: the preacher stamps his feet, perspires through his suit, mops his brow and shouts himself hoarse and the sermon communicates as a demonstration of religious commitment rather than an exercise in reason. It is in the Sunday school, therefore, that the basic tenets of pentecostal belief are taught.

The prestige of the office of supervisor within the pentecostal community and the significance attached to the Sunday school notwithstanding, the process of religious socialization is only partially effected within the Sunday school. In common with all other religious sects pentecost makes extensive temporal demands of its faithful and the young are inducted by systematic exposure within the cultural milieu of the church. They are dressed in Sunday best and brought to the meeting. They are given tambourines and are encouraged to clap hands and dance. When they sing or testify there is massive encouragement and applause and reticence is quickly overcome by the novice whose silence is broken by the voluntary praise phrases 'Alleluya' and 'Yes Lord' which fortify the little child as they do the practised orator. The behavioural skills of black pentecost are acquired by children with ease: if accommodation is available, they are practised two or three evenings a week as well as on Sundays and at conventions and it is on the basis of these rather than of doctrinal orthodoxy that induction is effected.

While the normative forms of participation are collective, there are institutional opportunities for individual performance and the standard of these is the 'testimony' or 'word'. An individual volunteers or is invited to go to the platform and give a brief sentiment of faith. Once again, the assembly makes the assignment less awesome by its manifest encouragement. It is usual to greet the congregation with 'Praise the Lord', sometimes repeated as 'Praise the Lord again' and 'Praise the Lord one more time'; the faithful respond in crescendo and this ritual both breaks the ice and gives the performer a sense of control. Against my wishes at the time, I was called to give a testimony at a convention of the Church of God Assembly in Clapton, east London, and found myself charged with unwonted confidence by the power of goodwill expressed in the behaviour of the assembly as I made my way reluctantly forward.

In this way the pentecostal churches, whether by accident or design, are to be found addressing important educational objectives in the affective domain: self-image and confidence enjoy immediate enhancements. The themes of dignity and self-respect feature prominently in pentecostal theology and legitimize personal aspirations of this kind: they sing the chorus 'From sinking sand he lifted me' and the preacher observes:

> We've got heart-aches, we've got persecutions on every hand. Inflation is knocking us all over. But Jesus came down, down, down, to raise us up, up, up. And this is why we can sing and we can shout.

Case 2: The Evening School

The Sparkbrook Islamic Centre in Birmingham came into existence in 1979. It occupies a former terrace of houses which has now been converted to accommodate a community mosque which is used for prayers five times daily as well as for Friday prayers and Eid prayers, a bookshop which serves local Muslims and has the purpose of disseminating an understanding of Islam among non-Muslims, and a *madraseh* or Islamic school. The Centre has been active in fostering good relations between communities and endeavours to promote a good understanding with local institutions, as by inviting local teachers to the Centre on a regular basis. The Centre at Sparkbrook is one of the largest and most active Islamic cultural centres in the United Kingdom.

The *madraseh* operates on five evenings a week between 5.00 p.m. and 7.30 p.m. and some of the students also attend on Sundays for extended studies. There is an enrolment of 400 children and the Centre has its own transport system for those who live beyond walking distance. Boys and girls are accommodated separately and their teachers are engaged on a voluntary basis.

The syllabus offered to students has three components: the Qur'an, Islamic studies and Urdu. Each of these subjects occupies about fifty minutes of the evening session. The sponsoring community organizes its own examinations on a regular basis and there are currently plans to sit public examinations (GCE Ordinary level) in Urdu and Islamic studies under the auspices of the centre. These subjects are in some but not all cases available in local day schools. The Islamic studies component is broad in conception and its main contents include the basic beliefs and duties of the Muslim, the life of Mohammed, the caliphs, duties to parents and the manner of worship; some of these themes, of course, also arise in the study of the Qur'an.

The scale and comprehensiveness of the Sparkbrook Centre and others of its kind prompts some challenging questions about the style and adequacy of state provision, for this is an expensive project in the midst of a community not distinguished by its affluence. Indeed, in addition to the *madraseh* there exists a network of homes to which children are sent by their parents for supplementary tuition.

A major reason for the sponsorship of alternative education in this way is the view held strongly by Muslims that Islam should only be taught by one who embraces it. In the Birmingham agreed syllabus for religious education, religions or 'stances for living' are presented in a non-confessional way and, in common with the general tenor of modern curriculum ideology, there is an encouragement of objectivity, critical thinking and intellectual detachment. The phenomenological study of religion with which the progressive conception of religious education is imbued does not appeal to conscientious Muslims.

In a similar way there is a conflict of educational organization and Muslim ethic. The devoted Muslim, I was told, would want to send his daughter to a single-sex school; yet the local authorities in whose areas Muslims have settled in a concentrated way invariably have co-educational schools as a matter of policy. The mixing of adolescent boys and girls is prohibited in Islam and institutionalized in the English education system. While in secular Western society divorce is increasingly asserted as a matter of right, in Islam 'divorce is permitted but is regarded as the most abominable of lawful acts.'[7] In the context of so direct a conflict on basic ethical principles the establishment of the Islamic cultural centre represents an introversionist sectarian response to a secularized Western society.

It is largely on grounds of expense that the withdrawal from the world has hitherto been restricted to the evening of the day. However, a Muslim day school has already been established with the support of Cat Stevens, a convert to Islam, and the day school model which is explored below is the logical development of the supplementary school. After all, segregation of sexes in the evening hardly undoes the supposed harm of mixing them during the day. Muslim teachers need to be trained in readiness, and the financial problems currently prohibiting this development are peremptorily addressed in the conclusion to this paper.

Case 3: The Day School

The John Loughborough middle and secondary school in Tottenham was founded in 1980 by the Seventh-Day Adventist Church. It has a current enrolment of 300 children of whom 98 per cent are black. Its opening marked the centenary of the coming to England of the American missionary John Loughborough.

The provision of education has long been a central function of the Adventist Church. Worldwide there are some 5000 Adventist schools, colleges and universities. In the United Kingdom, where urban Adventist congregations tend to be black and provincial churches to be white, there are secondary schools in Tottenham and Watford and primary schools in Leeds, Walthamstow, Plymouth and Bracknell. It is reckoned by Adventist leaders that these are established as a consequence of pressure from members that is a reaction to the inadequacies of state schooling at two levels. First, it is said that the state schools provide an uncongenial or unwholesome moral environment; and second, members are sensitive that teacher expectations are low and these in turn affect academic achievement.

It was around such concerns as these that in the late 1970s there was a concerted campaign among Adventists to establish and invest in a secondary school in the London area. Parents experienced a tension between home and school and the tendency for children to reject their home background and training. One instance of this conflict concerned the playing of school sports on a Saturday which is for Adventists the Sabbath, to be kept holy. Simultaneously there was widespread concern about the reported underachievement of West Indian children; this was recognized by the Select Committee on Race Relations and Immigration[8] and assigned in 1979 to the investigations of the Rampton Committee. When in due course the St Thomas More school in Tottenham became vacant, and after numerous feasibility studies, the Adventist Church acquired the premises and opened as a day school.

The Adventist philosophy of education differs markedly from that which prevailed in the pentecostal Sunday school reported above. Teaching is not catechetical. Doctrine is not the issue. No creed is taught. What is distinctive of Adventism is not the inculcation of denominational beliefs but the ethos which prevails. The example of moral life set by the teachers is paramount. Children will not find them smoking, nor drinking tea or coffee on which there are taboos. The ideals they emulate are to be ones of caring and of self-control. The teacher in the Adventist school will not be heard to swear. An assembly is held every morning, whether in the classroom or as a plenary session; it affords the opportunity to project

Christian principles and develop the person, and the emphasis is upon the moral rather than the theological dimensions of religious faith. Once a year, for a period of one week, there is a time of 'spiritual emphasis'. This preoccupation with moral environment commends itself not only to Adventist parents: one third of the children at John Loughborough school are from non-Adventist homes, including Roman Catholic families, and they travel to school from as far afield as Beckenham and Croydon.

The John Loughborough school represents the emancipation of a project in supplementary education, which was before its establishment practised in rented accommodation in Islington; there was an evening programme and a four-week summer school offering English, mathematics, music and other subjects. Clearly, the greater the catchment area of a school, the more prohibitive will be the problems of transport when it operates in the evening, and the day school is a preferred form. However, the costs concerned are partly referred to the parents and it is necessary to charge fees. The Church meets half of the costs of educating each child, be he or she of Adventist parents or not. This leaves a fee of £800 per annum for each child, to which further Church subsidies are available on the basis of a means test. The Church regards the whole project as a most worthwhile contribution to the community.

The story is told here of a black girl who was pursuing CSE courses in a state comprehensive school: her parents had higher aspirations and removed her to an independent school where just over a year later she passed seven GCE Ordinary levels. It is moving from a CSE climate to a GCE climate that many find to be the reward of John Loughborough schooling. Low expectations are renounced. The low status subjects which occupy those destined to perform badly in state comprehensives and which are widely applauded by educationists as models of curriculum development do not feature on the John Loughborough timetable. There are no concessions to relevance or immediacy of interest. History begins with the Wars of the Roses. There is no shunning of Shakespeare in English literature. Competence in standard English is expected and achieved. Black studies and its manifestations in the various traditional school subjects supplement rather than replace these. The dialect poet is read and enjoyed. There is a whole term of Caribbean history at the end of the second year. And the next school play, currently being written by one of the teachers, documents the history of the black people from slavery through colonialism to the present day.

So at John Loughborough school there are two routes to the objective of self-respect: that of high-level academic achievement is not exclusive of a considered study of black history and culture.

Interpretations

1 The Evolution of the Model

Not all forms of supplementary schooling imply by their existence a fundamental discontent with state provision. The language classes, for example, are organized in the recognition that no national system can provide for adequate tuition in all the mother-tongues represented by its students. In Ming Tsow's sample of 195 mothers/families whose children attended Chinese language classes, favourable assessments of day schools prevailed over unfavourable ones and respondants reported good progress, general satisfaction, good teachers and an absence of racial prejudice.[9] Indeed, on all academic criteria parents were more satisfied with their children's everyday school than with the language classes.[10] The language classes surveyed were confined very strictly to language teaching and dependence on transport and lack of accommodation meant that there was little development at the social level.[11] The tension is not to diversify activities within the language class but to establish Chinese language in the mainstream curriculum: such a course was favoured by 87 per cent of those whose children attended the language classes, 83 per cent of those whose children did not and thirty-five out of sixty-four language class teachers.[12]

In other institutions, however, instanced above by the cases of the Islamic Centre and the Adventist day school, dissatisfaction with the form and style of state provision is fundamental. This discontent is seen to have academic and moral themes. The establishment of evening, weekend or holiday schools serves, in principle at least, the purpose of compensation at the academic level, but there abides the problem that the self-image generated within the day school is normative in personal development while that which is projected in the evening is not necessarily transferable. The concern with moral environment runs still deeper and the rationale which applies in dissatisfaction with state schools is not satisfied by the provision of two or three controlled hours in the evening. What is done in an allegedly harmful way in the day-time — the mixing of the sexes, the exposure to teachers who might smoke or swear, the rejection of the notion that teachers should be moral exemplars, a contempt for the puritan ethic — cannot be undone in the evening. The logic argues for exclusive immersion in a controlled moral environment. In such communities the day school is the natural development of the supplementary school.

The constraints upon such a development are principally financial. Muslims expressed to me the judgment that they 'were not yet ready' to run their own day schools, recognizing thereby both the prohibitive cost and the problem of recruiting a sufficient range of qualified teachers. The Muslim day school, however, is a reality in London and is visible on the horizon in Bradford.

The John Loughborough school provides the case that has already undergone transition from supplementary to day school. Commencing with a limited school population at the lower age range, it has built up to fifth-year level. Once established, the ethos of such a school attracts pupils from outside its denominational base and it becomes recognized and sought after as a school which expects and secures high standards of its students.

2 Underachievement and the Myth of Relevance

The notion of a 'child-centred education' introduced by John Dewey has been normative in curriculum theory in post-war Britain and, still more, in the predispositions that teachers have in the selection of subjects for extended topic work and integrated study. In particular, it has been applied to the conditions of the urban school by Eric Midwinter who proposes a 'community curriculum'. In Midwinter's influential view, learning should begin with the here and now and work gradually outwards. Education is to take place in the butcher's shop and the fishmonger's on the corner. Midwinter is scornful of the teaching of French and of projects on Vikings which are in his judgment too spatially or temporally distant from the urban school to be educationally valid.[13]

Dewey and Midwinter have a lot to answer for. The modern world refers to schools an urgent agenda that includes international affairs such as arms, peace, development and multiculturalism; no worthwhile education can fail to explore problems of this order. Yet the criterion of relevance upon which Midwinter and others insist reinforces the very parochialism which it is the teacher's moral and political responsibility to break. The principle of immediate interest assumes that the child's existing motivations can properly dictate what is educationally justifiable. From the point of view of management and control there is some wisdom in this assumption; but if time in school is to be used as preparation for life thereafter we must have a more far-sighted vision of needs and interests. The child growing up in monocultural communities in Cornwall, Devon or Thanet will in due course come to enjoy life in a multicultural community; that child is poorly served by a teacher who panders to his or her currently limited interests. In the end, the only things defined by teachers as worth knowing are what the children already know.

We are touching here upon an important facet of teacher expectations. In a teacher-education seminar recently it transpired that only one of my students had read George Eliot and Jane Austen at school. She was a Kenyan Asian who was in Nairobi at the time while the others were in comprehensive schools in England. In practice the criterion of relevance constitutes an option for low status knowledge, for popular rather than classical, for the twentieth century rather than earlier times, for home rather than abroad, for the concrete rather than the abstract, and for those contents which do not lead to public examinations.

The hazard of cultural estrangement is an important consideration and the place of Islamic studies or of black history and literature will vary according to the aspirations of parents and, in state schools, the ethnic mix of the children. The practice at John Loughborough school as detailed above demonstrates the possibility of undertaking black history in a serious and systematic way alongside a conventional syllabus leading eventually to the GCE Ordinary level examination.

3 Patronizing Professionals: The Paralyzing Effect of Teacher Expectations

One of my erstwhile colleagues has for a daughter an infant Roald Dahl who when at home writes imaginative stories of book length. But when her book comes home from school it is found to have a whole page devoted to a single sentence written in handwriting three times her normal size. 'Today is my gran's birthday.' There is by way of an illustration an indeterminate blob waxed in the primary colours and decorated with what is interpreted to be a forest of candles, proportionate to gran's great age. 'You can do better than this,' says her mother. 'But that's what we have to do at school,' says Beatrix Potter.

This signifies more than an individual's mere lack of judgment: it is the manifestation of a profession in crisis. Teachers, like the clergy, are in a peculiarly depressed period of their professional history. There was a time when a clergyman was peerless in his parish: he alone understood the fabric of the church, he alone supervised the finances, he alone could manage the parish school, only he had been versed in that most exclusive of all disciplines, theology. Now he finds himself in the chair of an uncomfortably democratic institution, the parochial church council, on which there also sit specialists of every kind, architects, economists, headteachers and lay persons with full university degrees in theology to rival his college training. So it is with the teacher. The Taylor Report on the government of schools signalled the failure of teachers to exclude from the management of schools all lay persons including parents and employers. This was an effective assault upon teacher monopoly and the National Union of Teachers condemned it as 'a charter for busybodies'. The seal was put upon this by the Education Act of 1980 which made parent representation on school governing bodies a statutory requirement. While the movement toward an all-graduate profession has continued by the replacement of teachers' certificates with the Bachelor of Education degree, the traditional subject content of this is at most 50 per cent and its status is recognized in recent government policy which phases out the BEd degree in all but one or two subjects. The route to professional qualification now officially preferred is that of university degree followed by Postgraduate Certificate in Education.

The ideology that has pervaded teacher education in the last ten or fifteen years is structuralist. The intellectual apparatus with which teachers have been trained and sent into schools derives from the prominent educational research on social class and educational opportunity. Teachers in training have been trained in the view that there exists a stable deterministic relationship between class and educability and that working-class children may therefore be expected to perform badly or to fail because of their home background. The notion of underachievement which implies a discrepancy between performance and potential is a new idea and was not part of that mythology. The deterministic principle has in recent years been transferred from the working class to women and blacks and the predispositions of low expectations have been projected upon them.

Paradoxically, the intentions of those teachers who project debilitating expectations are benign. It was reported in interview that parents were disturbed that teachers were prepared to excuse poor work from black children which they would not accept from whites.

4 Progressives in Education: Lofty Intentions and Low Standards

In the debate on standards in education which was initiated by the *Black Papers* of Cox and Dyson, there has been no statement more damning or powerful than the sacrifices made by working-class parents to send their children to a fee-paying school which maintains a high moral tone and works to rigorous academic standards. Both of those values are unfashionable by the norms of progressive education. The posture of the teacher is open and informal and there is no sense that the teacher should provide an example of virtuous living for the children to emulate. Objective testing of academic performance, recognition of and organization according to ability differences, and the semblance of discipline are anathema to the new left in education:

> Scholastic achievement — merit of all kind — has become suspect; mass mediocrity is preferred. Worse, any badge of disadvantage — a black skin, a father in a manual job, a mother whose native tongue is not English — is taken as an omnibus excuse for failing to try. The anti-achievement dogma (a common but not inevitable feature of comprehensive organization) spreads through the classroom, the union meetings and the staff common room to be displayed in poor examination results and bad prospects for school leavers. Behaviour suffers and absenteeism mounts. In a dismaying cycle, discipline of the loosest kind is maintained only 'by the staff not demanding high standards of work and behaviour and allowing matters to drift'.[14]

That summary comes not — as well it might — from a plaintiff parent or the prospectus of a supplementary school justifying the case for withdrawal from mainstream education but from a *Times* leader; and the words enclosed by quotation marks are taken from the report by Her Majesty's Inspectors on schools in the London borough of Haringey, where spending per annum was £200 higher per pupil than in Liverpool and where teacher work loads were considerably less. The Inspectors found bad school attendance, unmarked homework, disturbances in lessons and a widespread concern on the part of parents. Anomie, of course, is not so much a principle of progressive education as an accident in which it is frequently involved. But even when we have disentangled what is attributable to ideology from what is attributable to incompetence, we are left with a fundamental dissonance between what minority group parents want for their children and what teachers in state schools want to give them. It was against such a background that Rampton found:

> The commitment shown by West Indian parents to (supplementary) schools and the encouragement that they give to their children to attend are impressive. The children have told us that they go willingly to supplementary schools because they are encouraged to work hard and made to feel they can achieve.[15]

5   *Financing Supplementary Schools: The Educational Voucher*

The problem of financing the supplementary schools is both a political question and a moral one. In the perceptions of the minority communities whose cases are considered above, the co-educational state school is inimical to fundamental religious principles. The moral environment provided by the modern school runs counter to that which is pursued as an ideal within the home and religious community, even to the point of causing serious offence. The so-called progressive ethos characterized above is mandatory except for those who can afford to liberate themselves from it: it is thus forced upon the poor and is avoidable by the not-so-poor only by sacrifice.

The right of denominations to offer their own education is historic and in recent years the costs of maintaining denominational schools have been largely borne by the state. The Church of England, the Roman Catholic church and various of the denominations control the provision of full-time education which is available to children free of charge.

It is widely urged that the supplementary schools be given every possible assistance in the way of facilities, advice and financial aid. The Rampton Committee urged local authorities to continue to make school premises available and to help with books and materials.[16] A report in Redbridge commends for support the Saturday Supplementary School established there.[17] And the Department of Education and Science is called upon to disseminate to local education authorities a clear commitment to help with the financial arrangements of voluntary language classes.[18]

To the extent that no greater expenditure is incurred by educating children in day schools administered by the minority communities than in those administered by the state, the case for public finance of minority day schools is a strong one. And on all the evidence of morale, behaviour and achievements, the minority day school has the potential of greater efficiency. Further, since there is already a financial commitment to the school by the sponsoring community (in the case of John Loughborough school amounting to 50 per cent), that subsidy can be used to reduce per capita charges.

The educational voucher, which is a means of placing in the hands of parents a token of value approximate to that of a child's education in a given year, has much to commend it in this context. The parents in Haringey whom Her Majesty's Inspectors found to be trapped in a system which was not offering 'the quality of education they need and have a right to expect' would have the possibility of taking their children to a school that was prepared to deliver the goods. The sponsoring communities, on the other hand, need not fear a flooding of their schools as they would always have the right to control entry by some criterion of denominational allegiance: their doors need not be opened more widely than they wish. But the assurance of finance would mean that more minority groups would be enabled to run their own schools. And the existing state schools could then be expected to make adjustments in their ethos and academic standards in order to be attractive to parents and children.

Notes

1 Homan, R. (1978) 'Political education in Bulgaria', in *Teaching Politics*, 7, 1, pp. 45–53.
2 Coard, B. (1971) *How the West Indian Child Is Made Educationally Subnormal in the British*

School System: The Scandal of the Black Child in Schools in Britain, London, New Beacon Books, p. 19.

3 *Ibid.*, p. 39.

4 Stone, M. (1981) *The Education of the Black Child in Britain: The Myth of Multiracial Education*, London, Fontana, p. 173.

5 Ming Tsow (1984) *Mother-tongue Maintenance: A Survey of Part-time Chinese Language Classes*, London, Commission for Racial Equality, pp. 10–11.

6 Calley, M.J.C. (1965) *God's People: West Indian Pentecostal Sects in England*, London, Oxford University Press, pp. 31–2.

7 Sarwar, G. (1983) *Islam: A Brief Guide*, London, Muslim Educational Trust, p. 6.

8 House of Commons, HC 180. 1. III (February 1977).

9 Ming, *op. cit.*, p. 24.

10 *Ibid.*, p. 23.

11 *Ibid.*, p. 36.

12 *Ibid.*, pp. 24, 29, 49.

13 For elaboration see Homan, R. (1981) 'The myth of relevance', in *International Schools Journal*, 2, pp. 17–21.

14 'Taught to fail', *The Times*, 13 July 1984.

15 HMSO (1981) *Interim Report of the Committee of Inquiry into the Education of Children from Ethnic Minority Groups: West Indian Children in Our Schools* (Chairman: Anthony Rampton), Cmnd. 8273, p. 45.

16 *Ibid.*

17 *Cause for Concern: West Indian Pupils in Redbridge* (1978) London, Black People's Progressive Association, p. 12.

18 Ming, *op. cit.*, p. 55.

12   Ethnicity and Educational Achievement

Sally Tomlinson

Central to the interminable debates surrounding the education of ethnic minority pupils in a system still largely designed for white majority society pupils is the debate on achievement. At its crudest level the question posed is: do ethnic minority children, particularly those of Caribbean origin, achieve educational skills and credentials on a par with white pupils, and if not, why not? The debate has had a variety of inputs — from minority parents and teachers, from academics of various disciplines, including some Asian and Caribbean academics, from practitioners at all levels of education, from local and central educational administration, from government appointed committees and from groups as varied as the National Association for Multi-Racial Education and the National Front. It is thus not surprising that the debate seems interminable and is likely to continue.

One of the reasons the debate will continue is that the factors responsible for educational achievement are held to be largely psychogenic, that is, factors such as ability, motivation and aspirations, plus limited sociogenic properties such as home background and occupational status of parents. If these factors continue to be regarded as of prime importance then dissension about the 'causes' of any 'low' achievement — whether defined as below-average reading age or failure to acquire a university place — is likely. If, however, achievement can be related systematically to wider social structures and processes, it may not be so easy to relate 'low' achievement simply to individual and family attributes.

In a society such as Britain, where much research has demonstrated inequalities of access to, and outcome from, educational structures, by social class and gender, 'achievement' itself becomes a problematic concept. Who defines what counts as achievement in a society where the highest achievers are white middle- and upper-class males? Who measures achievement and how? In whose interests is achievement actually defined? If these questions are raised then perhaps any lower, or 'under-achievement' on the part of ethnic minority pupils may be seen, as Reeves and Chevannes (1981) have suggested, to be an ideological construct on a par with theories of deprivation and disadvantage. In the USA several researchers have suggested that such ideologies or 'theories' can have the effect of absolving educators from their professional responsibilities to be effective teachers (Edmonds, 1979).

Weinberg (1977) has further suggested that, given the structural forces which have opposed the effective education of black children in the USA for so long, it is surprising that the children achieved at all, and Mullard (1982) in Britain has concluded that 'underachievement in a racist society is by many standards a massive achievement.' Certainly, to construct elaborate explanations for any low achievement of black children in societies which have built practices which disadvantage minorities, and beliefs which justify these practices, into their social institutions, could be held to be a pointless activity. On the other hand, if the educational achievement of minority pupils is slowly improving, as it now appears to be in the mid-1980s in Britain, does this mean that educators *are* beginning to change their practices and become more effective in their teaching of minority pupils? Since the education system is structured around hierarchies of achievement and attainment, and since research indicates that minority parents are anxious that their children acquire educational and vocational skills and qualifications (Tomlinson, 1984), and that the young people themselves also desire this (Brown, 1984), the debate on achievement must continue.

This chapter considers the changing situation with regard to the achievement of minority pupils from the 1960s to the 1980s and suggests that it might now be useful to examine in some detail the structures and processes of the education system which simply by working 'normally' could work to the educational disadvantage of ethnic minority pupils. The chapter then reviews some of the issues and critiques raised by the achievement debate.

'Underachievement': 1960–79

An open education system is a major means by which occupational and status mobility is made possible for migrants in any country, and there is certainly evidence that most parents who migrated to Britain from the Caribbean and the Asian sub-continent saw success in education for their children as of major importance (Rex and Tomlinson, 1979). It is worth noting that although most minority parents in Britain are, in crude socio-economic terms, 'working-class', their views and expectations of education have always approximated more to those of 'middle-class' white parents, but often without the detailed knowledge of the education system and its intricacies that middle-class parents usually possess. It was not surprising, therefore, that Caribbean parents should demonstrate their anxieties early in the 1960s, when their children did not appear to be well-placed to succeed in education. The North London West Indian Association voiced its anxiety over placement in low streams, remedial departments and ESN-M schools during the 1960s, and protested to the Race Relations Board. Black parents and teachers have continued to worry about the apparently lower achievement of black children — parents in Redbridge have conducted their own research (Redbridge, 1978), black parents in Haringey have pressurized schools to teach black children more effectively (Venning, 1983) and many parents have used supplementary education as a means of improving their children's attainments (Chevannes, 1982).

Between 1960 and 1979 there was a general consensus among educational practitioners, administrators and black parents that ethnic minority pupils, particularly those of Caribbean origin, 'underachieved' in schools. The concept of underachievement was seldom discussed in the literature of this period, but it was generally taken to mean that when comparisons were made between ethnic minority pupils and their white peers, minority pupils were likely to perform less well on standardized group tests of ability and attainment, and on individual 'IQ' tests such as the Stanford-Binet, that their school attainments were likely to be lower, particularly in reading and maths, and that they were likely to leave school with fewer or lower-level public examination passes. Evidence for these assumptions was provided by a variety of large- and small-scale research studies, and as Figueroa (1984) has noted, 'national data are sparse, and often tend to provide limited survey-type information. Other studies have been local small-scale investigations. Both national and local studies have often employed problematic methodologies and instruments' (p. 120). Several overviews of the literature on achievement have been made over the twenty-year period (Goldman and F. Taylor, 1966; F. Taylor, 1974; Tomlinson, 1980, 1983; M. Taylor, 1981, 1984), and have been criticized for not being more sceptical of these 'problematic instruments' (Figueroa, 1984; Troyna, 1984). It is certainly surprising that at a time when issues of culture-fair testing were being so hotly debated in the USA, and legal judgments made concerning the use of IQ and other tests for the allocation of ethnic minority pupils to different tracks and classes,[1] educational researchers in Britain continued to use the various tests with little or no reservations or critical discussions. Studies during the 1960s and 1970s which probably had most impact on practitioners' beliefs were the larger-scale studies whose findings were widely disseminated. The ILEA studies of transfer at 11 + (Little, 1975) and the literacy survey of 32,000 children at the ages of 8, 11 and 15 years (Mabey, 1981) showed that in inner-London Caribbean children appeared to score lower. The Educational Priority Area studies in London and Birmingham (Payne, 1974) showed Asian children scoring lowest on reading and listening tests. The National Child Development Study which followed the progress of a cohort of children from 1958 showed, as Bagley (1982) put it, 'underachievement by all of the children of immigrant parents and West Indian children in particular.'

Some smaller-scale studies during this period did provide counter-evidence that ethnic minority pupils were not necessarily underachieving, particularly when social class background was taken into account and more careful distinctions made between country of origin, rather than simply using the categories 'Asian' or 'West Indian'. For example, Bagley (1975) found that middle-class children of African origin scored above the national norm on the Stanford-Binet test, and (1982) demonstrated that Caribbean children performed very well on a Draw-a-Man test used to identify gifted children. Several Scottish studies demonstrated Pakistani boys achieving as well or better than Scottish boys (for example, Fowler et al., 1977). However, up to 1979 there were few studies which elucidated the achievements of minority pupils in passing public examinations at 16 +, presumably the most crucial measure of school 'achievement'. Taylor (1976) claimed that 'Asian pupils do better than white' from a small-scale study, but in fact at school-leaving age his white sample obtained slightly more qualifications — Asian pupils 'did better' by persisting in education and eventually entering higher education. Several studies of Asian pupils' achievements at O-level found little difference between white or Asian pupils who took O-levels at school, but Asian pupils were much more likely to go on to further education colleges to acquire more academic qualifications (Fowler *et al.*, 1977; Brooks and Singh, 1978). Up to 1979 there does not appear to be any published work on the school-leaving credentials of Caribbean pupils, but several studies had indicated that on attainment tests Caribbean girls performed better than boys (see Tomlinson, 1983, p. 41).

By the end of the 1970s the literature appeared to support the consensus that ethnic minority pupils, particularly those of Caribbean origin, were underachieving in the school system but some, particularly Asian boys, were persisting in education after 16 to acquire educational credentials. Heated debates as to the possible causes of this situation were under way and the government finally set up a committee of enquiry into the education of ethnic minority pupils in 1979.

Achievement: Post-1979

In January 1980 the consensus on underachievement was questioned when Driver published an article in *New Society* entitled 'How West Indians do better at school (especially the girls)'. This article raised the temperature of the achievement debate and, as Troyna (1984) has pointed out, it was ironic that only this study of achievement should have attracted exhaustive criticism of its methodology. Driver's study (1980b) examining O-level and CSE passes of pupils at five inner-city schools suggested that in at least two schools Caribbean pupils, particularly the girls, left with rather more passes than their white peers. Five years later, as more published work has appeared surveying the attainments and credentials of minority pupils and their persistence in education, Driver's work does not appear so controversial. For example, Roberts *et al.* (1983) found that black school-leavers in six areas had slightly more examination passes than whites; Rutter *et al.* (1982), following a cohort of pupils in twelve ILEA schools, found that black pupils were more likely to persist in education at sixth form level, to take O-levels and eventually to acquire rather more qualifications than their white peers. Murray and Dawson (1983), who studied the attainments, attitudes and characteristics of some 5000 pupils in Manchester in 1981, found that a larger proportion of both Asian and Afro-Caribbean pupils than white wished to go on to higher and further education: 46 per cent of Asians aspired to go on to polytechnic and university, 20 per cent of Afro-Caribbeans and 13 per cent of Europeans wanted higher education, but for the last two groups the major hope was to continue into further education. The 'Driver Debate' had scarcely died down before the 'Rampton Debate' began. The interim report by the Committee of Enquiry into the Education of Ethnic Minority Pupils (DES, 1981) published DES statistics collected in six LEAs in 1979, which showed that while both Caribbean and Asian pupils were doing well at the lower credential levels (particularly at CSE rather than O-level for the Caribbean pupils), only a small proportion of Caribbean pupils took A-levels and went on into higher education. The performance of Asian pupils in these six LEAs was comparable to white pupils, with Asians persisting more in further and higher education. Although the lower-level differences were not particularly large, a *Times* leader (6 August 1981) suggested that the 'striking differences in average achievement between West Indian and Asian children' could not be explained by poverty and discrimination and suggested deficiencies in Caribbean home background as a possible source for lower achievements — a suggestion designed to fuel controversy. Reeves and Chevannes (1981), in a stringent critique of the Rampton Report, suggested that if social class had been taken into account in the production of the tables 'Asians, too, might have been seen to be underachieving because of racism' (p. 39).

Troyna (1984) saw one result of the Rampton Committee's report as creating a 'myth of Asian over-achievement' and Tomlinson (1983), concerned that an apparent belief in the success of Asian pupils could be used as a 'stick to beat the West Indian community with', reviewed studies of Asian achievement from 1960 to 1980. These studies demonstrated that there was no 'overachievement', but there were certainly differences in performance of different 'Asian' groups and between Asian girls and boys. Tomlinson noted that in these research studies the explanations offered for lower Asian performance were far more limited than those offered for Caribbean performance and centred on language, culture and adjustment problems — which schools tended to regard as problems which could be overcome. Caribbean pupils' problems were regarded as more intractable. The conclusion could be drawn that 'the education system has incorporated and treated pupils of West Indian and Asian origin differently and that Asian children have been viewed more positively so that they have been given more positive educational assistance' (Tomlinson, 1983, p. 136).

Further studies have suggested that Asian pupils, while still not achieving as well as white children on a national level, are better placed than Caribbean pupils at school-leaving and that Caribbean pupils are not encouraged to stay on in sixth forms or channelled towards higher status GCE examinations. Craft and Craft (1983), in a study of 3000 pupils in an outer-London borough, found that, even when social class was taken into account, West Indian pupils did not achieve at O-level on a par with Asian or white pupils, but went on in larger numbers to take academic qualifications at further education colleges. No West Indians in the cohort achieved a university place, and Asians tended to get slightly lower A-level grades than whites and go to polytechnic rather than university. Figueroa and Swart (1982) found in a study of one comprehensive school that West Indian pupils tended to be entered for CSE rather than O-levels. As far as tests of ability and attainment go there are now indications that in inner-city schools both 'Asian' and 'Caribbean' pupils achieve on group tests of ability and attainment on a par with white pupils. Murray and Dawson, in their Manchester Study (1983), suggested that when social class was taken into account, differences between the groups on reading and maths tests were negligible.

The most recent research examining educational and vocational qualifications of ethnic minority and white adults aged 16 and over has been produced by the third

PSI Survey investigating the circumstances of the British black population via a questionnaire completed by some 5000 black and 2300 white people nationally (Brown, 1984). The education data indicate that to some extent the high aspirations of migrant parents for their children are being slowly fulfilled. Although older migrants have not improved their educational and vocational qualifications much (87 per cent of West Indian, 74 per cent Asian and 64 per cent white men having no academic or vocational qualifications), among 16-24-year-old young men only 35 per cent West Indian and Asians as against 27 per cent white young men now have no qualifications at all. It is worth reproducing the table from the PSI study on 16-24-year-old qualifications (see Table 1).

Table 1.   Informants Aged 16–24: Academic and Vocational Qualifications (percentages)

	Men			Women		
	White	West Indian	Asian	White	West Indian	Asian
Highest academic qualification: degree or higher degree	4	★	5	1	–	1
GCE A-level, HND/C, or above (no degree)	8	6	14	10	5	8
GCE-O-Level, ONCD	21	32	28	42	36	28
CSE and other academic qualifications below O-level	34	24	18	22	36	14
No academic qualifications but vocational or professional qualifications	5	3	1	1	2	★
Highest vocational qualification: Professional or clerical qualification	5	3	3	19	22	7
Apprenticeship	9	7	4	2	–	1
City and Guilds	8	8	3	5	5	–
No vocational qualification, but academic qualification	50	48	56	53	52	43
None of these qualifications	27	35	35	22	21	50
Age on completing full-time education: under 13	–	–	2	–	–	15
17 and over	29	41	58	47	51	50
Base: All adults (weighted)	483	476	718	470	495	684
(unweighted)	123	185	272	146	219	311

Source: Brown, C. (1984) Black and White Britain, Policy Studies Institute, p. 147, Table 76.

The most striking point illustrated by the table is that 'Asian' educational achievement does not appear to extend as far for young women as for men, 50 per cent of young Asian women (as against 21 per cent West Indian and 22 per cent white) having no qualifications. However, Brown does point out that this figure masks a difference between Asian girls in their teens and 20s: 70 per cent of Asian girls aged 16–19 in the sample did have academic qualifications. This PSI study, as other studies in the 1980s have found, suggested that educational qualifications were seen as valuable by both West Indian and Asian men and women, who were 'more likely to extend their education beyond the minimum school-leaving age than white men and women.' West Indian women in particular are more likely to study part-time than any other group.

The achievement debate now has much more up-to-date information available and much more relevant information as to the school-leaving and vocational qualifications of ethnic minority pupils. At the other end of the scale there is still no enquiry and little research into the numbers of ethnic minority pupils placed in the, now much larger, area of special education. Given the persistence of ethnic minority pupils in education after 16, debates have now moved on to such issues as: why Caribbean students do not or are not entered for higher-level academic examinations, and why Caribbean men in particular do not persist to the point of higher education, particularly when some Caribbean women do appear to persist via Access courses if necessary (Millins, 1981); how far the ideology of underachievement may still interfere with teachers' professional responsibilities to be effective teachers of all children; whether educational and vocational qualifications actually help minority youths to acquire employment (Troyna and Smith, 1983; Brown, 1984). These and other questions will not be answered on the basis of assertion; they will require research, which may prove as contentious as previous research on achievement issues. However, these newer questions will not be settled so easily on the basis of psychogenic factors; they will need to take account of wider sociological perspectives concerning the structures and processes of the education system and the links between education and the wider society, demonstrating how these processes and linkages actually affect minority pupils' and students' achievement.

Curriculum Option Choice

Since access to much further and higher education and training depends on the acquisition of O- and A-level GCEs or their equivalents, and since the acquisition of these certificates is currently rather more problematic for Caribbean students than for others, one school process which merits investigation is the way in which pupils are allocated or 'choose' their curriculum subjects and levels of study at 13 + .

The growth and development of option 'choice' has been a significant feature of comprehensive schools over the period that ethnic minority children have been absorbed into the education system. From studies of the procedures a clear conclusion has emerged that 'our option system quite dramatically, though not surprisingly, has led to considerable differences in the educational experiences of 14–16 year olds' (Schools Council, 1982, p. 10). Studies of option choice have also observed that there is a marked difference in subjects studied and levels of study according to social class and gender. There has been little research aimed at discovering how the processes affect minority pupils, although it is logical that if minority pupils are placed in lower-status, lower-level courses at 13+ they stand no chance of emerging at 16+ with many qualifications.

Schools operate elaborate advice and 'guidance' procedures at option time (Reid *et al.*, 1974) and the procedures allow schools to rationalize their beliefs that they are serving the individual differences, interests and abilities of all pupils. Ability is ostensibly a crucial determinant; many schools give standardized tests of both ability and attainment at this point — collect teachers' reports on pupils, and interview pupils and their parents. Early banding or streaming has a considerable effect on what courses and levels of study may be followed in the upper school, and placement here often depends on tests of ability and attainment given at the end of primary schooling or the beginning of secondary schooling. In any case, as Smith and Woodhouse (1984) have recently suggested, although much allocation at 13+ ostensibly depends on ability, 'the measures of ability used are shifting and ambiguous.' As with selection for particular kinds of special education, the allocation of Caribbean pupils at 13+ may depend on behavioural criteria, as much as ability. A study of upper-school allocation in a Yorkshire comprehensive school, carried out by Middleton (1983), illustrated the shifting criteria of 'ability'. Several black pupils, whose ability as measured by standardized tests would have warranted their inclusion in the 'A' band at 13+, were relegated to the 'B' band and thus had no chance of taking O-levels. This happened in spite of the headteacher's insistence that 'the B stream is not to be a dumping ground for badly behaved children.' One teacher's perhaps quite reasonable response to this was, 'you've got to face it, if you've got thirty pupils in an "A" class you've got to have order.' Middleton found that the black boys he interviewed were often 'proud to acknowledge their poor behaviour in the lower school', but did not realize that this had affected their chances of selection for O-level. Several teachers thought at least some of the boys misplaced in the B stream, and the boys themselves were not anti-school and did not truant. Middleton concluded that 'the use of behaviour as a major criterion for the induction of pupils into this administrative structure may be responsible for placing black pupils in the B band.'

A similar process has been observed during a study (currently in progress) of curriculum option choice in eighteen multiethnic schools.[2] Teachers' ambiguous criteria of 'ability', and their perceptions of the past and possible future behaviour of some pupils, did appear to affect their guidance of these pupils, who were ostensibly being offered a choice of what to study, and to what level. For example, in one interview with one Caribbean boy and his father the pupil was 'guided' away from his original choice of biology, technical drawing, art, CSE social studies and French, into basic skills, non-exam social studies, jewellery and the possibility of taking art and French if he could persuade the teachers to teach him. He had apparently been disruptive in these classes and both teachers had recorded him as 'unsuitable' for their subjects. There was some disagreement between the counselling teacher and the parent over whether the boy was 'disruptive' or 'mischievous' and whether this should preclude him being taught the subjects he had chosen.

It need not necessarily be the case that teachers are deliberately discriminating against particular pupils. Just by operating the 'normal' school procedures, within the normal assumptions that schools currently operate, some pupils may find themselves in options they would not have chosen freely. The ILEA Report on the Secondary School curriculum (Hargreaves, 1984) noted that teachers of over-subscribed subjects did have considerable power to exclude pupils they did not want to teach and that 'the less able and behaviour problems may be guided into undesirable subjects' (p. 57). It would seem reasonable to conclude that one school process — curriculum option choice at 13+ — might have considerable effect on numbers of Caribbean pupils entered for higher levels of study and 'academic' subjects and the subsequent outcome at 16+.

Issues and Critiques

Two recent critiques of the achievement debate take up the issue of the measures used to assess ability and attainment (Figueroa, 1984; Troyna, 1984), although, as the section above illustrates, even a higher measured level of ability is no guarantee of appropriate placement. Both these critiques, however, rightly point to the inadequacies and deficiences of many of the tests purporting to measure achievement. Figueroa points out that assumptions are still made that there *is* a measurable quality called 'ability', or 'general intelligence', that culture-fair methods do exist to assess both ability and attainment, and that all pupils have equal opportunities to learn and perform via an appropriate curriculum. These are all dubious assumptions. He suggests that tests of ability, particularly the revised Stanford-Binet test, do inevitably have cultural, linguistic and ideological bias built into them. He could have gone further, since there is a large literature which demonstrates how IQ tests have been used during the twentieth century to stigmatize whole social and racial groups. Kamin (1977) in particular examined how tests were used to prevent what were seen as 'degenerate hordes' entering the USA in the 1920s and has pointed out that Terman, who standardized Binet's tests at Stanford University, was a supporter of the eugenics movement which argued for 'racial purity' and regarded blacks, Indians and Mexicans as 'racially inferior'. Figueroa also pointed out that group tests of ability and attainment were inevitably culturally and linguistically biased and that in Britain examination boards have so far paid little attention to cultural bias in the subjects they examine. Certainly, despite the work of Hegarty and Lucas (1978) at the National Foundation for Educational Research, the popular Foundation tests have mostly been standardized on white middle-class populations. There are some signs, however, that psychologists are becoming much more critical of the bias in psychometric measures, and anxious about the way schools and teachers use tests (see Levy and Goldstein, 1984). There are also developments at examination board level; exam boards are now becoming aware that subject assessment in a multicultural society needs re-thinking (Schools Council, 1981).

However, while tests and testing procedures can be criticized, they are not about to disappear from education. Gipps *et al.* (1983) have recently indicated that more LEAs than ever are now implementing testing programmes for all their schools, and the current emphasis on 'raising standards' means that standards will continue to be 'measured' by tests. One dilemma for critics of tests used on minority pupils occurs when the pupils do achieve well on the tests. It is certainly not logical to criticize tests and examinations when minority pupils perform badly and accept them when the pupils do perform well. The problem may be that while sociologists of education have studied the way the education system grades and allocates pupils at every level and what the outcomes are in terms of social class, gender and ethnicity, they have seldom addressed themselves to the mechanism of this allocation, and the way in which within the dominant psychometric model of education testing procedures are seen as both necessary and justifiable. Testing and tests are certainly likely to continue to be an issue within the achievement debate.

A second issue of crucial importance to the achievement debate was raised by Reeves and Chevannes (1981), who questioned whether the theory of 'under-achievement' had become a more acceptable replacement for older theories of cultural deprivation and disadvantage. The assumption that the educational performance of all inner-city children was affected by inadequate families and environments and that these were intractable problems beyond the influence of education was certainly a powerful belief during the 1960s and 1970s. Reeves and Chevannes suggest that eventually as educators became conscious of a 'blame-the-victim' syndrome, and as minorities sought to assert their cultural traditions, explanations of achievement stemming from ethnic and class culture were no longer acceptable. 'Underachievement' became an acceptable theory to imply that some measure of achievement had occurred, but not all that an individual was capable of striving for. By implication, underachievement could be seen as 'self-inflicted and as resulting from a lack of exertion' (p. 39). They worry that educators may continue to feel absolved from scrutinizing their own practices and the structures and processes of education if the 'underachievement' of black pupils continues to be such a powerful common-sense belief.

Furthermore, there are signs that beliefs in the 'underachievement' of black youths are linked to the notion that this could contribute to social disorder. Troyna (1984) has pointed to the rather simplistic connections made by the Scarman Report (1981) and the Home Affairs Committee (1982) after the inner-city disorders: that the educational 'failure' of black youths contributes to their high unemployment level and therefore to their participation in social disorder. These beliefs are similar to those documented in the USA during the 1950s and 1960s that low educational achievement, and unemployment, of black youths constituted a threat to the social and political stability of the USA (Grace, 1984, p. 9). As far as Britain is concerned these are disturbing and empirically untrue connections. As noted earlier in this chapter there is now evidence that in some inner-city areas black youths leave school as well or better qualified than whites at the lower educational levels. They regard education as valuable and they are more anxious to achieve more qualifications than white youths. Their failure to acquire employment does not necessarily depend on their educational qualifications. As Brown put it, 'there is still a large difference between white and black job levels among those with and without qualifications, and we have to be careful not to overstate the differences of qualifications . . . there is a considerable proportion of the labour market where formal qualifications are not a major determinant of job level' (Brown, 1984, p. 294).

The achievement debate has reached a point where it can no longer be conducted solely on psychogenic levels — attempting to explain achievement and its consequences in terms of supposed individual or group characteristics. The structures and processes of the education system and the beliefs which sustain them must be examined more carefully. But in turn the relationship of educational structures and processes to the wider society, as they affect minorities, must be examined, otherwise there will continue to be misleading associations made between 'achievement' and the social behaviour of minority groups. There is currently a theoretical vacuity in this area, which makes it likely that the achievement debate will continue to be conducted on different levels and from different points of view for some time.

Notes

1 See Ysseldyke and Algozzine (1982) pp. 215–17 for a list of judgments. In particular Larry P. v. Riles (1970) enjoined the California State Department of Education from using IQ tests to place black pupils in classes for the educable mentally retarded. Hegarty and Lucas (1978) studied the possibilities of 'culture-fair' assessment in Britain and decided that it was probably not possible.
2 A study of curriculum option choice in eighteen comprehensive schools currently being carried out by the University of Lancaster.

References

BAGLEY, C. (1975) 'On the intellectual equality of the race', in VERMA, G.K. and BAGLEY, C. (Eds), *Race and Education across Cultures*, London, Heinemann.

BAGLEY, C. (1982) 'Achievement, behaviour disorder and social circumstances in West Indian children', in VERMA, G.K. and BAGLEY, C. (Eds), *Self-Esteem, Achievement and Multi-Cultural Education*, London, Macmillan.

BROOKS, D. and SINGH, K. (1978) *Aspirations Versus Opportunities: Asian and White School-leavers in the Midlands*, Walsall, CRC, Leicester CRC.

BROWN, C. (1984) *Black and White Britain: The Third PSI Survey*, London, Policy Studies Institute.

CHEVANNES, M. (1982) 'Interview on "Ebony" ', London, BBC, 17th Nov.

CRAFT, M. and CRAFT, A. (1983) 'The participation of ethnic minority pupils in further and higher education', *Educational Research*, 25, 1. February.

DEPARTMENT OF EDUCATION AND SCIENCE (1981) *West Indian Children in Our Schools: A Report of the Committee of Enquiry into the Education of Children from Ethnic Minority Groups* (the Rampton Report). London, HMSO.

DRIVER, G. (1980a) 'How West Indians do better at school (especially the girls)', *New Society*, 17 January.

DRIVER, G. (1980b) *Beyond Underachievement*, London, Commission for Racial Equality.

EDMONDS, R. (1979) 'Effective schools for the urban poor', *Educational Leadership*, Oct., pp. 15–24.

FIGUEROA, P. (1984) 'Minority pupil progress', in CRAFT, M. (Ed.), *Education and Cultural Pluralism*, Lewes, Falmer Press.

FIGUEROA, P. and SWART, L. (1982) 'Poor achievers and high achievers among ethnic minority pupils', Report to the Commission for Racial Equality, London.

FOWLER, R., LITTLEWOOD, B. and MADIGAN, R., (1977) 'Immigrant school leavers and the search for work', *Sociology*, 11, 1.

GIPPS, C., STEADMAN, C., BLACKSTONE, T. and STIERER, B. (1983) *Testing Children: Standardised Testing in Local Education Authorities and Schools*, London, Heinemann Educational Books.

GOLDMAN, R.J. and TAYLOR, F. (1966) 'Coloured immigrant children: A survey of research studies and literature on their educational problem and potential — in Britain', *Educational Research*, 8, 3.

GRACE, G. (Ed.) (1984) *Education and the City*, London, Routledge and Kegan Paul.

HARGREAVES, D. (1984) *Improving Secondary Schools*, London, Inner London Education Authority.

HEGARTY, S. and LUCAS, F. (1978) *Able to Learn: The Pursuit of Culture-Fair Assessment*, Slough, NFER.

HOME AFFAIRS COMMITTEE (1982) *Racial Disadvantage*, HMSO.

KAMIN, L. (1977) *The Science and Politics of IQ*, Harmondsworth, Penguin.

LEVY, P. and GOLDSTEIN, H. (Eds) (1984) *Tests in Education*, London, Academic Press.

LITTLE, A. (1975) 'Performance of children from ethnic minority backgrounds in primary schools', *Oxford Review of Education*, 1, 2.

MABEY, (1981) 'Black British literacy', *Educational Research*, 23, 2, pp. 83–95.

MIDDLETON, B. (1983) 'Factors affecting the performance of West Indian boys in a secondary school', MA (Ed.) Dissertation, University of York.

MILLINS, K. (1981) *Special Access Courses — an Evaluation*, London, Ealing College of Higher Education.

MULLARD, C. (1982) 'The Three R's: Rampton, Racism and Research', Paper presented to conference on the Research Implication of Rampton, Institute of Education, University of London, March.

MURRAY, C. and DAWSON, A. (1983) *Five Thousand Adolescents: Their Attitudes, Characteristics and Attainments*, Centre for Youth Studies, Faculty of Education, University of Manchester.

PAYNE, J. (Ed.) (1974) *Educational Minority: EPA Surveys and Statistics*, Vol. 2, London, HMSO.

REDBRIDGE, LONDON BOROUGH OF (1978) *Cause for Concern: West Indian Pupils in Redbridge*. Redbridge Community Relations Council and Black Parents Association.

REEVES, F. and CHEVANNES, M. (1981) 'The ideological construction of black underachieve-ment', *Multi-Racial Education*, 12, 1, pp. 22–41.

REID, M., BARNETT, B. and ROSENBERG, H. (1974) *A Matter of Choice*, Slough, NFER.

REX, J. and TOMLINSON, S. (1979) *Colonial Immigrants in a British City-a Class Analysis*. London, Routledge and Kegan Paul.

ROBERTS, M., NOBLE, M. and DUGGAN, J. (1983) 'Young, black and out of work', in TROYNA, B. and SMITH, D. (Eds), *Racism School and the Labour Market*, Leicester, National Youth Bureau.

RUTTER, M., GAY, M., MAUGHAN, B. and SMITH, A. (1982) 'School experience and achievement and the first year of employment', Report to Department of Education and Science, London.

SCARMAN REPORT, (1981) *The Brixton Disorders, 10–12 April 1981*, Harmondsworth, Penguin.

SCHOOLS COUNCIL (1981) *Examining in a Multi-Cultural Society*, Report of a Conference 25/9/83, London, Schools Council.

SCHOOLS COUNCIL, (1982) *Options for the Fourth*, London, Schools Council.

SMITH, I. and WOODHOUSE, D. (1984) 'Learning your place', *Newsletter 52*, Economic and Social Research Council, June, pp.16–18.

TAYLOR, F. (1974) *Race School and Community*, Slough, NFER.

TAYLOR, J.H. (1976) *The Half-Way Generation*, Slough, NFER.

TAYLOR, M.J. (1981) *Caught Between: A Review of Research into the Education of Pupils of West Indian Origin*, Slough, NFER.

TAYLOR, M.J. (1984) *The Best of Both Worlds: A Review of Research into the Education of Pupils of Asian Origin*, 2 vols, Slough, NFER.

TOMLINSON, S. (1980) 'The educational performance of ethnic minority pupils', *New Community*, 8, 3, pp. 213–34.

TOMLINSON, S. (1983) *Ethnic Minorities in British Schools*, London, Heinemann.

TOMLINSON, S. (1984) *Home and School in Multi-Cultural Britain*, London, Batsford.

TROYNA, B. (1984) ' "Fact and artifact?" The educational underachievement of black pupils', *British Journal of the Sociology of Education*, 5, 2, pp. 153–66.

TROYNA, B. and SMITH, D. (1983) *Racism, School and the Labour Market*, Leicester, National Youth Bureau.

VENNING, P. (1983) 'Menace warning sent to Haringey heads over exam', *Times Educational Supplement*, 11th Feb.

WEINBERG, M. (1977) *A Chance to Learn: A History of Race and Education in the United States*, Cambridge, Cambridge University Press.

YSSELDYKE, J.E. and ALGOZZINE, B. (1982) *Critical Issues in Remedial and Special Education*. Boston, Houghton Mifflin.

13 Comparative Studies of Cognitive Styles and Their Implications for Education in Plural Societies*

John Berry

Introduction

It is obvious to any traveller that cultures and individuals differ from place to place; these differences have been the stuff of tales of exploration and of anthropology, and need no elaborate documentation here. The general position taken in this paper is that these differences arise because peoples around the world develop cultural and psychological characteristics which help them to adapt to the kinds of problems which they frequently encounter. These characteristics serve people well when they remain in the place where they developed; however, when individuals migrate to other settings, and meet other kinds of problems, there may be a mismatch between the individual and the requirements of living in the new place.

This paper is concerned with one kind of behaviour, the 'cognitive' (or intellectual) functions, and to some extent it ignores other important features of human development, such as emotional and social life. It asks the question: 'What do we know about cognitive variation across cultures, and about the sources of this variation?' For some this may be a dangerous, even a subversive question; but set in the context of the issue of human adaptation, it becomes a small but natural part of our attempts in the social and behavioural sciences to understand the nature and function of human variation.

The *way* in which we understand cognitive behaviour is an important element in our approach. If one accepts uncritically the notion of 'general intelligence', then serious problems arise when we work cross-culturally. However, if one moves away from such a rigidly quantitative approach, to a more qualitative notion of 'cognitive styles', then many of the problems disappear (Berry and Dasen, 1974).

* This chapter is reprinted with permission from Samuda, R. and Woods, S. (Eds) (1983) *Perspectives in Immigrant and Minority Education*, New York, University Press of America.

The effects of ecological and cultural factors on the development of cognitive styles will be examined, using as an example the Field Dependent-Field Independent cognitive style (FD-FID) of the late Hy Witkin (Witkin and Goodenough, 1981), and the eco-cultural model of Berry (1976). The effects of cultural change on these styles will also be considered. Experiences both prior to and after migration are known to alter the behaviour of individuals. What do we know about the effect of 'Westernizing' influences in the various countries of origin, and of acculturation in host countries, on the cognitive styles of migrants (Berry, 1983)?

A final issue to be addressed is that of the educational implications of these observations and arguments. If people develop differently in their cultures of origin, and if these differences persist to some extent over their life-span in the new culture, what needs to be done to the educational and other social systems of host countries in order to meet the needs of immigrants?

Culture and Cognition

Three general positions may be discerned in current work on cognition cross-culturally. All three share an interest in describing and interpreting the *cognitive performance*, the *cultural context* of that performance, and the *relationships* which may exist between them. They differ in a number of ways, which are illustrated in Figure 1.

The conventional approach has been to take a standard test of general ability or 'intelligence' and to administer it to all and sundry. Usually the only modification to the test has been its translation, or to make some minor variation in content. Two assumptions are typically made: one is that the cultural life of the test developer and the cultural life of the test taker differ in only one important respect, that of language. The other is that the cognitive abilities which are characteristic of the cultural life of the test developer and those of the test taker differ in only one respect, that of the *level* of development.

These two assumptions are illustrated in the upper portion of Figure 1. First, elements in the cultural context are treated more or less as a unit (solid boundary around elements on the left), and, second, the cognitive abilities are assumed to be a single package (solid boundary on right). Test scores are then usually interpreted in terms of populations having bigger or smaller packages. For example, Vernon (1979, p. 7) has noted that it is commonly assumed that intelligence is a 'homogeneous entity or mental power that, like height or weight, can vary in amount or in rate of growth or decline . . .' His own empirical work (Vernon, 1969) illustrates these assumptions.

With respect to the first assumption, it is clear to me that cultural differences have not been taken seriously in the debate on population differences in intelligence. With respect to the second assumption, little attempt has been made to find out what (perhaps different) cognitive abilities are actually in place in various groups, and how they are structured. Given these two errors of omission, the great logical error of commission is then performed: if the cultures are not really different, if the abilities

Figure 1. *Schematic Diagram of Three Approaches to Relationships between Cultural Contexts and Cognitive Performances*

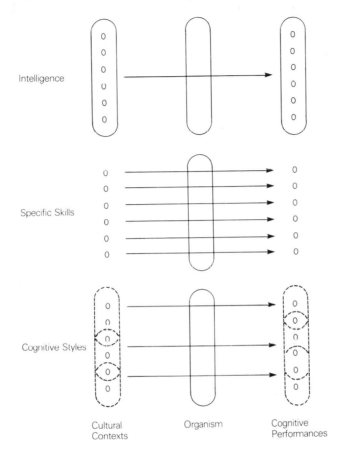

are not really different, then the differences in test performance must be due to different levels of development. However, from the point of view of cultural relativism, if cultural differences are real and large, and if abilities develop differentially in adaptation to these differing contexts, then differences in test performance cannot logically be claimed to be differences in levels or amount of development.

An alternative to this approach is that taken by workers in 'cognitive anthropology' (e.g., Cole *et al.*, 1971). From their perspective, a single feature of the context (such as a specific role or a particular experience) is linked to a single performance (such as performance on a categorization task, or accuracy on a test of quantity estimation); this approach is illustrated in the mid portion of Figure 1. They contrast their 'notion of culture specific skills' with general ability theory (Cole *et al.*, 1971, p. xiii), which often asserts that in some cultures cognitive development is pushed further than in some other cultures (i.e., that levels or amounts of intelligence differ). Assuming that cognitive processes are universal (Cole *et al.* 1971, p. 214; Cole and Scribner, 1974, p. 193), they argue that 'cultural differences in cognition reside more in the situations to which particular cognitive processes are applied, than in the existence of a process in one cultural group and its absence in another' (Cole *et al.,* 1971, p. 233). This emphasis on the particular, and culturally relative, nature of cognitive skills has meant that Cole and his co-workers do not search for *patterns* in their data. Generally, they appear unconcerned whether performance 1 is related to performance 2, or whether cultural element 1 tends to be experienced along with cultural element 2 in their sample. Unlike intelligence testers, they do not assume any universal pattern or structure in their skill data; indeed they seem uninterested in the question. Similarly, they also seem uninterested in how the numerous cultural elements may be organized in a cultural system in which the individual develops.

The two approaches to understanding the relationships between culture and cognition thus far considered have differed in their acceptance of cultural relativism and in their concern for systematic relationships. The approach taken by *intelligence* testers ignored cultural relativism but assumed a universal structure in relationships; the approach taken by those interested in *specific skills* assumed the position of cultural relativism, but ignored systematic relationships. The approach taken by researchers into cognitive styles also assumes the position of cultural relativism, but, in addition, searches for systematic relationships among abilities, among elements of the cultural context, and between patterns of contexts and abilities (see lower part of Figure 1).

One basis for this approach is in the work of Ferguson (1954, 1956) who argued that 'cultural factors prescribe what shall be learned and at what age: consequently different cultural environments lead to the development of different patterns of ability' (1956, p. 121). Further, he argued that through overlearning and transfer, cognitive abilities become stabilized for individuals in a particular culture. Both cultural relativism and systematic relationships are thus implicated in this approach, and these have been adopted in much of the work on cognitive style.

A recent review of the research on various cognitive styles (Goldstein and Backman, 1978) makes it clear that while sharing a general approach, there are many important differences among the numerous research traditions. This need not be a problem here, for only one has received any substantial treatment in the cross-cultural field, that of field dependence-field independence (Witkin *et al.*, 1962; Witkin and Goodenough, 1981).

This particular cognitive style includes not only cognitive (intellectual or perceptual), but also some social and emotional characteristics; this makes it a particularly useful approach to understanding the individual as a whole. The central feature of this style is the 'extent of autonomous functioning' (Witkin, Goodenough and Oltman, 1979); that is, whether an individual characteristically relies on the external environment as a given, in contrast to working on it, is the key dimension along which individuals may be placed. As the name suggests, those who tend to accept or rely upon the external environment are relatively more Field Dependent (FD), while those who tend to work on it are relatively more Field Independent (FID). The construct is a dimension, the poles of which are defined by the two terms,

FD-FID; individuals have a characteristic 'place' on this dimension, reflecting their usual degree of autonomy (Witkin and Goodenough, 1981). However, individuals are not 'fixed' into this usual place, since relatively more field-independent people may shift to a more field-dependent approach as the situation warrants; this 'mobility' of cognitive style is an important feature. Moreover, specific training has also been shown to affect one's usual style or approach.

This most recent conceptualization, which draws together perceptual, cognitive and social characteristics, is much broader than the original use of the term by Witkin *et al.*, (1962). Over the course of research the field dependent-independent dimension has referred to a series of components which has evolved as the research programme advanced. Initially it included only the contrasting ways in which individuals establish the upright in tests involving tilted frames or tilted rooms; more field dependent people tended to rely upon the external frame, while more field independent persons tended to rely upon internal standards. Later on it came to include the tendency to separate or disembed a small item from a larger context; more field dependent individuals had difficulty in overcoming the embedding context, while those more field independent found it easier to overcome the influence of the organized complex. Later still, the dimension grew to include the articulated-vs-global field approach. Here, cognitive tasks were presented whose solution depended upon taking an essential element out of the context in which it was presented, and on restructuring the problem material so that the element became used in a different context; more field-dependent persons were less likely to restructure (and hence not solve) the problem, whereas more field independent persons did restructure and more often arrived at a correct solution. Most recently the whole area of autonomy in social behaviour and interpersonal competencies has come to be included in the FD-FID cognitive style as well; those who are more field dependent tend to accept social influence more, and to be more competent in social relations, while those more field independent tend to be more independent of social influence, and to exhibit less social competence.

The current conceptualization of the field dependent-field independent cognitive style, which we employ in this study, is that arrived at by Witkin and Goodenough (1981): autonomy of external referents in perceptual and social behaviour. It has two indicators or components which are termed 'restructuring skills' and 'limited interpersonal competencies'. The field dependent-independent cognitive style is thus a pervasive dimension of individual functioning, showing itself in the perceptual, intellectual, personality and social domains (Witkin and Goodenough, 1981), and it tends to be relatively stable over time and across situations. It 'involves individual differences in process rather than content variables; that is to say, it refers to individual differences in the "how" rather than the "what" of behaviour' (Witkin and Goodenough, 1981, p. 57). Since it refers to the 'how' of one's behaviour, the field dependence-independence construct avoids some of the difficulties of the 'ability' approach, where the focus is on the 'how much'; this is particularly important in our use of the dimension cross-culturally.

Individual and group differences in the FD-FID cognitive style have been traced to two broad categories of influence: eco-cultural and acculturational. In the first, a cognitive style is viewed as a way of behaving which helps individuals and groups to cope with (adapt to) prevailing problems in their immediate environment. In the second, the style which has developed under these traditional conditions becomes altered to respond to new cultural influences; for the immigrant these typically are initial 'Westernization' while still at home (e.g., by education, telecommunications), and the whole set of new influences which inundate him on arrival in the new setting. The reason for distinguishing these two broad sets of influences is that what may be adaptive in the traditional setting may not be adaptive in the new one.

What do we know about these two types of influence? In Table 1 are outlined some of the important influences: beginning with the ecological variables, an ecological approach asserts that interactions between an organism (in pursuing satisfaction of its primary needs) and its habitat will generate characteristic patterns of economic, demographic, sociocultural, and biological adaptations. The relationships in such a system are probabilistic rather than guaranteed productions. One pervasive set of adaptations has been that of the 'nomadic style', and incorporates a nomadic settlement pattern, a low concentration of population, and a hunting and gathering subsistence base. An adaptation in sharp contrast to this may be termed a 'sedentary style', and includes a sedentary settlement pattern, a higher population concentration, and an agricultural economic base. Other subsistence activities, such as herding and fishing, have variable relationships to these demographic elements (see Berry, 1976, p. 119). This basic contrast in settlement style is evident in much of the background literature of studies of cultural ecology.

Table 1. *Variables Influencing the Development of Field Dependent-Field Independent Cognitive Style*

Influence	Prediction of cognitive style	
	Field independent	Field dependent
Ecological		
Subsistence pattern	Hunting, gathering	agricultural
Settlement pattern	nomadic	sedentary
Population density	low	high
Cultural		
Stratification	low ('loose')	high ('tight')
Family type	nuclear	extended
Socialization emphases	assertion	compliance
Acculturation		
Western education	high	low
Wage employment	high	low
Telecommunications	high	low

In adaptation to these contrasting settlement styles are a set of cultural variables. In those societies with a nomadic style, there are likely to be relatively low levels of role diversity and sociocultural stratification; these have been termed 'loose' by Pelto (1968). In contrast, those societies with a sedentary style are likely to have higher levels of role diversity and stratification; these have been termed 'tight' by Pelto. Also lying along the dimension are the characteristic socialization practices examined by Barry, Child and Bacon (1959). In their classical analysis they were able to demonstrate that societies with a nomadic style tended to foster 'assertion' during child rearing, whereas those with a sedentary style tended to foster 'compliance'.

The importance of these contrasting socialization emphases is that Witkin *et al.* (1962) have shown such emphases to be systematically related to the development of cognitive style among individuals within Western society. In the Western studies reviewed by Witkin and Goodenough (1981), socialization practices that emphasize strict rules and overprotection (cf. 'compliance') tend to foster field dependence. In contrast, those practices that encourage separation from parental control (cf. 'assertion') tend to foster the development of higher levels of field independence. In the cross-cultural studies reviewed by Witkin and Berry (1975) a similar relationship was evident. But, in addition, there is strong evidence that differences in the broader societal pressures emanating from tight and loose structures may reinforce such specific socialization emphases.

A final set of variables (in Table 1) deals with the impact of other cultures on both the traditional culture and individuals in it. These acculturative influences include education (very often of a Western type), a shift from traditional economic activity to wage employment, and an increase in settlement size and population density (urbanization). It is considered that both education and wage employment often encourage the analytic activity included in the field independent cognitive style. Thus, an increase is likely in field independence with increasing acculturation. However, in some cases there is a persistence of the traditionally adaptive cognitive style for many generations during acculturation (Berry, 1983).

Both the ecological and cultural factors found among subsistence-level peoples are predictive of greater FD among agriculturalists and greater FID among hunters and gatherers. The evidence presented by Berry (1976) and the bulk of the evidence reviewed by Witkin and Berry (1975) support this generalization. Whether analyzed at the sample or individual level, eco-cultural adaptation clearly accounts for a high proportion of group and individual differences in cognitive style development. In other words, samples that were nomadic and hunting and gathering in subsistence pattern were relatively FID in contrast to the sedentary agriculturalists. Influences stemming from acculturation also contribute to the distribution of scores on these tests. In all cases, though, acculturation (mainly through a form of Westernization) is less strongly related than is eco-cultural adaptation.

In the outline of the concept of cognitive style, mention was made of 'social autonomy' being theoretically related to 'restructuring' within the FID cognitive style, and of 'interpersonal competencies' being related to the FD end of the dimension. Social behaviours may also thus be included within the framework. More specifically, it may be predicted that individuals who grow up in a tight, stratified, and densely populated society, such as those often found in agriculturally-based groups, will be more sensitive to group needs and more responsive to group requirements. In contrast, those developing in loose social units might be expected to be more independent of authority and less conforming to group pressure. A first examination (Berry, 1967) of this prediction contrasted samples from two cultures on a conformity task. This involved a situation where individuals are requested to judge the length of a line in the face of a false social norm. Differences between the two groups were as expected: in the tight samples judgments were significantly closer to the suggested group norm than in the loose samples. At this group level of analysis, there was correspondence between the two behavioural domains that are theoretically related in the FD-FID cognitive style (Berry, 1979).

In summary, it should be clear that *individuals* are different from one another in cognitive style; to the extent that ecological and cultural factors play a communal role, we may also say that *groups* are likely to differ in cognitive style as well. Acculturational influences may work, both before and after immigration, to reduce these large cultural variations; however, cultural groups do tend to persist in traditional patterns of behaviour in their new home (see Berry, 1983, for an overview of patterns of acculturation). Host societies are thus likely to encounter nearly the full range of these cross-cultural differences among immigrant peoples. What does this mean for the educational process?

Implications for Education

In plural societies institutions must increasingly 'open up' to accommodate the broadening variety of clients. In some countries (for example, Canada and Australia) there are official national policies of *multiculturalism*, which recognize cultural diversity to be a resource rather than a problem, and which encourage the maintenance and development of numerous cultural traditions within the framework of the larger society. For schools, this policy and ideology raises many questions, some of which are now receiving substantial attention (Samuda, Berry and Laferriere, 1984). One of these issues is how to work with such a variety of culturally-based cognitive styles in an educational system.

A major review of the educational implications of the FD-FID cognitive style was completed in 1977 by Witkin and his colleagues. The review is an extremely valuable source, and this section follows its structure closely. In that review Witkin *et al.* (1977) examined four major questions: how students learn, how teachers teach, how students and teachers interact, and the role of cognitive style in career differentiation.

Student learning styles are known to vary in relation to cognitive style. First, relatively FD students tend to be better than FID students at learning and remembering social material. There is no known difference in sheer learning ability or memory; however, the relevance of social materials to FD students gives them the edge in this domain. Second, reflecting their external orientation FD students are likely to learn better with external reinforcements, while FID students tend to learn better under conditions of intrinsic motivation. Third, FID students have been shown to learn better than FD students when the material lacks organization; however, the level of learning does not differ when the materials are already structured. All three differences in learning styles are directly predicted by the known orientations of students with differing cognitive styles. A foreknowledge of the likely style of individuals or groups of students, then, will be useful in the choice and presentation of educational materials.

Turning to the second area, that of teaching style, Witkin *et al.* (1977) have shown that relatively FID teachers are more likely to assume the responsibility for directing the teaching situation, while FD teachers favour teaching situations that allow interaction with students. Furthermore, FID teachers, but not FD ones, 'feel' that informing the student when a response was incorrect, was effective in enhancing student learning' (p. 29). Thus the cognitive style of the teacher is also important, and this raises the question: what happens during student teacher *interactions*, when there is a stylistic match or mismatch between them?

A few answers have been indicated by Witkin *et al.* (1977). When the cognitive styles of students and teachers are matched, they view each other more positively than when they are not matched; this differential evaluation includes views about personal and about intellectual characteristics. Moreover, when cognitive styles are matched, evaluations of student performance are higher than when they are mismatched. This latter finding may not indicate bias but simply better actual performance (of both teaching and learning) when cognitive styles are similar.

Finally, Witkin *et al.* (1977) have brought together substantial evidence that a student's cognitive style is an important factor in career paths; thus, it is not only general ability which is operating here, but also the profile or organization of these abilities which is important (see Figure 1). With respect to vocational interests, relatively FID students tend to prefer positions where analysis is required, but social relations are not; in contrast FD students tend to prefer a job with a 'people emphasis'. Actual vocational choices are also related to cognitive style: in the academic setting, relatively FD students tend to specialize in the humanities, languages, clinical psychology, nursing and social or human services; FID students tend to choose the sciences, mathematics, engineering and experimental psychology. Despite these general orientations, overall achievement is not related to cognitive style. Thus, there is evidence for better performance in the 'appropriate' special area, but across the board it is not possible to claim that one is, for example, a better linguist than another is an engineer.

In addition to these observations about teaching and learning, similar arguments may be made in other educational spheres. In the design of school programmes and the development of curriculum, it should be possible to make the material relevant to student interests, and to 'pitch' the material in the appropriate way. In the areas of testing, selection, guidance and counselling, an appreciation of stylistic differences, and their possible cultural roots, should permit a more sensitive, less rigid and less quantitative approach to student needs in a culturally plural system.

In summary, there are clear and documented implications of the cognitive styles of individuals in the educational process. While large individual differences are normally present in all cultural or ethnic groups, it is true to say on the basis of the section on cultural influences that we are likely to find more FD persons from those societies which are traditionally tight agricultural groups than in looser social structures. Similarly, based upon acculturational influences, we are likely to find more FID persons in those societies which have been more exposed to 'Westernization' than in those which were more traditional before emigration.

Armed with these general relationships, it should be possible to provide educational services which take the students' (and their families') cognitive style into account, rather than attempt to treat all as if they were identical culturally and psychologically. To ignore these stylistic differences is to court the incorrect (and unjust) interpretations which have stemmed from the unilinear 'general intelligence' position — that differences are deficits, rather than qualitative variations which can enrich a school, a community and a nation.

References

BARRY, H., CHILD, I. and BACON, M. (1959) 'Relation of child training to subsistence economy', *American Anthropologist*, 61, pp. 51–63.

BERRY, J.W. (1967) 'Independence and conformity in subsistence-level societies', *Journal of Personality and Social Psychology*, 7, pp. 415–18.

BERRY, J.W. (1976) *Human Ecology and Cognitive Style: Comparative Studies of Cultural and Psychological Adaptation*, New York, Sage Halsted.

BERRY, J.W. (1979) 'A cultural ecology of social behaviour', in BERKOWITZ, L. (Ed.) *Advances in Experimental Social Psychology*, Vol. 12, New York, Academic Press.

BERRY, J.W. (1983) 'Acculturation: A comparative analysis of alternative forms', in SAMUDA, R. and WOODS, S. (Eds), *Perspectives in Immigrant and Minority Education*, New York, University Press of America.

BERRY, J.W. and DASEN, P.R. (Eds) (1974) *Culture and Cognition*, London, Methuen.

COLE, M. and SCRIBNER, S. (1974) *Culture and Thought*, New York, Wiley.

COLE, M. *et al.* (1971) *The Cultural Context of Learning and Thinking*, New York, Basic Books.

FERGUSON, G.A. (1954) 'On learning and human ability', *Canadian Journal of Psychology*, 8, pp. 95–112.

FERGUSON, G.A. (1956) 'On transfer and the abilities of man', *Canadian Journal of Psychology*, 10, pp. 121–31.

GOLDSTEIN, K. and BACKMAN, S. (1978) *Cognitive Style: Five Approaches and Relevant Research*, New York, Wiley.

PELTO, P. (1968) 'The difference between tight and loose societies', *Transaction*, April, pp. 37–40.

SAMUDA, R., BERRY, J.W. and LAFERRIERE, M. (Eds) (1984) *Multiculturalism in Canada: Social and Educational Perspectives*, Toronto, Allyn and Bacon.

VERNON, P.E. (1969) *Intelligence and Cultural Environment*, London, Methuen.

VERNON, P.E. (1979) *Intelligence: Heredity and Environment*, San Francisco, Calif., Freeman.

WITKIN, H.A. and BERRY, J.W. (1975) 'Psychological differentiation in cross-cultural perspective', *Journal of Cross-Cultural Psychology*, 6, pp. 4–87.

WITKIN, H.A. and GOODENOUGH, D.R. (1981) *Cognitive Styles: Essence and Origins*, New York, International Universities Press.

WITKIN, H.A., DYK, R.B., FATERSON, H.F., GOODENOUGH, D.R. and KARP, S. (1962) *Psychological Differentiation*, New York, Wiley.

WITKIN, H.A., GOODENOUGH, D.R. and OLTMAN, P.K. (1979) 'Psychological differentiation: Current status', *Journal of Personality and Social Psychology*, 37, 7, pp. 1127–45.

WITKIN, H.A., MOORE, C.A., GOODENOUGH, D.R. and COX, P.W. (1977) 'Field-dependent and field-independent cognitive styles and their educational implications', *Review of Educational Research*, 47, pp. 1–64.

14 Equality of Opportunity and the Ethnic Minority Child in British Schools

John Rex

In some ways the discussion of 'multicultural education', or that of minority children in British schools, presents a typical case of the kind of problem which confronts sociologists in policy-oriented and politically relevant research. I should like to suggest that it can be approached in an objective way which cuts through the confusion, the obfuscation and the ideological loading which are its usual character- istics. That objective way was outlined by Gunnar Myrdal in his classical study of American race relations (1944), but actually has a more general relevance for large areas of research on policy.

Myrdal, it will be remembered, was called in to make a factual and objective study of what was then called, interestingly enough, the 'negro problem'. He responded to this, first of all, by calling into question the notion of 'fact'. Obviously he did not want to deny that there were facts to be recorded. What he did do, as I understand him, however, was to point out that what he was really being asked to record were not simple facts of this sort, but what might be called 'necessary facts'. On this issue he replied with the question: 'necessary from whose or from what point of view?' As he saw it, a 'fact' which was necessary from, say, the point of view of the southern white was by no means necessary from the point of view of southern blacks. His conclusion, therefore, was that the social scientist should always make the viewpoint or value standpoint, from which he judged facts to be necessary, unnecessary or obstructive, clear and explicit. Putting this in a slightly different way, what he was asking for was that we should clarify the ends or goals which we regarded as necessary and then ask which institutions, practices or empirical states of affairs were conducive to the attainment of those goals.

This methodological approach or plan of study led Myrdal to suggest two alternative and complementary types of sociology of race relations. The primary one was a critical sociology, which looked at the 'facts' from the point of view of the American constitution as interpreted by the Courts. Admittedly this standpoint was not totally clear and unambiguous. But it was not entirely woolly either. It did provide a definition of goals in terms of which existing political practice could be judged. The other, more empirical, sociology was based upon the bringing together of the conflicting perspectives of participants in the political struggle, especially of those with a realistic chance of affecting the outcome, and judging what was likely to emerge as a result of their conflict (Myrdal, 1958).

What this paper undertakes to accomplish is an outline of a critical approach to the problem of multicultural education. With this accomplished it would then be possible to go on to a more empirical sociology in which existing practice and policy were seen no longer as the means of realizing mushy and ill-defined consensual goals but as deviating from the ideal which a critical sociology outlines in directions which were explicable in terms of the actual interests and goals of the participants.

The viewpoint, the value standpoint, the goal or the end-state in terms of which I propose to judge multicultural education and the treatment of the minority child in school is that of equality of opportunity within a very competitive credentialling system of education and social selection. Some may say that this is a very limited goal and that equality of outcome rather than merely equality of opportunity should be the standard in terms of which education is judged. There is certainly an argument for this. It is, however, based upon long-term goals of an essentially utopian kind. There is no effective political force which is capable of realizing 'equality of outcome' in the immediate future. It is a goal which is only ambiguously part of the goals of the labour movement, amongst which it co-exists with the assertion of an entitlement to mobility opportunities. The goal of equality of opportunity on the other hand is one which is very realistic, in that it is accepted by wide sections of the population including the more disadvantaged groups, and it is one which is admitted as central by those who, like Roy Jenkins when he was Home Secretary, are concerned with relatively immediate political problems. What is important is that the introduction of the notion of equality of opportunity effectively ruled out those practices which acknowledged cultural difference but allowed for an inferior role for minority groups in British society.

There are, of course, many who will object to this approach as simply 'reformist'. This is understandable, and perhaps the more so in view of the subsequent political career of Jenkins. The problem, however, for those who wish to leave out the notion of equality of opportunity is that if it is left out, in what will for the foreseeable future be a competitive and credentialling system, minorities are liable to be fobbed off with the recognition of their right to be culturally different without their being given a fair chance to compete.

The International Experts Committee which met in Paris in 1967 was well aware of this issue. They actually rejected the notion of a 'right to be different' because they saw that insistence upon it would be used by every oppressive government seeking to justify policies of racial domination. It was unfortunate that a subsequent statement by Unesco responding to pressure from black and Third World governments did include a reference to this right (Montagu, 1972). In the absence of a strong insistence on equality of opportunity, it left the door open to those who wished to justify inequality in terms of difference. Again, that shrewd critic of colonialism, J.S. Furnivall, found it necessary in responding to those who called for a more practical education for Indians to point out that Indians who wanted certificates in a society which gave jobs to people with certificates were asking for the most practical education of all (Furnivall, 1948). A similar response might be made to those who in England have called for a more practical education in inner-city areas. This is something that those who believe in inequality are all too willing to concede in their own fashion.

It may, of course, be unfair to those who criticize the notion of equality of opportunity to try to saddle them with responsibility for an unequal form of multiculturalism, What does happen in practice, however, is that those who are not committed to equality of opportunity are quite prepared to form an unholy alliance with anyone who opposes this goal, including the advocates of equality of outcome, so long as it is clear that their ideals remain on a purely utopian level. The ground is then cleared for policies which do nothing to achieve either equality of outcome or equality of opportunity.

Another line of criticism of the Myrdalian approach which is adopted here is almost the opposite of that which I have been discussing. It is not that the use of equality of opportunity as a critical value standard does not go far enough, but rather that the use of any such value standpoint is irrelevant in a society which cannot be expected to pursue such an aim. According to this view, what we have to do is simply to ask the realistic sociological question: 'what educational policies would you expect in an unequal, capitalistic and racist society?' What then follows is simply a functionalist account of the so-called state apparatuses.

The problem with approaches of this kind is not that they are necessarily untrue. It is simply that they do not prove what they assert. What is proposed here is that we test existing policies against what is after all a moderate and realistic goal and, in so far as it can be shown that this goal cannot be realized in this way, prepare the ground for asking what goals are in fact being pursued. A critical sociology therefore prepares the ground for an empirical sociology which askes concrete and specific research questions, rather than simply making unproved dogmatic aassertions. What may well turn out to be the case is that there is a conflict of goals, and the upshot of the research may be to show whose goals are dominant in the system, what alternative goals are being realistically pursued and which policies are conducive to the attainment of which goals.

What follows is an attempt to set out the kind of specific policies which would be relevant to the attainment of equality of opportunity within the present educational system or some modified version of that system which one may realistically expect to come into being. Not all of these policies, or discussion of the issues relevant to these policies, form a normal part of the agenda of the multicultural education debate. They include the allocation of school places particularly in secondary schools, the medium of instruction at the moment of entry to school, the teaching of mother tongue, the teaching of English as a second language at basic levels, the maintenance of minority cultures, the teaching of English as a second language at more sophisticated levels, the provision of courses at examination levels in minority languages, history and culture, specific teaching to combat racism and the modification of the curriculum as a whole and for all children in ways that give recognition to minority cultures.

The allocation of school places, or the allocation of children to specific schools, has interestingly dropped off the agenda so far as ethnic minority children are concerned. There was, of course, and still is, a debate which goes on about the assignment of native-born, working-class children to schools. Middle-class parents have usually taken care to locate their homes within the catchment areas of schools where there are fewer rough working-class children and the system as a whole has always involved some degree of segregation. What has happened in recent years, however, is the emergence of further differentiation within what are largely working-class schools between problem inner-city schools and those in longer established and often suburban working-class schools. The children of immigrant minorities have been heavily concentrated in the worst of the inner-city schools.

It might be thought that the proposal for bussing which arose in Ealing when the first classes with 30 per cent or more of Asian students emerged was precisely the sort of policy which could be said to be promoting equality of educational opportunity. The policy certainly seemed to have a respectable pedigree in the American Civil Rights movement. Study of the cases in which bussing was proposed in England, however, serves to throw doubt on this. What was being discussed was not that Asian and West Indian children in local schools were not enjoying equality of opportunity, but that there were increasing numbers of schools in which English working-class children were being held back by the problem of having non-English-speaking classmates and suffering the stigma of being educated in black schools. The basic answer to the question as to where the surplus of black children should go was really simply 'away'. When 'away' was seen to mean that they would crop up in other schools as well, and that they would have had to be replaced by other children bussed to inferior schools, the pressure for bussing quickly died away.

As matters are at present, ethnic minority children are likely to suffer one of two undesirable fates. Either they form a small minority in white schools or they find themselves heavily segregated in black schools. So far as the former is concerned, the schools have rarely been able to respond to the variety of problems faced by the minority children. Faced with growing resource constraints, they have barely been able to cope with numbers, they may not be eligible for the so-called 'Section 11' money which government provides for the education of minority children and may be forced to assign minority children and their problems to whatever problem-solving organizations they have. There may be more or less sophistication in the way in which different headteachers approach this problem, but the temptation must surely be to see the problems of minority children as remedial problems. Classification and labelling of this kind will appeal particularly if the teachers involved are predisposed to make racist judgments. There are very slight signs indeed of the problems being addressed in terms of some professional ethic.

If what has just been said is true, some might then be inclined to argue that the problems of West Indian and Asian children — or more strictly the children of West Indian and Asian immigrants — will be best dealt with in functionally specialized and segregated schools. Unfortunately one cannot accept this quietly complacent view. We now have schools in inner-city areas of London and the Midlands where the precentage of these children is between 90 and 100. American experience reminds us that in the fifty-eight years between the Plessey v. Ferguson and the Brown v. the Board of Education judgments the American Courts concluded that education which was separate was inherently unequal. That conclusion was reached in the light of a huge weight of evidence. We have no such evidence here, partly because social scientists have not yet made up for the deficiency of centralized records by systematically researching the schools. What is allowed to count as evidence is usually the teachers' own estimates of their performance. In arguing about this 'evidence' we would no doubt concede that there are some devoted and skilled teachers who want above all to ensure that all their children have a fair chance. But, prima facie, since the teaching is hard and unrewarding even where there is some inducement provided by way of special increments, many of the teachers who gravitate towards these schools are simply those who cannot get better positions. There are surely also likely to be some racists and paternalists who see the role of the 'slum teacher' and the teacher of blacks as quite removed from that of teaching for academic success in a 'normal' school. Quite often teachers in these schools see themselves as running 'remedial' schools, or as providing special teaching directed towards passing Certificate of Secondary Education Mode 3 examinations.

Apart from anything else the segregation of Asian and West Indian children together in the same schools means that two quite different sets of ethnic minority educational problems are being dealt with simultaneously. Asian children, whether successful or not, face problems of a linguistic and cultural kind and come from families with a strong positive attitude towards the instrumental aspects of British education. The West Indian children come from a culture which is a regional variant of English culture marked and marred by the heritage of slavery. Moreover, within each of these groups and within the sub-groups amongst them there are numerous variations. It is surely absurd to suppose that there is something called 'black-education' which can deal with all of these diverse problems. Quite probably there are teachers within the system who know how diverse the problems are, but they will be aware more than anyone how unsophisticated the response of their schools has been in understanding the diversity.

Obviously problems of disadvantage and inequality arise for ethnic minority children because of the kinds of institution in which they find themselves. But with that understood, there is an additional problem of language. Even if there were not such questions of disadvantage, therefore, some ethnic minority children, especially Asian children, would face problems at the moment of entry. These problems are of three kinds. There is the problem for the non-English-speaking child of approaching his school work with the linguistic capacity he or she actually commands; there is the problem of maintaining his or her skill in the mother tongue; and there is the problem of acquiring sufficient English to be able to work with English as the medium of instruction. These require separate consideration.

Three approaches have been adopted regarding the language of instruction at the moment of entry into the school: children have been sent to special centres for English instruction; peripatetic teachers have serviced schools with non-English-speaking children; and finally and worst of all, the children have simply been left to cope with English as best they can. All of these techniques work to some extent, but surely they are all unsophisticated, callous and cruel. They fail to cope with the basic problem facing all school children which is that at the outset they have not merely to learn but to learn to learn. A child who has to cope within the first years of his schooling both with acquiring a new language and with starting the learning process lives in something of a nightmare world. No doubt the nightmare becomes less and less frightening as time goes on, but at best the outcome will be that the child no longer presents such a severe problem to the school. His capacity for future learning may in the process have been permanently damaged. Certainly his situation mocks the very notion of equality of opportunity.

There is, of course, an alternative. It has been quite widely adopted in countries such as Sweden, has existed for some time in England as far as non-English-speaking European children are concerned, and is just beginning to exist in one or two areas for Asian children. This is that at the outset the non-English-speaking child receives his education in the medium of the mother tongue. The learning process then starts and within that it is possible to introduce English as a second language by stages. In that way the language acquisition takes place within the learning process and not in opposition to it. It should be noted that the aim of education in the mother tongue here is not to try to create linguistic apartheid, but its very opposite, namely to help the child eventually to learn much more effectively in English.

Still under this same head of the use of mother tongue, we have to note what has been the major linguistic problem in England, namely that of the late entrant to the system. Here, however, the same principles would apply. To first be withdrawn from a class to learn English and then be placed back in it and left to catch up with the work means that, although the minority child learns to speak English, he is virtually guaranteed a place near the bottom of the class. What would be necessary to ensure equality of opportunity would be a continuation of instruction in the mother tongue with the gradual introduction of English to the point at which the child could be placed in a normal class on something like equal terms.

To suggest the establishment of institutions which could cope with educational problems as well as language teaching on this scale would immediately produce the replay that resources were not available on this scale. Yet the problems posed by the assimilation of tens of thousands of non-English-speaking children are such that, were equality of opportunity taken seriously as a goal, institutions of this kind would be credible. The existing type of provision clearly fits the need to train an underclass without disturbing the day-to-day routine of lower-class schools too much. Since, together with the discussion of bussing and then the de facto acceptance of segregation, the provision of language teaching in withdrawal classes has been the main form of policy response to immigration, it seems that the creation of such an underclass is all that has been envisaged.

A quite different question from instruction in the mother tongue is that of mother-tongue maintenance. This has a quite literal meaning in that it deals with the problem of enabling Asian children to continue to talk to their mothers. As matters stand, many Asian children, having to use English to deal with the major matters of education and life, lose the facility to speak the language of their parents, with considerable disruption of their home life and the imposition of severe strain on the cultural and personality level. There has been some debate about whether the maintenance of bilingualism retards learning. Common sense suggests to many administrators that it does. Research in the area, however, points in the opposite direction. As in the case of instruction in the mother tongue, so in this case it is interesting that the need has been far more readily recognized for Italian and other European children. Different standards seem to have been applied in assessing the needs of Asians.

The third problem mentioned above, that of acquiring sufficient English, has already been implicitly dealt with. Emphasis upon mother-tongue teaching as a problem by no means implies that there is not a serious problem of providing for instruction in English as a second language. The aim of achieving equality of opportunity implies the development of sophisticated teaching methods and of ensuring that this does not mean a retardation in the general educational process. Possibly it could be argued that those who have to surmount the hurdle of learning a new language should go back a year at school. What is not compatible with equal opportunity is a policy which places the non-English-speaking child at the bottom of the class. Generally speaking, provision in this area is such that those authorities which have simply provided withdrawal centres are thought to be in the vanguard. All that these centres can do by themselves, however, is to solve the administrative problems of school. They do not solve the problems of ethnic minority children in a competitive educational system.

The problems of Asian children in the language area are reproduced in a weaker but still significant form for West Indian Creole-speaking families. One might not argue here for instruction in Creole, except perhaps in infant classes, but the stresses and strains of West Indian life are such that effective operation at school and in the home and community requires the development of a healthy bilingualism.

There is obviously a cultural problem parallel to the linguistic problem which we have been discussing. A case can and should be made for culture maintenance along with language maintenance. There are, however, real difficulties here because of the place usually occupied by social and cultural studies in the curriculum, particularly at the lower secondary levels. It is already the case in a school that such studies are provided simply to solve the problem of the less bright children, then fitting Asian and Caribbean studies into the curriculum in that particular slot could simply be a way of reinforcing any tendency to inequality. If, moreover, the subject is taught in a paternalistic way, i.e., by white teachers, it can have little positive value.

A particular set of problems relates to the teaching of black studies to West Indian children in schools. It is here that the problems of paternalism are at their most acute. The movement which goes under the name of 'black consciousness' in all its many forms is of the most profound importance in the West Indian islands and in migrant West Indian communities. It is a movement which seeks to rectify the cultural damage done to those forcibly transported from Africa to the plantations and, inevitably, it involves an element of political resistance. It is extremely unlikely that white teachers in a white school setting will understand and be able to interpret this culture in its full significance. What tends to be offered, therefore, under the heading of 'black studies' is a castrated form of this culture, which lays emphasis upon its safe and stereotypical products such as steel bands. Not surprisingly, serious students of the educational problems of West Indian children have seen education of this type in schools as a distraction which at worst labels West Indian children as different and inferior, and at best is a distraction from the more serious aspects of education.

The conclusion to which one is led is that the maintenance of ethnic minority culture is best left to those who believe in it, that is, to the adult members of the community concerned, through supplementary education. Unless, in rare cases, there are schools in which the subject is understood and the place given to it in the curriculum is such that it does not imply inferiority. Supplementary schools, on the other hand, can have a very important role to play in the educational system and deserve financial support from any government committed to equality of opportunity. Not merely do they guarantee a healthy biculturalism which is beneficial to the society as a whole as well as to the educational progress of the children involved; they also provide a valuable setting in which successful remedial education can occur. Not surprisingly, many West Indian supplementary schools have found a function for themselves, not so much in teaching black studies courses, but much more in teaching basic skills in an atmosphere free of the cultural biases and sometimes implicit racism which inhibit children's progress in schools (Stone, 1981).

Nothing said above on these issues should be taken to suggest that all children of West Indian and Asian parents should be forced into following a bicultural educational programme. Increasingly these children in schools insist that they are British and want to be treated as such. While some of them and their parents may see such biculturalism as an essential value to be maintained, the matter should be one of choice. Skin colour should not determine educational rights: what should determine them are the changing values of the children involved. What they most want, if they are given equal opportunity and have attained the necessary skills, is to gain full recognition amongst their peers and by their teachers.

So far we have been discussing the provision of the kind of setting in which young children in primary schools or in the early stages of secondary education are protected from unnecessary psychological strains so that they can cope adequately with the learning process. This, however, is only a starting point. In the crucial selective stages of secondary education, and perhaps particularly in new comprehensive schools, it is essential that children should not merely have English, but that their English should become more sophisticated so that they can use the language in a discriminating way in order to cope with high-level arts and science courses. To learn to speak a language in a basic way and to gain acceptance in the majority culture and the society of school children is by no means to be able to compete at the higher academic levels. The sociology of education in Britain has dealt extensively with the difficulties faced by English working-class children in acquiring the kind of language necessary to succeed at the higher levels. The child from an ethnic minority community finds that he has to make a double transition, first from his own language and culture to that of the English school and peer-group culture, and then from that position to one in which he has the linguistic capacity to cope with work at the higher levels. The answer to this set of difficulties lies clearly in the development of an adequate English as a second language, 'stage two', programme. Yet, as Little and Willey (1981) found in their survey, this aspect of provision for ethnic minority children has, as yet, hardly been developed. Asian children do, in fact, cope with these difficulties and, if the Rampton evidence is to be taken seriously, cope well enough to do as well, or even slightly better than their English peers. This degree of competitive success, however, by no means shows that there is not a great deal of ability being wasted because of linguistic deficiency.

The final set of problems which a programme of multicultural education has to face deals not simply with the elimination of technical and psychological barriers to competitive success at the levels of the system, but rather with the school's evaluation of ethnic minority peoples and their culture. Taking for granted that the schools must evaluate the success of children in coping with the demands of British society, and without any wish to create a kind of cultural apartheid, we must now ask whether the educational system can ensure that minority cultures have their place within the total system. Clearly we do not have (and will not have) the kind of cultural situation which exists in, say, Brussels or Quebec, in which two or more cultures have actual political equality. But to say this is by no means to say that our society cannot be multicultural in the sense of giving academic validation to minority cultures.

In a perceptive piece written for the Association of Teachers of Social Science, Jennifer Williams (1979) has pointed out that minority cultures have been given a place in the low-status uncertificated parts of the curriculum only. The obvious answer to this is that they should be given their place at high-status and certified levels. What is not wanted, clearly, is that Asian and West Indian children should be offered soft options so that they can get O- and A-levels of some kind. Such qualifications would be of little value in the world of work anyway. To say this, however, is by no means to say that there is not a place for academically rigorous courses in Asian and Caribbean languages and culture which merit equal respect with courses in European languages and culture. If courses are provided at this level the effect on such education as exists in minority languages and culture lower down the school would be immediate. They would no longer simply imply a way in which the less-bright child might fill in his time, but would have their place in a sustained programme of academic training. It would also be possible at this level to take on board some of the political difficulties which beset courses in minority culture at the lower levels. The test of acceptability would not be a political one of whether or not cultural values are subversive. (It might be argued that it is in the nature of cultural values to be subversive.) Rather, the clash of political standpoints would be rigorously subjected to scrutiny within an academic discipline. For all the anti-working-class bias of history courses in Britain in the past, it has been possible to develop history syllabuses in which central themes of working-class struggle have found their place in a rigorous academic curriculum. Similarly, courses in Asian and Afro-Caribbean studies would give serious and critical attention to the themes of colonialism, slavery and racism.

Pure language courses would also have their place in this curriculum. Just as those who study French history are advised to learn French language at the higher levels, so Asian children will naturally want to learn their own languages along with courses in their history and culture. Some may even wish to learn related scholarly languages, just as English children learn classics, and it is not surprising that some Muslim educationalists call for provision and recognition of courses in Arabic. Of course, not every Asian child would wish to take these courses any more than every English child who survives to O- and A-level wishes to take modern languages or classics. But it would be an option and the existence of such an option would do much to institutionalize respect for the minority culture.

On the whole it is not the examining boards which stand in the way of these developments. They already provide examinations in Asian languages and would be open to proposals to develop examining in the area of Asian and Afro-Caribbean culture and history. The problem is basically one of resources and teacher initiative. While there are resource constraints in providing for minority subjects of all kinds, it should not be impossible to ensure within a local authority area that courses of the kind envisaged are provided on a centralized basis.

It has been suggested here that the provision of higher-level courses in minority languages and culture will have a beneficial effect upon courses lower down the school. Equally, they might have a powerful effect on the two other types of provision which we have to discuss, namely, teaching against racism and the 'deracialization' of the curriculum as a whole. Nothing could accelerate the development of the curriculum in these directions more than the accreditation of minority cultures within the credentialling system.

Teaching against racism can have a similar beneficial effect within the system as a whole. Every British school has a problem of racism. The Rampton Committee dwelt upon teacher racism and perhaps overrated the importance of its more overt forms. But we are faced with the fact that we live in a culture in which, although it is formally and legally regarded as undesirable and illegitimate, racism is implicit in the thinking of many British parents and children as well as teachers.

A poor answer to the problem is to provide what might be called 'Sunday-school lessons' in anti-racism. Such research as there is suggests that lessons of this kind are, if anything, likely to be counter-productive (Stenhouse, 1979). We must, however, recognize that some kind of political education has its part to play in the curriculum at all levels and, given the formal commitment of our society to anti-racism, it is surely not far-fetched to suggest that within government and politics courses this theme should have a reasonably central place. It accords both with the socialist theme of the brotherhood of man and with the Tory theme of 'one nation'. Here, as in the case of the teaching of minority cultures, what is required is the institutionalization of a theme through its inclusion at the most serious and recognized points in the curriculum. It is a theme which belongs in the 'core' of the curriculum and one which should be found at the highest levels.

Finally, it has to be noted that the response of many educationalists to suggestions about structural reform of the curriculum to accommodate ethnic minority children is to say that what is wanted is not special and separate provision but reform of the curriculum as a whole and for all children to take account of the fact that we are living in a multicultural society. This can be very misleading. Unless the thrusts of multiculturalism and equality of opportunity for ethnic minority children are deliberately institutionalized, it is unlikely that anything will happen to the syllabus as a whole, and the protestations of those who talk in general terms about a suitable syllabus for a multicultural society are all too often a cover for an intention to do nothing.

If, however, all the other elements of a programme to ensure equality of opportunity and respect for the ethnic minority child have found their place within the system, the more general problem of curriculum reform remains. Textbooks, syllabuses and examination schemes have to be revised. What one would like to hear are concrete and specific proposals for doing this rather than general affirmations. Much better that we should hear of concrete proposals for revision of the history and literature syllabuses to give due weight to the problems of the Indian sub-continent and the Caribbean than that we should be invited to agree that even the mathematics syllabus should be revised in the direction of mathematics for all mankind'. This problem should be dealt with seriously. What we have at present is simply a concern for developing multicultural books and materials, usually for use at the lower levels. Is it not possible that some of the many resource centres which are growing up to meet this demand could enlarge their scope and become the centres in which precise proposals for syllabus reform could be developed?

What we have set out here is the sort of agenda which would have to be tackled if the question of equality of opportunity for the minority child, including the theme of equality of respect for minority communities and their culture, were taken seriously. It should be absolutely clear that in terms of these goals actual provision falls woefully short. What we see on the whole is a system which has responded by addressing those areas in which ethnic minority children pose problems for its own continuance rather than the new and specific problems of the ethnic minority child. Still worse, the effect is to provide a system in which many ethnic minority children actually fail by the criteria which matter and through failing are forced into the situation, if not of an underclass, at least of an excluded class. It could be argued that if this were the acknowledged aim of the system it could be regarded as highly effective, and it is this point which is often made by sociologists of education and Marxists in what appear to practitioners to be cynical comments on their work.

It is certainly not the aim of this paper to deny the genuine idealism of many practitioners. What we have sought to do here is simply to apply systematic critical standards to their achievements rather than question their ideals and to show how the constraints of the system drive even their most idealistic aims in unintended directions. This is even more true when we turn to a consideration of the effective as distinct from the ideal debate about multicultural education as represented by the deliberations of the Rampton-Swann Committee (1981).

One theme which has been noticeably missing from the agenda outlined above has been assessment of the performance of ethnic minority children. It is no accident that this has been the main theme of most public discussion. If it could be shown that there are so many defects in the existing *system* of provision, so many obstacles standing in the way of equality of opportunity for the immigrant child, the fact of unequal performance would not appear problematic. We should deal with the systems problems first and then go on to see what the effect of changes in areas of performance were. We should not begin with low 'West Indian' performance as an intractable problem and then go on painfully to explore its correlates in the home and community as well as the school.

The Rampton Committee represented a formal response to all the confused issues which have been thrown up by the presence of ethnic minority children in our schools. It based itself upon a confused consensus. It was supposed to be *the* inquiry which dealt with the problems of ethnic minority children and with multicultural education; but all the more general problems were subordinated to the one question which had been thrown up by the Parliamentary Select Committee, namely that of low 'West Indian' performance. A first volume was devoted to this special theme before the Committee got on with its more general job, and the signs are that, even with this task completed, the same theme will take precedence over others in the second volume.

In many ways the Rampton Committee interim report and the manner in which it reached its conclusions should itself be regarded as a central topic for research, rather than as the work of a body of researchers arriving at objective and practical conclusions. It represented an attempt by a society marked by a confused amalgam of racism and idealism to reach a consensus on a practical problem. Its personnel were selected by a Labour Minister of Education and drawn from educational administrators, teachers and race relations practitioners, including a minority of black members. Its composition and its conclusions were not, however, entirely acceptable to the Conservative Minister who was to receive its first report, and the publication of that report took place in politically charged circumstances. According to an inspired leak in *The Times* before the publication of the report, the Chairman, Mr Anthony Rampton, had been unable to control the blacks and radicals of his committee, who had attributed West Indian failure to teachers' racism rather than to home background. In this glossed version of the report, West Indian failure was assumed and the issue was whether the teachers or the home and community were to blame.

In fact the report, whatever its inadequacies, was more complex than the press leaks suggested. Taking a sample of English, Asian and West Indian children from a selection of schools, it showed that in terms of ethnic background Asian children were doing slightly better than English children in their attainment of O- and A-levels and CSEs, while West Indian children were doing very much worse. There was no attempt to break down these statistics by such factors as actual country of origin, parents' occupation or parents' education, but the report discussed a wide variety of possible factors which might have produced these results. Both teacher racism and home background were discussed as possible contributory factors, but they were discussed along with a variety of factors in educational administration and provision which it was thought might be improved.

The report cried out for criticism, not in terms of one political interpretation of the 'causes' having been given pre-eminence over another, but in terms of the inadequacy of its statistics and its purely speculative account of the causes and correlates of failure by black children. One had only to look at the occupational breakdown of the English, Asian and West Indian populations in the 1971 census, or the differing educational backgrounds of parents in the different ethnic samples, to see that the results in terms of performance were to be expected, and even if the broad conclusion about performance were accepted, there was little in the report to suggest any social scientific investigation of the weight to be attributed to various contributory factors.

There was no debate of this kind, however. A new chairman acceptable to the Minister was appointed with considerable lack of clarity as to whether he was now to turn his attention to the Asian children or whether he should produce some more substantiated evidence on the causes of black failure (thought of now as a general problem, despite the surprising evidence about Asian performance). The radical elements on the Committee and their friends, on the other hand, argued that what was happening was that the findings of the Rampton Report were being buried and that it was their duty to take their stand on the Rampton recommendations, backing their position with better evidence.

Those who see state interventions such as the setting up of the Rampton Committee as a functionally efficient method through which a ruling class seeks to achieve its objectives of subordinating minority groups have a difficult case to prove. The way in which the Committee's conclusions were arrived at and received was all too messy for that. At most it could be said that it created conditions of such intellectual confusion that nothing to the benefit of either ethnic minority children or the educational system was likely to occur. What it clearly did not do was to make its value standpoints explicit, or systematically to consider the institutional arrangements within the schools which facilitated or inhibited the realization of these values.

From the standpoint of this paper it was misleading for the Committee to have begun with the statistics of performance on an ethnic basis, but assuming this starting point and assuming realistically that the Committee will continue to work on the problem with which it started, we may do well to ask what it would have to do in order to provide evidence which would help in promoting equality of opportunity.

The first thing to notice is that crude racial and ethnic statistics are always misleading. Clearly it should be a general rule that in all statistical matters 'third variables' should be explored, and in this case the question which cries out for an answer is what it is about being 'West Indian' which leads to low performance. The mere assertion of ethnic difference shares with recent announcements of differential crime rates by the Metropolitan Police the possibility that those who put forward the statistics will be charged with attributing undesirable characteristics to the genes or the culture of the minority group involved. Where such a conclusion is drawn, it is all too easy to draw the inference that the best thing to do is to get rid of those involved. Obviously it is not the case that this was in the minds of the Rampton Commissioners, but in the sort of political climate which exists in Britain, its conclusions, like those of the Metropolitan Police, could be used to fuel repatriation propaganda.

An exploration of third variables, on the other hand, would include such factors as parents' occupation, parents' education, membership of one-parent families, housing conditions, children's experience of not only teachers but also other white professionals (including the police), the selective processes as they actually operate in schools and other similar factors. These could not be discussed in terms of a debate about whether white racism or parental influence and community were to blame. What would be particularly worth exploring is whether white children with similar social characteristics to the 'West Indians' who do badly also fail within the system. It would at least be worth hypothesizing that these social factors go far to explain what is represented as a simple ethnic difference. In so far as such studies showed that there was a difference between West Indian, Asian and British children from carefully controlled samples, it would then be possible to focus sharply on any specifically ethnic element.

In such a statistical analysis both school system factors and extra-school factors would have to be sharply defined and considered. It would be wrong to exclude either from a serious sociological analysis. But in so far as what we are talking about is the contribution made by schools to promoting equality of opportunity, it is the school system factors which would have to be given priority. There is little, after all, that the Department of Education can do to alter the extra-school factors, but it can draw these to the attention of other government departments. Unless it takes these steps, the suspicion must linger that discussion of both factors, particularly when they are ill-defined in emotionally loaded ways, is simply part of a process of 'blaming the victim'.

This brings us back to the agenda for a critical evaluation of educational practice, which has formed the main substance of this paper. If we are to choose factors which are likely to be worth investigating as possibly playing a causal role in low performance, we must have some theoretical criterion of relevance. That criterion of relevance should be the possible contribution made by any particular arrangement or lack of arrangement in schools to furthering equality of opportunity. Where such arrangements are inadequate, inequality of outcome is to be expected.

At the outset of this paper it was suggested that what was necessary in the study of the position of minority children in schools was both a critical and an empirical study of institutions and practices in order to see what institutions and practices were conducive or otherwise to the attainment of given goals and values, and also what goals existing practices actually served to attain. Much of what we have written has come under the heading of a critical study. It remains only to indicate what existing practices are likely to achieve.

Many of our contemporary sociologists of education tend to work within a framework of functionalism or Marxism: they start by assuming a system with certain needs and then seek to show that existing arrangements fit within that system. Too often they do this in terms of simple theoretical dogma. The necessity of existing educational arrangements is accepted as inevitable, given certain purposes malign or otherwise, which are attributed to the system as a whole, with little attempt being made to look at what does actually occur.

This is not the position taken here. Neither the existing practice of schools nor the enquiry into the causes of low performance by some ethnic minority children seems totally explicable in such terms. What we can show is that neither existing practice nor the attempt to improve that practice by the sorts of inquiry which have been conducted measures up to our critical standards. Certainly, their failure to do so turns in part upon the malign intent of those in power who permit some lines of inquiry and some practices and discourage others. But it would be an incomplete account which left out of the picture the pressures emanating from practitioners and politicians whose aims are very much at odds with those of the powerful. The outcome in practice is likely to be the result of conflicting pressures. Such a result is as subject to criticism as is any set of deliberate arrangements. The important thing which social scientists have to do in these circumstances is not simply to work within a particular political compromise, but, having made their value standpoints clear and explicit, to show what the system is achieving and failing to achieve.

It is not claimed that this paper represents the outcome of research in which a set of empirical conclusions has been proved. What it attempts to do is to set out a systematic framework within which research studies could be pursued. The kind of framework which it suggests, moreover, is more objective than that of most practitioners and polititians who, though they are quite inexplicit about their goals, nevertheless ask social scientists to address themselves to the technical problem of how these goals are to be attained.

References

Committee of Inquiry into the Education of Children from Ethnic Minority Groups (1981) *Interim Report: West Indian Children in Our Schools*, Cmnd 8273, London, HMSO.

Furnivall, J.S. (1948) *Colonial Policy and Practice*, Cambridge, Cambridge University Press.

Little, A. and Willey, R. (1981) *Multi-Cultural Education: The Way Forward*, London, Schools Council.

Montagu, A. (1972) *Statement and Race*, London, Oxford University Press.

Myrdal, G. (1944) *An American Dilemma: The Negro Problem and Modern Democracy*, New York, Harper.

Myrdal, G. (1958) *Value in Social Theory*, London, Routledge and Kegan Paul, pp. 157–8.

Stenhouse, L. (1979) 'Problems and effects of teaching about race relations', *The Social Science Teacher*, 8, 4, Stevenage College of Further Education, Stevenage, Hertfordshire, p. 128.

Stone, M. (1981) *The Education of Black Children in Britian: The Myth of Multi-Cultural Education*, London, Fontana.

Williams, J. (1979) 'Perspectives on the multi-cultural curriculum', *The Social Science Teacher*, 8, 4, Stevenage College of Further Education, Stevenage, Hertfordshire, p. 151.

15 Multicultural Education and Its Critics: Britain and the United States*

James A. Banks

The Ethnic Revival

During the forties and fifties social scientists predicted that ethnicity would wane in nation-states as they became increasingly modernized. Race relations scholars believed that interest groups would be related primarily to social class and to other voluntary and achieved affiliations in modernized nation-states. When ethnic protest movements emerged in nations such as the United States, Canada and the United Kingdom in the sixties and seventies, it was clear that existing theories were unable to explain the complex nature of ethnicity in Western democracies. Ethnicity in most Western nations was far from disappearing when the seventies began. It was experiencing a renaissance.[1] Ethnic discrimination, immigration and the need for individuals to have cultural group attachments in modernized societies are some of the reasons why ethnicity persists in Western nations.[2]

The Rise of Multicultural Education

The demand for reform of the national education system has been an integral part of ethnic revival movements in Western nations.[3] A major goal of most ethnic revival movements is to attain equality for the excluded ethnic group. The school is usually viewed by the victimized ethnic group not only as an important vehicle that can help it to attain equality, but also as an institution that contributes to the group's exclusion because it reinforces the dominant anti-egalitarian ideologies and values of the

* An earlier version of this paper was presented at a symposium at the University of Nottingham, 22 June, 1983, during my lecture tour to British universities and polytechnics. The lecture tour was supported by the British Academy and hosted by Sunderland Polytechnic. I wish to acknowledge the thoughtful comments made on an earlier draft of this paper by a group of my colleagues in the United Kingdom and the United States.

nation-state. Since the school is viewed by ethnic reformers as an important institution in their oppression, they attempt to reform it because they believe that it can be a pivotal vehicle in their liberation.

The reforms that schools have implememented in various nations to respond to the ethnic revival movements are known by a variety of names, including multiethnic education, multiracial education and multicultural education.[4] The varied names used to describe the reform movements reflect the myriad goals and strategies that have been used to respond to the ethnic movements both within and across different nations. While multicultural education within the various Western nations shares some important characteristics, in each nation there are significant differences in the histories and nature of the groups that have led the ethnic movements, in the kind of responses that have been given by national leaders, in the entitlements articulated by ethnic groups and in the political contexts from which the ethnic revival movements emerged. It is important to keep these differences between nations in mind when multicultural education is studied cross-nationally.

The Nature of Multicultural Education

Multicultural education is an inclusive concept used to describe a wide variety of school practices, programs and materials designed to help children from diverse groups to experience educational equality. It is therefore not unlike many educational innovations when they first emerge. When a new educational reform movement arises and is in search of its *raison d'être*, disparate programs and practices emerge and claim the new label. This happened when reforms such as progressive education, career education, inquiry teaching and education for the gifted first arose in the United States. During its formative stages, when it is defining its boundaries and formulating its basic principles, an educational reform movement is highly vulnerable and susceptible to criticism. During this period many concepts which its leaders are formulating are violated by practitioners who become involved in the reform movement but who are neither adequately informed about its basic philosophy and aims, nor skilled in implementing its major components.

A reform movement such as multicultural education, which deals with highly controversial and politicized issues such as racism and inequality, is especially likely to be harshly criticized during its formative stages because it deals with serious problems in society, and appears to many individuals and groups to challenge established institutions, norms and values. It is also likely to evoke strong emotions, feelings and highly polarized opinions.

Scholars from both the right and the left criticize multicultural education. However, the radical left critique is primarily British rather than American. Some of the most acid and perceptive critics of multicultural education in Britain are radical scholars. American critics of multicultural education are primarily conservative and neo-conservative. Radical American scholars such as Apple, Katz, and Bowles and Gintis have not focused their analyses and criticisms on multicultural education but on the general nature of schooling.[5]

It is difficult to explain why multicultural education has been a target of radical critics in Britain but not in the United States. This may be due to the unique nature of multicultural education in the two nations and to their different histories of race relations. Kirp points out that America has historically had more explicit race relations policies than Britain.[6] Multicultural education in the United States may have dealt more explicitly in its early stages with institutional racism and inequality than multiracial education in Britain. The American multicultural education movement may therefore be viewed more kindly by radical critics than its British equivalent.

The radicals criticize multicultural education because they believe that it fails to promote structural reform of societal institutions. The conservatives criticize it because they perceive it as a threat to the status quo, are afraid that it will reinterpret the national experience, create Balkanization, help to splinter the nation, and prevent minority youths from developing the skills needed to participate in the national civic culture. Radical scholars criticize multicultural education for not doing what the conservatives are afraid it will achieve: significant reform of the social structure.

The Radical Critique of Multicultural Education

The radical left critic argues that multicultural education is a palliative to keep excluded and oppressed groups such 'as blacks from rebelling against a system that promotes structural inequality and institutionalized racism.[7] Many radical scholars believe that capitalism is a basic cause of inequality in Western nations.[8] By focusing on cultural differences and human relations in the classroom, multicultural education, they claim, promotes the myth that all cultures are equally valid. This fiction is designed to make oppressed groups content with the status quo and with the system that oppresses them.

Multicultural education, argue the radical critics, does not deal with the real reasons for ethnic and racial groups being oppressed and victimized. It does not promote an analysis of the institutionalized structures that keep ethnic groups powerless and victimized. It avoids any serious analysis of class, institutionalized racism, power, capitalism and the other systems used to keep excluded groups powerless. Multicultural education, they further argue, diverts attention from the real problems and issues. Instead, it focuses on the victims as the problem. It describes the characteristics of powerless groups that supposedly cause their problems, such as their low self-concepts, confused identities and linguistic deficiencies.

Rather than multicultural education, the argument continues, we need serious analyses of the institutionalized racist and class systems that keep ethnic groups powerless and victimized. We need to focus on the institutions and structures of society rather than on the characteristics of minority students. some of the radical critics of multicultural education in Britain tend to emphasize anti-racism as the major strategy needed to deal with the problems caused by the structural exclusion of ethnic groups.[9] An important group of radical critics argues that the school is one of the social institutions that both reflect and perpetuate social class, ethnic and racial stratification. Consequently, because it is a part of the problem, it is impossible for it to promote anti-racism and social equality.

The radical critics of multicultural education tend to be cogent and explicit when they criticize the school but vague and ambiguous when they propose strategies for school reform. Bowles and Gintis, whose arguments are frequently used by the critics of multicultural education to support their positions, are perceptively critical of the school but are vague when they describe school reform strategies. In their chapter on 'Strategies for Change', they write, 'How do we get there? ... Indeed, we have no firm, strongly held, overall, and intellectually coherent answer to the central issue. ... The overriding strategic goal of a socialist movement is the creation of working-class consciousness.'[10] Neither in these statements nor in other parts of their chapter on change strategies do Bowles and Gintis delineate specific reform strategies. Their discussion of change strategies typifies radical criticism of multicultural education.

If you follow the radical critique to its ultimate conclusion, you must abandon the school as a vehicle to help bring about equality. If the school merely reflects the social structure (which the critics claim is both racist and class stratified), then it is futile to try to promote change within it. This leads reformers to abandon the school and to try to implement a structural revolution outside it. In this role educators have forsaken their function. The radical critique, if logically pursued, can become an alibi for the educational neglect of ethnic issues. Multicultural education alone cannot make structural changes within society. It can, however, facilitate and reinforce reform movements that can take place outside schools. The schools can promote social criticism and help students to develop a commitment to humane social change.

The Conservative Critique of Multicultural Education

In both the United States and the United Kingdom there is concern about the eroding quality of the common schools. This concern is especially acute in the United States. Many reports have called for increased emphasis on teaching basic skills and have emphasized the eroding quality of American schools.[11] As concern for teaching basic skills increases, the commitment to multicultural education wanes because most back-to-basics advocates see it as a frill that diverts attention from the main goal of the school — the teaching of basic skills. This trend is evident in the Twentieth Century Fund Report which emphasizes the primacy of teaching English and recommends that the federal funds now allocated for bilingual education 'be used to teach non-English-speaking children how to speak, read, and write English.'[12]

The back-to-basics critics of multicultural education often perceive it as a mushy movement which is more concerned about raising children's self-concepts and making their racial attitudes more positive than it is about helping students to master basic skills. Maureen Stone is one of the most erudite back-to-basics critics of multicultural education in Britain.[13] She argues that in their eagerness to raise the self-concepts of black children and to teach them black history and culture, teachers in Britain often act like counsellors rather than teachers, and have consequently largely failed to teach black students the basic skills.

Conservative critics of multicultural education believe that the school should help all students to develop the attitudes, skills and knowledge needed to participate in the shared national culture. The school, they argue, should promote allegiance to the overarching idealized values of the nation-state and competency in the national language and culture.[14] If ethnic groups want their children to learn ethnic cultures and languages, these should be taught by the groups themselves and not by public institutions such as schools. We should, the conservatives argue, make an important distinction between the function of public institutions such as schools and the role of private agencies such as ethnic institutions.

The Tactics of the Critics

Critics to the right and left use a similar and effective method to criticize the multicultural education movement. Rather than analyzing the goals of the movement as stated by its theorists or describing the best school practices that exemplify these goals, the critics have chosen some of the worse practices that are masquerading as multicultural education and defined these as multicultural education. They have then proceeded to criticize multicultural education as they have conceptualized and defined it. The critics create straw men whom they then destroy.

The radical critics of multicultural education in Britain, for example, have not studied carefully the works of American multicultural education theorists such as Mildred Dickeman, Geneva Gay and Barbara A. Sizemore. As early as 1973 these scholars delineated goals of multicultural education related to the analysis and reform of the major social, economic and political institutions of society.[15] Writing in what became a highly influential book published by the National Council for the Social Studies, Dickeman, Gay and Sizemore provided analyses of the schools and society that helped teachers to understand better institutionalized racism and structural inequality.[16] These authors also suggested ways that teachers could help raise students' consciousness about these concepts and problems — a goal consistent with the reform strategy proposed by Bowles and Gintis.

Critics of multicultural education have focused on some of the most questionable practices and dubious assumptions associated with it. Ethnic holiday celebrations, the making of multiethnic calendars and other kinds of superficial practices are often assumed to constitute the essence of multicultural education. The fact that many teachers also have this conception of multicultural education merely confounds the problems of this nascent reform movement. Stone argues that the major goal of multicultural education in Britain is to increase the self-concept of black students, which she views as inappropriate and harmful to their education.[17] Yet theorists of multicultural education in Britain, such as Craft, Lashley and Lynch, conceptualize goals for multicultural education that are more theoretically and empirically sound.[18]

There is a wide gap between theory and practice in multicultural education in both Britain and the United States. Critics such as Stone frequently derive their conceptions from misguided school practices rather than from the theoretical and empirical work of multicultural education scholars. A top priority for multicultural education in the coming years is to close the wide gap between theory, research and practice.

The problems of multicultural education have also been confounded by the fact that its theorists are still in the process of reaching consensus on goals. However, this is developing at an impressive pace, and although important disagreements still exist (such as which specific ethnic, racial, social class and cultural groups should be included in multicultural education), there is consensus among theorists about the field's major goals and boundaries.[19] Most theorists and researchers in multicultural education, for example, agree that *total* school reform is needed to create a school environment that promotes educational equality for minority youths. They also agree that among the important variables in the school environment that influence the academic achievement and emotional development of minority youths are the learning styles favored by the school, the languages and dialects that are sanctioned, the teaching materials and the norms toward ethnic diversity that permeate the school environment.

Responding to the Radical Critics

Multicultural theorists need to study seriously the critics of the field, evaluate their arguments for soundness and validity and incorporate those ideas which will contribute to the main goals of multicultural education. These goals include reforming the total school environment so that students from diverse racial, ethnic and cultural groups will experience educational equality. Realistically, goals for multicultural education must be limited. Educators have little control over the wider society or over students when they leave the classroom. Educators can teach students the basic skills and help them to develop more democratic attitudes by creating school and classroom environments that promote cultural democracy. However, schools alone cannot eliminate racism and inequality in the wider society. They can reinforce democratic social and political movements that take place beyond the school walls and thus contribute in important ways to the elimination of institutional racism and structural inequality. The multicultural curriculum can give students keen insights into racism and inequality within their societies and help them to develop a commitment to social change.[20]

Multicultural theorists need to think seriously about the radical argument which states that multicultural education is a palliative to contain ethnic rage and that it does not deal seriously with the structural inequalities in society and with important concepts such as racism, class, structural inequality and capitalism. During the early stages of multicultural education in the United States, when it focused primarily on teaching the cultures and histories of non-white ethnic groups, the attention devoted to concepts such as racism and structural inequality was salient.

Yet, as the ethnic studies movement expanded to include more and more ethnic groups, and eventually to include feminist issues and other cultural groups, increasingly less attention was devoted to racism and to the analysis of power relationships. Gay has expressed concern about the wide boundaries of the field:

> Another potential threat to multiethnic education comes from within. Although any educational idea must grow and change if it is to stand the test of time, such growth must remain within reasonable boundaries and retain a certain degree of continuity. If many new dimensions are added to an idea too rapidly, the original idea may be distorted beyond recognition. This may be beginning to happen to multiethnic education.[21]

The radical critique of multicultural education should stimulate multicultural educators to devote more attention to issues such as racism, power relationships and structural inequality. Radical writers are accurate when they argue that racism and structural inequality are the root cause of many of the problems faced by ethnic groups in modernized Western nations such as the United States and the United Kingdom. However, as Green has perceptively pointed out, multicultural educators must live with the contradiction that they are trying to promote democratic and humane reforms within schools, which are institutions that often reflect and perpetuate some of the salient anti-democratic values pervasive within the wider society. Green writes, 'Contradiction is the essence of social change.'[22]

The school itself is contradictory, since it often expounds democratic values while at the same time contradicting them. Thus radical scholars overstate their case when they argue that the schools merely perpetuate and reproduce the inequalities in society. The influence of schools on individuals is neither as unidimensional nor as cogent as the radical critics claim. The school, both explicitly and implicitly, teaches both democratic and anti-egalitarian values, just as the wider society does. Thus schools, like the society of which they are a part, create the kind of moral dilemma for people that Gunnar Myrdal described when he studied American race relations in the forties.[23] Myrdal believed that this moral dilemma made social change possible because most Americans felt a need to make the democratic ideals they inculcated and societal practices more consistent.

Multicultural education can help students to become more aware of the inconsistencies between democratic ideals and societal practices in Western societies, to develop a commitment to reflective and humane social change, and to acquire the skills needed to become efficacious in promoting social reform. Some creative work has been done by scholars in the United States such as Fred Newmann and Harold Berlak on social action projects designed to help students to develop political efficacy and civic action skills.[24] The major goal of ethnic studies teaching, as conceptualized in my previous works, is to help students develop a sense of political efficacy and the knowledge and skills needed to influence public policy in order to increase equity within their societies.[25] Craft, a British multicultural education theorist, believes that the school can contribute to the reformation of society:

> While schools quite clearly devote much of their efforts to social, economic and political continuity, they also contribute to social change. They

generate an output of social criticism in each generation, and an element of original thinking across a broad spectrum. It is perhaps too simple an analysis of the social process to argue that education has only a conservative function.[26]

Responding to the Conservative Critics

A main assumption of the conservative critics of multicultural education is that there is an inherent contradiction between responding to the cultural characteristics of students, teaching ethnic content, and teaching basic skills. Multicultural educators need to demonstrate the fallacy of this assumption and reveal how multicultural education is designed to help minority students to achieve better, and not less well, in school. A major assumption of multicultural education is that a curriculum that is consistent with the learning and motivational styles of ethnic youths, and that validates their cultures, identity and worth will enhance their ability to master the basic skills. More conceptual and empirical work is needed to test the validity of this assumption. Teaching minority youths basic skills is one of the most important goals of multicultural education.

Many conservative critics believe that the goals of multicultural education are un-American and that lessons taught in the multicultural curriculum undercut patriotism. This is a serious misconception. Multicultural education promotes goals that are highly consistent with American democratic ideals. A key goal of multicultural education is to help all students, including majority group students, to develop more democratic attitudes, values and behaviors. This should be an important goal of citizenship education since a major aim of schooling in a democracy is to help students to develop the attitudes and values needed to be successful citizens in the national civic culture. Much evidence indicates that most students, from an early age when they first come to school, have anti-democratic racial attitudes.[27] Their attitudes tend to harden if steps are not taken to make them more democratic.[28] Helping students to develop more democratic values and attitudes is highly consistent with the goals of citizenship education in democratic nation-states. Educational practitioners as well as the lay public need to become more aware of the ways in which multicultural education tries to create a better education for all students.

Multicultural Education and the American Democratic Tradition

Multicultural education in the United States emerged out of the conflicts and struggles of the sixties and seventies. Thus it is a legitimate child of American participatory democracy. It is consistent with the American democratic tradition that views the school as an important socializing institution that helps the nation's youth to acquire the democratic values, knowledge and skills essential for the survival of participatory democracy. Because multicultural education has aims that are highly consistent with United States' idealized values and goals, there is a much greater possibility that it will become institutionalized within American schools than more radical conceptions of school reform, such as those envisioned by the radical critics. Radical reform movements have rarely succeeded in American educational history, in large part because educators are mainstream Americans who perceive themselves as gatekeepers of the nations' sacred democratic traditions, symbols, heroes, myths and institutions. Movements that appear to threaten the nation's democratic ideals, such as neo-Marxist notions of school reform, are likely to be summarily rejected by most American educators.

The rich potential of multicultural education, despite its problems and brief, troubled history, is that it promises to reform the school within the context of the basic assumptions about schooling held by most teachers and to help schools better to realize American democratic values. Thus multicultural education does not envision new goals for schools, but rather asks schools to expand their concepts of political and cultural democracy to include large groups of students who have been historically denied opportunities to realize fully American democratic values and ideals. It is for these reasons that I believe that educators who wish to change the schools so that they will better promote educational equality should opt for reformist approaches, such as those known as multicultural education, and reject radical proposals for the reconstruction of American society and schools. I suspect that reformist rather than radical approaches will also be more successful in reforming British schools. However, my colleagues across the Atlantic, rather than I, are in a position to argue the case for the reform of British schools. While radical scholarship has a richer tradition in Britain than in the United States,[29] the British schools that I have observed are just as conservative, if not more so, than those in America.

Multicultural Education: A Troubled Future

Multicultural education has a rough road ahead in both Britain and the United States. While it is being harshly criticized by both left and right, it is searching for its soul and *raison d'être*. It is plagued by internal problems that must be solved quickly before it is dismissed by many educators as just another promising fad that failed. Conservatives damn multicultural education because they fear that it will revolutionize society. Radicals dismiss it as useless and harmful, as simply another tool of the ruling elite to contain ethnic rage. Yet, as the debate escalates, the problems of minority groups in the schools and society deepen. The new advocates of excellence in American schools are largely silent about equality. A quest for excellence without equality will increase the problems of minority students. New immigrants continue to flock to America to fulfil their dreams at a time when the dreams of many Americans are shattered. Ethnic tension in Britain has been exacerbated by the new wave of conservatism and rigid social class structure. Despite its problems, multicultural education provides sensible and concrete guidelines for action, within the existing context of schools and society, that can lead to increased equity for all students. Its biggest problem is that we have not had the will and vision to give it a chance to succeed.

Notes

1 Glazer, N. and Moynihan, D.P. (Eds) (1975) *Ethnicity: Theory and Experience*, Cambridge, Mass., Harvard University Press.

2 Banks, J.A. (1981) *Multiethnic Education: Theory and Practice*, Boston, Mass., Allyn and Bacon.

3 Banks, J.A. (1978) 'Multiethnic education across cultures: United States, Mexico, Puerto Rico, France, and Great Britain', *Social Education*, 42, March, pp. 177–85; Bullivant, B. (1981) *The Pluralist Dilemma in Education: Six Case Studies*, Sydney, George Allen and Unwin.

4 Bullivant, *ibid.*

5 Apple, M.W. (1982) *Education and Power*, Boston, Mass., Routledge and Kegan Paul; Katz, M.B. (1975) *Bureaucracy and Schools: The Illusion of Educational Change in America*, Expanded Edition, New York, Praeger; Bowles, S. and Gintis, H. (1976) *Schooling in Capitalist America: Educational Reform and the Contradictions of Economic Life*, New York, Basic Books.

6 Kirp, D.L. (1979) *Doing Good by Doing Little: Race and Schooling in Britain*, Berkeley, Calif., University of California Press.

7 A thoughtful critique of multicultural education is presented in Carby, H.V. (1980) *Multicultural Fictions*, The University of Birmingham, Stencilled Occasional Paper, Race Series: SP NO. 58. For discussions of race, culture and schooling in Britain see: Barton, L. and Walker, S. (Eds), (1983) *Race, Class and Education*, London, Croom Helm; and Tierney, J. (Ed.), (1982) *Race, Migration and Schooling*, London, Holt.

8 See Barton and Walker (1983) *op. cit.*, and (1982) *The Empire Strikes Back: Race and Racism in Britain*, London, Hutchinson.

9 This conclusion was gleaned from my discussion with British educators and from the popularity among the British anti-racism advocates of Judy H. Katz's work. See Katz, J.H. (1978) *White Awareness: Handbook for Anti-Racism Training*, Norman, University of Oklahoma Press; and Dodgson, P. and Stewart, D. (1981) 'Multiculturalism or anti-racist teaching: A question of alternatives', *Multiracial Education*, 9, Summer, pp. 41–51.

10 Bowles and Gintis (1976) *op. cit.*, pp. 282 and 285.

11 The National Commission on Excellence in Education (1983) *A Nation at Risk: The Imperative for Educational Reform*, Washington, D.C., US Government Printing Office; The Twentieth Century Fund Task Force on Federal Elementary and Secondary Education Policy (1983) *Making the Grade*, New York, The Twentieth Century Fund; Boyer, E.L. (1983) *High School: A Report on Secondary Education in America*, New York, Harper and Row.

12 Twentieth Century Fund Task Force (1983) *op. cit.*, p. 12.

13 Stone, M. (1981) *The Education of the Black Child in Britain: The Myth of Multiracial Education*, Glasgow, Fontana.

14 Thernstrom, A.M. (1980) 'E pluribus plura: Congress and bilingual education', *The Public Interest*, 60, pp. 3–22.

15 Dickeman, M. (1973) 'Teaching cultural pluralism', in Banks, J.A. (Ed.), *Teaching Ethnic Studies: Concepts and Strategies*, 43rd Yearbook, Washington, D.C., National Council for the Social Studies, pp. 1–25; Gay, G. 'Racism in America: Imperatives for teaching ethnic studies', in Banks, *ibid.*, pp. 27–49; Sizemore, B.A. 'Shattering the melting pot myth', in Banks, *ibid.*, pp. 73–101.

16 Banks (1973) *Teaching Ethnic Studies, ibid.*

17 Stone (1981) *op. cit.*

18 Craft, M. (1981) *Teaching in a Multicultural Society: The Task for Teacher Education*, Lewes, Falmer Press; Lashley, H. (1981) 'Culture, education and children of West Indian background', in Lynch, J. (Ed.), *Teaching in the Multi-Cultural School*, London, Ward Lock Educational, pp. 227–48; Lynch, J. (1983) *The Multicultural Curriculum*, London, Batsford Academic Educational.

19 Banks, J.A. (Ed.), (1981) *Education in the 80s: Multiethnic Education*, Washington, D.C., National Education Association.

20 Hannan, A.W. (1983) 'Multicultural education and teacher education: The British case with some American comparisons', *European Journal of Teacher Education*, 6, 1, pp. 81–2.

21 Gay, G. (1983) 'Multiethnic education: Historical developments and future prospects', *Phi Delta Kappan*, 64, April, p. 563.

22 Green, A. (1982) 'In defense of anti-racist teaching: A reply to recent critiques of multicultural education', *Multiracial Education*, 20, Spring, p. 34.

23 Myrdal, G. (1944) *An American Dilemma: The Negro Problem and Modern Democracy*, New York, Harper and Row.

24 Newmann, F.M. (1975) *Education for Citizen Action: Challenge for Secondary Curriculum*, Berkeley, Calif., McCutchan Publishing; Berlak, H. (1977) 'Human consciousness, social criticism, and civic education', in Shaver, J.P. (Ed.), *Building Rationales for Citizenship Education*, Washington, D.C., National Council for the Social Studies, pp. 34–47.

25 Banks, J.A. (1984) *Teaching Strategies for Ethnic Studies*, 3rd ed., Boston, Mass., Allyn and Bacon; Banks J.A. (1983) (with Clegg, A.A., Jr.) *Teaching Strategies for the Social Studies: Inquiry, Valuing and Decision Making*, 3rd ed. New York, Longman.

26 Craft, M. (1982) 'Education for diversity: The challenge of cultural pluralism', Inaugural Lecture, University of Nottingham, 26 February, p. 4.

27 Williams, J.E. and Morland, J.K. (1976) *Race, Color and the Young Child*, Chapel Hill, N.C., University of North Carolina Press; Milner, D. (1983) *Children and Race: Ten Years On*, London, Ward Lock Educational.

28 Glock, C.Y. *et al.* (1975) *Adolescent Prejudice*, New York, Harper and Row.

29 Lazarsfelt, P.L. (1973) *Main Trends in Sociology*, London, George Allen and Unwin.

Index

French migration to, 104–5
ideology regarding minority groups in, 55
immigrants to, 104–5
immigration policy of, 55, 102–3, 104, 105
languages in, 7–8, 105, 106
migrants' achievement of goals in, 53
Minister of State for Multiculturalism in, 51, 105
multiculturalism in, 6, 7–8, 34–5, 45, 51–7, 101–9
occupations of immigrants to, 107
Official Languages Act (1969) in, 105
origins of immigrants to, 104, 105, 106
Quebecois nationalism in, 104–6
racial discrimination in, 103–4
race in, 49–57
race relations policy in, 51
schools in, 107–8, see also Canada, multicultural education in
selection of immigrants by, 55
separatist movement in, 104–6
social class in, 52–7
teachers and multiculturalism in, 7–8, 107
Ukrainians in, 104, 105
'Vertical Mosaic' in, 107
capitalism, 6, 49–50, 53–5, 56–7, 125, 133–5
Caribbean
see also West Indian children; West Indians; West Indies
migrants from, 53
Caribbean children
see West Indian children
Church of God of Prophecy, 170–1
Coard, B., 168–9
cognition
cultural context of, 14–15, 196–204
cognitive dissonance, 82
cognitive styles
see also field dependent-field independent cognitive style
acculturation and, 200–2
and career choice, 203
comparative studies of, 14–15, 195–204
and ecology, 14–15, 196–204
education and, 14–15, 202–4
and pupil learning styles, 202–3
and socialization, 200–1
and teaching style, 203
Commission for Racial Equality, 10, 40
Committee of Inquiry into the Education

of Children from Ethnic Minority Groups [Rampton Committee], 11–12, 173, 179, 184–5, 214, 215–18
community
and schooling, 167–80
Community Relations Commission, 152
Council for the Accreditation of Teacher Education in England and Wales, 150
Council of Europe, 150
Council for National Academic Awards, 150–1, 155
Craft, M., 154–5
Creole, 13
cultural capital, 69
cultural context
of cognition, 14–15, 196–204
cultural deprivation, 190
cultural pluralism
see pluralism
culture
and curriculum, 6–7, 69–71
definition of, 43–4, 77–8
and educational performance, 68
and ethnicity, 50–7, 211–12
and ethnography, 6–7, 68–75
and identity, 92–3
of minority groups, 50–7, 211–12
and multicultural education, 12, 15–16, 20, 27–8, 33–47, 69–71, 213–15
and multiculturalism, 6–7, 12, 50–7, 61–73
of poverty, 84
subjective, 85–8, 93, 95
curriculum, 2–16, 20–31, 33–47, 72, 77–99, 151–2, 175–6, 187–9, 213–15
choice of options in, 187–9
and culture, see culture, and multicultural education
model of, 37–44
as mono-cultural, 20–31
relevance and the, 175–6
tensions in the, 37–44

Daily Express, 4
Daily Mail, 4
Day Schools, 169, 173–4
Deifenbaker, John, 105
Department of Education and Science (DES), 2, 4, 9, 155
Dewey, J., 175
'Driver Debate'
on underachievement, 184
Drysdale, R., 118
Durkheim, E., 129